The Son of
Man Glorified

Book #1 of the Son of Man Series

Jeff Reintgen

WESTBOW
PRESS
A DIVISION OF THOMAS NELSON

WestBow Press books may be ordered through booksellers or by contacting:

WestBow Press
A Division of Thomas Nelson
1663 Liberty Drive
Bloomington, IN 47403
www.westbowpress.com
1-(866) 928-1240

ISBN: 978-1-4497-7403-5 (e)
ISBN: 978-1-4497-7404-2 (sc)
ISBN: 978-1-4497-7405-9 (hc)

Library of Congress Control Number: 2012920770

Printed in the United States of America

WestBow Press rev. date: 11/27/2012

Contents

Preface

Jesus Christ -- Messiah and the Son of Man. These two titles, found uniquely in God's counsels, show forth all the working of God for the accomplishing of His eternal purpose and glory; that purpose being, the gathering together of all things, both in heaven and on earth – in Christ (Eph. 1:9-10).

It is my hope that you will find, as you read through the pages of this book, that this is truth from God, inspired by enlightenment from the Holy Spirit, and not representative of the doctrinal systems of men. It is an explanation of the counsels of God that are and will be carried out according to His purpose and will, and all for the exaltation of His glory.

In this book you will learn important Biblical principles and truths, such as, how God truly views man, and how man was fully tested by God in responsibility and failed. We will discover what it means to God that Israel was chosen and separated by Him, and why God sends a Messiah to this nation twice, and how He remains faithful to the Jews, as Jehovah, to fulfill all His promises to them. In this testing of man, and Israel as privileged of God representing man, is the understanding of the real reasons God had for the giving of the law to the Jews, and simply, once given, leaving it there with them.

Also then we will see that the Son of Man came for one purpose, the suffering of death. The absolute glorifying of God is accomplished in the redemptive work of this Man, the second Adam, and results in God exalting Him to His right hand in glory. God kept a mystery from His Jewish prophets that He now, by the sending down of His Spirit, reveals through a specially chosen instrument of His glory (Eph. 3:1-5). The believer's place and position in Christ is fully developed and explained, especially in our association and relationship to this glory, the very glory of God. The Son of Man glorified, has entered into the glory on our behalf. Believers are placed in this position by faith, and we possess the knowledge and power of it by the Holy Spirit given to us.

Personal thoughts from the author concerning the reading of this book

This book is written for the purpose of Biblical study. It is written for the purpose of explaining and understanding Scripture. It is not a Christian novel or a self-improvement teaching. It is not intended to read like a story being crafted with suspense and intrigue. You will find that it is not an undertaking of the grand use of the English language, although I did my best to use the language properly with correct grammar and spelling. The overall purpose is to enhance the believer's knowledge of God's Word.

There are many general Biblical principles in the ways and counsels of God that are fundamental to understanding the detail of Scripture. Without mastery of the general principles that run through the entire Bible, the study of Scripture becomes onerous and frustrating. This book is my feeble effort to bring real understanding of these important truths.

From start to finish this book deals with the explanation of these spiritual principles. As the reader progresses through the book you will see that the teaching of many of these principles is repeated from chapter to chapter. It becomes redundant, especially for someone who is familiar with these truths. Yet that is the issue. I would estimate that the majority of believers are not familiar with them, do not understand their explanation, and reject them outright without much thought. Yet without understanding and accepting them as truth from God, a definite human viewpoint of Scripture will always pervade your thoughts and study. So the teaching of the principles is often repeated, usually with a different twist, further insights, or a more developed perspective. Please forgive me for any annoyance and frustrations that my redundancy may cause you.

The chapters of the book could very well stand on their own as individual papers and teachings. Many of them were written that way, as one complete thought, and then accumulated and placed into the whole work. This is a further reason why many of the principles are found in multiple places. If the truth could be applied to the subject of the chapter to enhance its understanding, then the explanation of the principle was inserted along with it. As a consequence the later chapters of the book grew in size, and as my editor remarked, they became complete books unto themselves. Again my apologies.

My last explanation for the redundancy is just to say it is the way my mind works. I love to fully and completely explain things. My mind barely stops thinking of these Biblical truths and principles, and how the detail of Scripture is now easily understood by them. I am amazed to find that God does not make any mistakes. I am not simply agreeing to this as an intellectual premise, but I have actually found God to be so. I find the enlightenment of Scripture by the Spirit of truth to be exciting and wonderful.

If you use this book for Biblical study, please have a good Bible translation by your side. Most of the quoted scriptures in the book are out of the New King James Bible. But there are many scriptures listed, not quoted, that you will need to look into yourself. And always pray, asking that the eyes of your understanding be opened to the things of God. It is the mind and thoughts of God that the believer should be seeking.

This is my humble task on your behalf, as given to me by God and directed by the Spirit of truth, that all believing readers may begin to see and understand with me the very counsels of God. May the Father of glory, in the name of His Son, Jesus Christ, enlighten you by His Spirit and bless you in your efforts to study and understand.

Chapter 1:
The Counsels of God

ow much do we understand about God? How well do we know Him? For a lot of people these are big questions; too big to give an adequate answer. God is, in a sense, incomprehensible. His wisdom, His knowledge, His power is infinite in character and nature, and reaches well beyond the understandings of our finite minds. This is true and will always be true and I would think most believers know and accept this without argument. But when I ask, how much do we understand about God, I'm not referencing His incomprehensible and infinite attributes. What I point to are God's counsels -- His purposes and plans. I reference what He has already revealed concerning Himself, and these counsels. And what God has revealed is ours as believers to understand and comprehend. It certainly is -- all of it. As a Christian, do you truly believe this?

Deut. 29:29

"The secret things belong to the LORD our God, but those things which are revealed belong to us and to our children forever, that we may do all the words of this law."

Moses, by the Spirit of God, is saying that there are hidden things concerning God. *However* what God reveals belongs as a possession to the nation of Israel. I realize this speaks of the law given to Israel and their performing it, but what we also see is the principle that what God reveals is to be known and understood by those He reveals it to. Now in this light and with this understanding, let us look at this next verse, which shows the same principle, but has a different object and source of revelation.

John 1:16-17

"...for of his fullness we all have received, and grace upon grace. For the law was given by Moses, but grace and truth came through Jesus Christ."

The overall principle stays the same -- *what God reveals is to be known and understood by those He reveals it to.* The object of revelation is certainly different -- *the law* came by Moses, but this revelation is *grace and truth* by Jesus Christ. It is distinct and quite different, as is the instrument God uses as the source to bring forth this new revelation. I will not go into the details of these distinctions now, but simply make the point that they are obviously here. I will point out this one difference as a further insight in understanding -- the group to whom He reveals has changed; the Law of Moses was to Israel, but grace and truth to believers in Christ. This distinction becomes an important one, and is fully explained as we go through the entire book. But first, we need to understand more about God's ways in revealing His truth.

Believers have a more Intimate Relationship with God

Ps. 103:7

"He made known his ways unto Moses, his acts unto the children of Israel."

God showed Israel His works (deeds), but to Moses His ways. This scripture alludes to an intimacy of relationship between Moses and God that Israel, as a nation did not have or benefit from. The believer has an intimate relationship with God as well, of which Moses was a prefiguring (a type). The believer/church has this intimacy through Christ -- we are sons of God, we are His body, we are His bride (Eph.

5:26-32). We are bone of His bone and flesh of His flesh, and every bit united to Him.

John 15:14-15

"You are my friends if you do what I command you. I don't call you servants any longer, because servants don't know what their master is doing. Instead, I call you friends, because everything I heard from my Father I have made known to you."

The believer has been invited by God into His counsels. It is God's desire that we know His plans and purposes. In showing forth this relationship in scripture, God uses Abraham also as a type prefiguring the believer concerning this. Abraham had a more intimate relationship with God than that of his nephew Lot. God said to him, *"shall I hide from Abraham what I am about to do?" (Gen 18:17).*

God Gives His Spirit, so the Believer may know and understand

God's purpose in giving revelation is for the church to gain understanding of it by the Spirit, the revealer of truth. It is never for the purpose of confusion or to maintain a state of mystery. We also have definite statements that encourage the believer that the revelation from God can be understood in its fullest.

I Cor. 2:6-16

"We speak the wisdom of God in a mystery, the hidden wisdom which God ordained...for our glory,...but God has revealed them to us through His Spirit...yes, the deep things of God...no one knows the things of God except the Spirit of God. Now we have received...the Spirit who is from God, that we might know the things that have been freely given to us by God. These things we speak...in words...which the Holy Spirit teaches, comparing spiritual things with spiritual...but we have the mind of Christ."

Again I'll say this -- the believer has been invited into the counsels of God. Sure, God is infinite, and His knowledge and wisdom is light-years beyond our finite minds, and there is mystery associated with God; but what God reveals is ours to understand, as sons and not servants in the house of God (John 15:14-17). And this is all the difference, we are sons and not servants. We have not been left in the dark. We have been given the mind of Christ, and the plans and ways of God are ours to know and understand, as sons in the household of our Father. It is the believer's privilege. And it is God's good pleasure to do so.

Eph. 1:7-9

"In Him we have redemption through His blood, the forgiveness of sins, according to the riches of His grace, which He made to abound toward us in all wisdom and prudence, having made known to us the mystery of His will, according to His good pleasure which He purposed in Himself."

It is important for us to know and believe this. It is the reason I have for writing this book. I believe the Holy Spirit can work in the hearts and minds of believers to open up understanding of the Scriptures. In these days it is sad to see how little comprehension and clarity Christians possess of God's Word. And it is even more so to see ministers in the church struggle to rightly divide the word of truth (II Tim. 2:15). Often confusion and frustration reign. However it should not be like this. I find that God is willing, no, more than willing -- it is His good pleasure to reveal His thoughts and purposes to us.

Seek only God's thoughts from His Word

There is a tremendous difference between God's thoughts, found in God's Word, revealed by God's Spirit, and the thoughts and teachings of man. All teachers should have the desire and goal to only share and teach His thoughts, as they are revealed in His Word, unfolded by the Spirit. We must be able to separate out, by the same Spirit, the ways of men, and the erroneous teachings of the carnal mind.

The difference between the two ways is real. Man's failure in his responsibility in the church to seek only God's thoughts, has been the cause of much confusion and blindness. The house of the living God, the body of Christ, is the pillar and ground of the truth (I Tim. 3:15). The revelation of truth from God is simply not found anywhere else, not in its entirety. And we know that it is easier to wrongly divide the scriptures due to a lack of effort and diligence, than it is to rightly divide scripture (II Tim. 2:15).

As believers, we should desire to be enlightened by the truth, to possess the true light of scripture taught by the Spirit of God. Knowledge of God's thoughts, intentions, and plans should distinguish the church. Will we ever possess the ability to calmly and soundly judge, as believers, all that is presented to us? We have this godly ability, for God says He has given to us the mind of Christ (I Cor. 2:16).

The Christian World turns to Unsound Doctrine

If a believer is too busy in his life to examine scripture for himself, then I feel sorry for him. It's as if one becomes so busy with the world they have no time to be a disciple. In this position the Christian is totally dependent on other men for his spiritual food and growth. Inevitably, whether innocently done or not, there will be a seeking out for what is comfortable and pleasurable. There will be desires for what is appealing to the flesh.

2 Timothy 4:3-4

"For the time will come when they will not endure sound doctrine, but according to their own desires, because they have itching ears, they will heap up for themselves teachers; and they will turn their ears away from the truth, and be turned aside to fables."

This is a definite statement of truth and reality that characterizes Christendom in the last days. This passage, this prophecy if you will, is a reality now in Christianity, and will only get worse as we close to the end. It brings out two unsettling understandings. First is that professing Christianity, as a whole, judges and analyzes based on their desires and comforts. God's truth, and the diligent seeking of that truth, doesn't even enter into the equation for many. And this is very dangerous, especially in these days. Second, the truth of God will not be endured. This is evident in the above scripture.

And so then, what will remain in Christianity? It will be comfort and pleasures, convenience and emotions, a tickling of the ears and a certain form of godliness, a getting along with this world. Maybe most telling, it will be the gathering of crowds around talented men in the flesh, a show in the flesh.

Have you ever asked yourself, as a biblical principle -- when has the truth of God ever gathered a crowd? Miracles and wonders may have attracted crowds, and then the feeding of thousands did as well (John 6:26), but when the truth was taught, men walked away and returned to the comforts of their homes (John 6:60, 66). Jesus Christ was the embodiment of God's truth and grace. In the end He was left alone, only His Father with Him (John 16:32). The teaching of the real truth of God never, ever attracts a crowd. This is an important understanding for the believer. The church world has turned in the past, and will continue to turn away from the truth of God.

A more accurate examination of God's Word is needed. We should always adhere to the scriptural rule in I Thess. 5:21, 'to prove all things, and hold fast that which is good.' This is what I would urge all believers to do, before adopting or rejecting any teaching of ministers and men. Apply yourself for your own benefit to the testimony of scripture, to draw ideas directly and simply from them -- draw out God's thoughts. But trust no man's mind; adopt nothing unexamined, reject nothing unexamined.

Colossians 2:2-3

"...to the end that their hearts may be encouraged, being united together in love, and unto all riches of the full assurance of understanding, to the full knowledge of the mystery of God; in which are hid all the treasures of wisdom and of knowledge."

Col. 3:10

"...and having put on the new, renewed into full knowledge according to the image of Him that has created Him."

Believers are the new creation of God. This creation is likened after the image of the one doing the creating. The full knowledge of the counsels of God concerning this image is this new creation's means and common ground. The storehouses of God's eternal wisdom and glory have been opened up to the child of God. The full purpose of God in Jesus Christ on our behalf has been revealed and declared by the Holy Spirit.

God's Purposes, Will, and Plans

Ephesians 1:9-10

"...having made known to us the mystery of His will, according to His good pleasure which He purposed in Himself, that in the dispensation of the fullness of the times He might gather together in one all things in Christ, both which are in heaven and which are on earth—in Him."

This passage reveals to us the general thought of what is contained in the counsels of God. It includes all the work of God to accomplish His purpose -- to fully glorify Himself. This work results in the gathering of all things in Jesus Christ, who becomes the center of all the glory of God. We will soon realize it is a distinct gathering – of things in heaven, and then things on earth. But we also must understand that the work of God had need of a foundation – a basis, on which all these thoughts and all this work are to be accomplished. This is Christ Himself. As we continue on in this study we should realize that God has finished a sovereign work through Jesus Christ, the Son of Man. By this work God has identified Himself with man, and more specifically, the believer.

What the Spirit reveals from God's word must be the believer's delight to know and understand. God certainly reveals His truth for this purpose – the saints' understanding. And we should always find that what is revealed carries with it a sanctifying influence for our walk, for it more fully reveals the character of God.

So come along with me into this study of the counsels of God. We will look at some principles and truths from God's Word that, I believe, are birthed by the Spirit of God. These principles, if understood, can give clarity and enlightenment to the whole of scripture. If you are a believer, God desires you to understand His Word. As a son in the household of the Father (Gal. 4:5-7, Rom. 8:14-17, I Cor. 2:7), He has privileged you with the Spirit of adoption. The Holy Spirit is also the Comforter, that leads us into all truth, and who reveals the hidden wisdom to us which God has ordained for our glory! I believe the eyes of our understanding will be enlightened, if we will simply seek the thoughts of God. "Now we have received...the Spirit who is from God, *that we might know the things* that have been freely given to us by God." (I Cor. 2:12).

Chapter 2:

Messiah, Promise to Israel

W e should be able to make certain connections and distinctions concerning the general overall principles and purposes of God found in scripture. In God's counsels, what I share next becomes a very important understanding. *Jesus Christ, in the title and role of Messiah, was always a specific promise in Old Testament prophecy to Israel, the physical descendants of Abraham.* As such, Messiah was never a promise to the Gentile nations, and they were never instructed to specifically look for Him. I believe we will find, if we search and know the scriptures, and allow the Spirit of God to show us, that the title and role of Jesus Christ as Messiah, has little direct application to the Body of Christ, or the individual believer. Messiah speaks to Israel, as do all the Messianic scriptures (that is, if we can agree as to which scriptures are Messianic). There are very distinct promises connected to Messiah -- the throne of David, the Promised Land, setting captives free, declaring the acceptable year of the Lord (Luke 4:17-21), and a kingdom over the twelve tribes of Israel (Is. 9:6-7).

The Counsels of God and the Two Titles of Jesus Christ

The majority of the Word of God, its proper interpretation and understanding, depends on clarifying the distinctions between the two titles of Jesus Christ - that of "Messiah" and that of "Son of Man." I believe this to be the most important understanding concerning the counsels of God, and I want you to be able to see how God's Word makes these distinctions clear and obvious. This is a time in which the proverb, "can't see the forest, for the trees," will come into play. In studying the statements of Scripture, the believer has to be able to truly step back and see the bigger picture God is bringing out that the details are hinting at, or describing, or even obscuring. This is one of those times, and I am really hoping you will clearly see the 'forest' with me. When we examine these two titles and roles, as we will do extensively in this book, we want to particularly pay attention to their *nature and character.*

Now I'm sure some skepticism is already starting. I've made a somewhat grand statement that these two distinct titles of Christ lead to an understanding of a majority of scripture. But consider this -- in eternity past, before the foundations of the world, God had a purpose and a plan already, and the grand emphasis of this plan is the glory of God. These counsels centered in on the exaltation of Jesus Christ (Eph. 1:9-10). I do not believe many Christians would argue this point. But again allow me to point out some scriptural support. Adam, in the beginning in paradise, is a type of the second Adam, who is Jesus Christ, the Son of Man (Rom. 5:14). Then, when man fell in sin, in God's cursing of the serpent afterward, we see the declaration of the Seed of the woman (who is Jesus Christ) that would eventually come and crush the power of the serpent (Gen. 3:15). Also, when God confirmed the covenant of promise to Abraham, it was confirmed in his one Seed, who is Christ (Gal. 3:16-18, Gen. 22:18). So it is easy to see in God's word, that His counsel and plan from the foundation of the world, *centered on Christ.* This can be clearly traced through the scriptures.

Ephesians 1:9-10

"...having made known to us the mystery of His will, according to His good pleasure which He purposed in Himself, that in the dispensation of the fullness of the times He might gather together in one all things in Christ, both which are in heaven and which are on earth—in Him."

The two titles of Jesus Christ, "Messiah" and "the Son of Man", are very distinct in how scripture makes use of them. And the promises of God associated with both titles are also very distinct, as are the people to whom these promises are made. *These two titles, found uniquely in God's counsels, show forth all the working of God for the accomplishing of His eternal purpose and glory; that purpose being, the gathering together of all things, both in heaven and earth – in Christ (Eph. 1:9-10).*

Jesus Christ and the Title of Messiah to Israel

First let us consider Christ as Messiah --this is always related to a specific people, the descendants of Abraham after the flesh, the Jews. Messiah was to come to Israel, and the Jews had, and still have, this expectation. And there were, and still are, promises associated with this expected coming. These physical promises concern the restoration of Israel, the Promised Land, and the throne of David. There will be a son of David, after the flesh, reigning forever out of Zion's hill in Jerusalem over the twelve tribes of Israel.

Psalm 132:10-18

"For Your servant David's sake,
*   do not turn away the face of Your Anointed.*
The LORD has sworn in truth to David;
*   He will not turn from it:*

For the LORD has chosen Zion;
*   He has desired it for His dwelling place:*

"This is My resting place forever;
*   here I will dwell, for I have desired it.*
I will abundantly bless her provision;

11

I will satisfy her poor with bread.

I will also clothe her priests with salvation,
And her saints shall shout aloud for joy.
There I will make the horn of David grow;
I will prepare a lamp for My Anointed.
His enemies I will clothe with shame,
but upon Himself His crown shall flourish."

Also in Psalm 89:2-4,

"For I said, Loving-kindness shall be built up forever; in the very heavens wilt thou establish thy faithfulness.

I have made a covenant with mine elect, I have sworn unto David my servant:

Thy seed will I establish forever, and build up thy throne from generation to generation."

And in Psalm 2:2, 6,

"The kings of the earth set themselves, and the princes plot together, against Jehovah and against his anointed.... And I have anointed my king upon Zion, the hill of my holiness."

The First Presentation of Messiah to Israel and His Message and Work

I believe that from these verses we should be able to make a few connections. Messiah is the Anointed One, and also, is associated with Jehovah choosing Zion as a dwelling place for ever. I see in the title "Messiah" a connection of the idea, God coming in the flesh or Jehovah among Israel, all of which describes Jesus Christ. He came to the Jews as their Messiah, He came unto His own (*John 1:11*). He presented Himself to Israel as their Messiah, and we find this presentation clearly in Luke's gospel. And further, there is a distinct message (gospel) and work associated with the coming and mission of Messiah, quoted by Jesus from the book of Isaiah,

Luke 4:18-21

> *"The Spirit of the LORD is upon Me,*
> *Because He has anointed Me*
> *To preach the gospel to the poor;*
> *He has sent Me to heal the brokenhearted,*
> *To proclaim liberty to the captives*
> *And recovery of sight to the blind,*
> *To set at liberty those who are oppressed;*
> *To proclaim the acceptable year of the LORD."*

Then He closed the book, and gave it back to the attendant and sat down. And the eyes of all who were in the synagogue were fixed on Him. And He began to say to them, "Today this Scripture is fulfilled in your hearing."

At this presentation of Messiah, the people in His hometown became enraged. They forced Him out of the synagogue and to the edge of a cliff to throw Him down to His death. Why? He was claiming to be Israel's long awaited Messiah, now come in the flesh. He took the book of Isaiah and found a passage referencing the Anointed One, declared to them its fulfillment in their hearing by His presence. Every Jew would have clearly known to whom this passage was referring. However, it is disappointing that many in the Body of Christ don't know the same. The passage from Isaiah not only speaks of the Anointed One, but also the ministry Messiah would have in Israel. It is the fulfillment of promises and prophecies centered on the Messiah. Also in Luke the Lord says;

Luke 4:43

"...but He said to them, "I must preach the kingdom of God to the other cities also, because for this purpose I have been sent."

Luke 9:1-2, 6

"Then He called His twelve disciples together and gave them power and authority over all demons, and to cure diseases. He sent them to preach the kingdom of God and to heal the sick.

So they departed and went through the towns, preaching the gospel and healing everywhere."

It says,"...preaching the gospel..." This *gospel* that was preached by Christ and His disciples at first, was one of promises of physical blessing, physical healing, and physical restoration to Israel, *and Israel alone (Luke 4:43, Matt. 10:5-8, Luke 9:1-2).* The gospel preached in *Luke 9:6 and Luke 9:11* is the gospel of Messiah, *and did not contain thoughts or references to suffering, crucifixion, death and resurrection.* When He delivered those in Israel from demon possession, He was proclaiming liberty to the captives, and doing so in a literal and physical way. The feeding of the five thousand is a partial fulfillment of *Ps. 132:15,* the physical blessing of the Messiah to Israel.

From the outset of this study, I want to re-emphasize to the reader the importance of clearly seeing and understanding these distinctions and differences made by the scriptures. The two titles of Jesus Christ are distinct – I write to prove this argument from the scriptures to you. The gospels – the messages – attached to each title are quite distinct and different from each other. The gospel of Messiah is one of promises and blessings to Israel, in the flesh, and on the earth. We will see how different the gospel associated with the Son of Man is as we move along through the book.

The Kingdom of God and the Kingdom of Heaven

Also notice that Jesus said He must preach the kingdom of God, as well as sending the disciples forth to do the same. The kingdom of God was at that time present. The kingdom of God was among them because Emmanuel was there, as their Messiah. We may see this clearly also in Luke;

Luke 11:20

"But if I cast out demons with the finger of God, surely the kingdom of God has come upon you."

God was present working among them (John 5:17-20) and therefore the kingdom of God was also, and so, it was preached as the gospel of Messiah to Israel. He sent His disciples early in His ministry from town to town, saying to them, go only to the house of Israel, and they returned rejoicing that even unclean spirits were subject to them in His name.

There is a distinction made in scripture between the kingdom of God and the kingdom of heaven. As we have seen already, the kingdom of God is present anywhere God is present. However, when Jesus and John the Baptist spoke of the kingdom of heaven, it was always not yet, but at hand. We will discover, as we go further on in our study that the kingdom of heaven could only exist after the Son of Man went away to heaven. This kingdom is so named because the King of this kingdom, the Son of Man, is away in heaven. The kingdom of heaven is related to the Son of Man title. The kingdom of God is a broad and general term, and speaks of the direct working of God. We see these points clearly made again in Matthew.

Matt. 10:1, 5-8

"And when He had called His twelve disciples to Him, He gave them power over unclean spirits, to cast them out, and to heal all kinds of sickness and all kinds of disease…. These twelve Jesus sent out and commanded them, saying: "Do not go into the way of the Gentiles, and do not enter a city of the Samaritans. But go rather to the lost sheep of the house of Israel. And as you go, preach, saying, 'The kingdom of heaven is at hand.' Heal the sick, cleanse the lepers, raise the dead, cast out demons. Freely you have received, freely give."

It is physical blessing all the way here, it would be hard not to see that. And then in Acts, the disciples ask at that time for the restoration of Messiah's kingdom in Israel;

Acts 1:6

"When they had come together, they asked Him, saying, "Lord, will You at this time restore the kingdom to Israel?"

This was a kingdom described to them, as well as to all the Jews in Isaiah -- Messiah's kingdom.

Isaiah 9:6-7

"For unto us a Child is born,
Unto us a Son is given;
And the government will be upon His shoulder.
And His name will be called
Wonderful, Counselor, Mighty God,
Everlasting Father, Prince of Peace.
Of the increase of His government and peace
There will be no end,
Upon the throne of David and over His kingdom,
To order it and establish it with judgment and justice
From that time forward, even forever.
The zeal of the LORD of hosts will perform this."

Jesus clearly was the Messiah come to the house of Israel, come unto His own. And the gospel of Messiah was that which He and His disciples preached. He did many signs and wonders among them, fulfilling at least partially the promises associated with Messiah concerning physical blessing and restoration. He was of the lineage of David, the son of David according to the flesh, and called as such by many at that time.

Messiah's Mission to the House of Israel Only

But now, let us look at a passage of scripture in Matthew that makes very little sense, or may even be offensive, without having an understanding of Messiah's mission.

Matt. 15:21-28

"Then Jesus went out from there and departed to the region of Tyre and Sidon. And behold, a woman of Canaan came from that region and cried out to Him, saying, "Have mercy on me, O Lord, Son of David! My daughter is severely demon-possessed."

But He answered her not a word.

And His disciples came and urged Him, saying, "Send her away, for she cries out after us."

But He answered and said, "I was not sent except to the lost sheep of the house of Israel."

Then she came and worshiped Him, saying, "Lord, help me!"

But He answered and said, "It is not good to take the children's bread and throw it to the little dogs."

And she said, "Yes, Lord, yet even the little dogs eat the crumbs which fall from their masters' table."

Then Jesus answered and said to her, "O woman, great is your faith! Let it be to you as you desire." And her daughter was healed from that very hour."

In verses 21-24 you have the "big picture" concerning the title and mission of Messiah. He is referenced as Lord, Son of David (v. 22). Then Jesus speaks of the scope of His mission as Messiah, or better yet, He speaks of the limits of His mission -- *"I was not sent except to the lost sheep of the house of Israel."* This is fairly emphatic; as the Messiah, He was sent by God to Israel only. And in verses 25-26, He says, *"It is not right to take the children's bread and throw it to the dogs."* Are you uneasy with the Lord's statements here? This may seem somewhat rude and heartless. He says, "It is not right..." What we need is an understanding of the Messiah title and mission in relation to the counsels of God. Jesus is saying this would not be proper or appropriate concerning the reasons and limitations of His mission as Messiah. He says,"...the children's bread..." The Jews are always the children of God according to the flesh, descendants of Abraham after the flesh.

Israel, as a nation, always has a wall of partition up around them; this was placed there by God Himself, separating them from the Gentiles. Their law, rites, and ordinances kept this partition in place. There is an obvious separation from this woman having to do with her being a Gentile – this separation was always part of the Jewish law. Messiah and His mission are related to the Law of Moses, and you see part of this association here. There was still this wall of separation present (vs.24-26). The "bread" is the promise of physical healing and deliverance to the physical descendants of Israel -- the children -- given by Messiah. He says,"...throw it to the dogs," further identifying the existence of this wall of partition between Jews and Gentiles -- the Gentiles being the dogs. When understanding comes concerning this portion of scripture, it is quite enlightening.

Prophecy and the Two Presentations of Messiah

Here are some further connections of Christ and His title of Messiah, as to the Jews only. In Malachi there is the promise of Elijah being sent before the great and awesome day of the Lord.

Malachi 4:1-5

"For behold, the day is coming,
Burning like an oven,
And all the proud, yes, all who do wickedly will be stubble.
And the day which is coming shall burn them up,"
Says the Lord of hosts,
"That will leave them neither root nor branch.
But to you who fear My name
The Sun of Righteousness shall arise
With healing in His wings;
And you shall go out
And grow fat like stall-fed calves.
You shall trample the wicked,
For they shall be ashes under the soles of your feet
On the day that I do this,"
Says the Lord of hosts.

"Remember the Law of Moses, My servant,
Which I commanded him in Horeb for all Israel,
With the statutes and judgments.
Behold, I will send you Elijah the prophet
Before the coming of the great and dreadful day of the Lord."

We know that for the Antichrist, the beast, the ten kings, and all the armies at Armageddon, it will be judgment (*Mal. 4:1*). But for the Jewish remnant in the end (*Rev. 7:1-8, Rev. 14:1-5, Rom. 9:27-29, Rom. 11:25-29, Mal. 4:2*) it will be their Messiah come from Zion, their Deliverer *(Rom. 11:26, 27, Rev. 14:1)*. However before His return in the end, there will be two witnesses in Jerusalem for a period of 3 ½ years during the coming tribulation *(Rev.11:1-12)*. One of the two witnesses comes in the power of Elijah. This is the actual fulfillment of this prophecy from Malachi. One will stand witnessing in Elijah's character and ministry (I don't feel it is coincidence that Moses is mentioned by Malachi as well), preceding what we know to be the second coming of Messiah to Israel. But there was a partial fulfillment of this same prophetic passage at the first coming of Messiah, which was preceded by the appearance of John the Baptist, heralding the coming of the Lord. So Malachi promises Elijah coming, and the revelation of scripture stops -- then the next thing is John the Baptist on the scene, who, if you will, is Elijah come *(Matt. 11:13-14)*, preparing the way of Messiah to Israel.

In keeping things straight, we have a partial fulfillment of the Malachi prophecy concerning Elijah coming before the great and terrible day of the Lord, and a partial fulfillment of Messiah coming to Israel; all this in John the Baptist and Jesus Christ, at first. This was not the real entire fulfillment of the Malachi prophecy, nor did Messiah take the throne of David and reign. Only in the end, in the last days, will this prophecy completely be fulfilled. So we have the prophecy given by Malachi, then years later a prefiguring partial fulfillment, and in the end, there will be the full development of the prophecy.

Another important point to be made is the two comings of Messiah are quite different in character. The first was in grace and humility, at a time when Israel was being tested; the second will be in righteous judgment and sovereign power when Israel will be saved and established. This is an important understanding about the title of Messiah in the counsels of God. Messiah will have two different presentations to Israel. The first one has already past. The second one is in the future.

The Physical Blessings of Messiah to Israel

In Matthew we have another interaction between John and Jesus that emphasizes both the title and work of Messiah.

Matt. 11:2-5

"And when John had heard in prison about the works of Christ, he sent two of his disciples and said to Him, "Are You the Coming One, or do we look for another?"

Jesus answered and said to them, "Go and tell John the things which you hear and see: The blind see and the lame walk; the lepers are cleansed and the deaf hear; the dead are raised up and the poor have the gospel preached to them."

The Messiah was the Coming One; coming to Israel. The works of this One were physical healings, deliverances, and feeding the poor. The gospel preached to the poor was not crucifixion and death of Messiah, but one of Messiah blessing the poor and restoring. In Matt. 9:27 the two blind men followed Him, crying out, "Son of David, have mercy on us!" This is another reference to Christ as Messiah, as every Israelite would understand. He heals them of their blindness, but forbids them to tell anyone; again foreseeing His rejection as Messiah by the nation. Another portion of scripture in Matthew emphasizes the same or similar things;

Matt. 12:15-23

"But when Jesus knew it, He withdrew from there. And great multitudes followed Him, and He healed them all. Yet He warned them not to make Him known, that it might be fulfilled which was spoken by Isaiah the prophet, saying:

"Behold! My Servant whom I have chosen,
My Beloved in whom My soul is well pleased!
I will put My Spirit upon Him,
And He will declare justice to the Gentiles.
He will not quarrel nor cry out,
Nor will anyone hear His voice in the streets.

A bruised reed He will not break,
And smoking flax He will not quench,
Till He sends forth justice to victory;
And in His name Gentiles will trust."

Then one was brought to Him who was demon-possessed, blind and mute; and He healed him, so that the blind and mute man both spoke and saw. And all the multitudes were amazed and said, "Could this be the Son of David?"

Jesus heals the multitudes, but warns them not to speak of Him as Messiah. The prophecy from Isaiah 42:1-4 (Matt. 12:18-21) is mostly Messianic in character. When God is saying, My Servant whom I have chosen, and I will put My Spirit upon Him, He is identifying the Messiah. However, when God speaks of His Beloved, He is referring to the Son of God (Matt. 3:17, John 1:18).

The Son of God – not a Title Taken Up by Christ

Jesus is the Son of God, always has been, and always will be. This is who He is. Messiah however, is a title He takes up in the working out and fulfilling of the counsels of God. When He takes up the Messianic title it is as the Son of God. This is because He never stops being the Son of God. But it is the Messianic title alone that is associated with the counsels of God in this passage, not the fact that He is the Beloved Son. When we speak later in the book of Jesus setting aside the Messiah title and turning to the Son of Man title and role, He does so as the Son of God as well. The two titles, whether taken up or set aside by God, have their meaning and involvement in God's counsels. In His counsels there is a particular work of God associated with each title. Also there is a distinct message or gospel linked to each title, as well as a distinct future kingdom to each of varying scope and influence. But Jesus is the Son of God. This is His divinity. Therefore, Jesus as the Beloved Son is not the working out of the counsels of God.

This prophecy is much like the one we considered from Malachi; it has a partial fulfilling presently with Christ, but a final and complete fulfillment in the end at Messiah's return. That is how the Gentiles are involved with Messiah, in the end, for some of the Gentile nations are spared in the separating judgment of the sheep and the goats (Matt. 25:31-32). The prophecy, in part, points to the end, for that is the only time Messiah sends forth justice to victory (it certainly wasn't a consequence of His first coming), and the Gentiles will be gathered to a restored Israel in blessing. In v. 22 He delivers another captive of Israel by healing the blind and mute, and in v. 23 they marvel, "Could this be the Son of David?"

Messiah's Connection with the Physical Earth

There are two very important connections that are to be made from all the above material concerning the title of Messiah that I am hoping we all will see and clearly understand. First, it is that Messiah strictly connects with Israel, the physical seed of Abraham; and second, that Messiah strictly connects with this physical earth, in physical blessing, physical restoration, physical land, physical descendants of Abraham, and the throne of David on which the physical Seed of David will sit. It is all Israel and the earth when we know the nature and character of the title of Messiah in God's counsels, and for that matter, the nature and character of prophecy.

But the Messiah was not received in His first coming. He was persecuted and hated by the leaders and elders of Israel. They gnashed their teeth at Him and conspired to put Him to death. The people in general were dull of hearing, hard of heart, and blind to any insight into whom He really was. Instead of a Deliver come out of Zion at this time, God laid a stone of stumbling, and a rock of offense. Jesus was the stone that the builders rejected. But this happened that the word might be fulfilled which is written in their law, 'They hated Me without a cause.' (John 15:22-25). Who has believed the report? To whom has the arm of the Lord been revealed? Israel did not believe in Him (John 12:37).

Chapter 3:

The Rejection of Messiah

*J*esus came to Israel as Messiah, as Jehovah among them, Emmanuel, God in the flesh, and as King of the Jews. All these reference basically the same thing, that Israel's long awaited Messiah had come, heralded by the baptism and ministry of John.

John 1:11

"He came to His own, and His own did not receive Him."

But it is clear from this verse in the first chapter of John's gospel, that when Messiah came, He was not well received. And if not received, we may say that Messiah was rejected by the nation of Israel as a whole. They would not have Him as their King, the King of Israel, the King of the Jews, but rather instead said, *"We have no King, but Caesar!"* (John 19:15)

And so Messiah was soundly rejected in His first coming, and in Zion, the place associated so much with the Anointed of Jehovah, He became a stone of stumbling, and a rock of offense;

Rom. 9:32-33

"Wherefore? Because it was not on the principle of faith, but as of works. They have stumbled at the stumblingstone, according as it is written, Behold,

I place in Zion a stone of stumbling and rock of offence: and he that believes on him shall not be ashamed."

Jesus Christ as Messiah became a source of stumbling for the nation. They were offended at Him, and would not receive Him. In Matt. 21:42 the Messiah is the "stone that the builders rejected..." Further we see that they would not come to Him;

John 5:39-40

"Ye search the scriptures, for ye think that in them ye have life eternal, and they it is which bear witness concerning me; and ye will not come to me that ye might have life."

Because His own people, the Jews, rejected Him, the nation of Israel suffered certain consequences and judgments from God.

Messiah Rejected – Israel Set Aside and Made Desolate by God

In Matt. 23:37-39, Jesus describes how the rejecting of Messiah, in turn, brought about Israel being rejected by God, and set aside as a nation. Also all the Messianic promises to Israel of physical blessing and restoration would be set aside as well.

"O Jerusalem, Jerusalem, the one who kills the prophets and stones those who are sent to her! How often I wanted to gather your children together, as a hen gathers her chicks under her wings, but you were not willing! See! Your house is left to you desolate; for I say to you, you shall see Me no more till you say, 'Blessed is He who comes in the name of the LORD!'"

The promises associated with Messiah would have to wait. Messiah had been rejected and Israel would be judged and left desolate by God. Jerusalem would be destroyed as well as the temple, and the people scattered into the nations. All things associated with the title of Messiah would be set aside.

In another portion of scripture (John 12:12-50) we may see clearly the rejection of Messiah and the transition to the title, character, and mission of the Son of Man.

John 12:12-15

"The next day a great multitude that had come to the feast, when they heard that Jesus was coming to Jerusalem, took branches of palm trees and went out to meet Him, and cried out:

"Hosanna!
'Blessed is He who comes in the name of the Lord!
The King of Israel!"

Then Jesus, when He had found a young donkey, sat on it; as it is written:

"Fear not, daughter of Zion;
Behold, your King is coming,
Sitting on a donkey's colt."

In this euphoric moment the people gathered in Jerusalem, cried out after Jesus, declaring Him the King of Israel. This is definitely referencing the Messiah of Israel, and we see daughters of Zion associated with the King. But things soon change, and in this same chapter we see...

John 12:23

"But Jesus answered them saying; The hour is come that the Son of man should be glorified."

Here I believe we see something entirely different from the celebratory reception He received. We can see in the Lord's mind a transitioning from the role of Messiah -- His triumphal entry into Jerusalem -- to that of the role and character of the Son of Man. When the Greeks come wanting to see Him (v. 20), He knows it would be the distinct mission of the Son of Man that would be God reaching out to the Gentiles. The thought of Gentiles and the Son of Man would be under the scope of the kingdom of heaven, which was at hand, but not yet present. Messiah is a promise to the Jews and Jesus knows that any fulfillment of these promises is now not possible. It was in the idea of fulfilling all righteousness that God had to present Messiah to Israel because of the promises to the patriarchs. This had to be done first, in the counsels of God, to the physical seed of Abraham, before God sets the title of Messiah and the promises aside. God then turns to do an entirely different and distinct work among the Gentiles.

The Testing of Israel – God Looking for Fruit

The history of Israel as a nation is for the most part, a story of failure. From the time Israel stood before Jehovah at Mt. Sinai to the coming of Messiah, the pages of Old Testament scripture tell of their rebellion and sin (Ez. 20:1-44). This did not change with the coming of Messiah to them. As a people they were being given one final exam, but all that resulted was failure. In a remarkable way, Jesus tells this story of the history of Israél, in a parable in Matthew.

Matt. 21:33-41

"Hear another parable: There was a householder who planted a vineyard, and made a fence round it, and dug a winepress in it, and built a tower, and let it out to husbandmen, and left the country. But when the time of fruit drew near, he sent his bondmen to the husbandmen to receive his fruits. And the husbandmen took his bondmen, and beat one, killed another, and stoned another. Again he sent other bondmen more than the first, and they did to them in like manner. And at last he sent to them his son, saying, They will have respect for my son. But the husbandmen, seeing the son, said among themselves, This is the heir; come, let us kill him and possess his inheritance. And they took him, and cast him forth out of the vineyard, and killed him.

When therefore the lord of the vineyard comes, what shall he do to those husbandmen?

They say to him, He will miserably destroy those evil men, and let out the vineyard to other husbandmen, who shall render him the fruits in their seasons."

Whenever God is looking for fruit in the scriptures, it is the measuring of responsibility in man. God had done much for Israel in setting them up, choosing them for Himself, separating them from all other nations and building up a wall around them in the world -- Israel was blessed of God and had every advantage God could give man in the flesh, as in the first Adam. With all this blessing comes responsibility and God comes looking for fruit in the vineyard He planted (Isaiah 5:1-7). Earlier in this same chapter, it is the same principle (Matt. 21:18-19). Jesus comes to the fig tree looking for fruit, and finding none, curses the tree saying, "Let no fruit grow on you ever again." The fig tree is a type of man in the flesh, but more specifically the nation of Israel. All that the Lord found was leaves, the outward adorning of the flesh by the religion of the Jews. They had borne no fruit and they were judged and cursed as a nation for their failure in responsibility.

God sent many prophets to Israel, and they were beaten and abused. God then sends more, and the same happens to them. Finally, at the end of the testing of Israel, God sends His Son, saying; 'They will respect my son.' Messiah, the Son of David, is rejected (the stone that the builders rejected – v. 42). This represents the end and finality for Israel as far as responsibility. It is over, it is finished. God is done looking any longer for fruit from Israel. And what do the scriptures say upon the rejection of the son? "Therefore, when the owner of the vineyard comes, what will he do to those vinedressers?" Israel as a nation is judged in consequence of their failures, Jerusalem is destroyed, and they are left in desolation. "And he that falls on this stone shall be broken, but on whomsoever it shall fall, it shall grind him to powder." This statement is all judgment. As for Israel, and for that matter, all of mankind, it was proven that man in Adam could not produce fruit. Israel was given every advantage, given the law and the oracles of God (Rom. 3:1-2), and yet they were only found disobedient. The works of man in the flesh did not produce fruit unto God, but rather is reserved only for judgment and condemnation.

Israel Restored in the End

It is not that God cannot restore Israel. This He will certainly do in the end, for God is ever faithful to all His promises. This same Messiah, Jesus Christ, will come to Israel again, a second time, the true son of David. He will be their Deliver out of Zion, to remove all their transgressions and sins (Rom. 11:26-27). He will defeat all their enemies. He will sit on the throne of David, forever reigning over the twelve tribes of Israel restored and prospering in the Promised Land. These are God's promises to Israel attested to by the prophets of old. And they will surely all come to pass, for God remains faithful and true, even in the midst of abject unfaithfulness in man (Rom. 3:1-4).

But simply said, this will all happen in the end, based on an entirely different principle. It will not be the principle of responsibility in Israel, but rather the principle of sovereign grace in the faithfulness of God. I will not go into the details of this now. Suffice it to say in the end, and surely not until then, God fulfills every promise and word to Israel. He does so strictly by His own infinite power and integrity. This future fulfillment by God has absolutely no dependence on anything Israel has ever done in responsibility.

But the parable (Matt. 21:33-41) tells the story of the history of Israel in its failure in responsibility, as does the cursed fig tree that had no fruit. Messiah was not received, but rejected, and that is clear also from the testimony of scripture in John;

John 12:37-40

"But although He had done so many signs before them, they did not believe in Him, that the word of Isaiah the prophet might be fulfilled, which he spoke:

"Lord, who has believed our report?
And to whom has the arm of the Lord been revealed?"

Therefore they could not believe, because Isaiah said again:

"He has blinded their eyes and hardened their hearts,
Lest they should see with their eyes,
Lest they should understand with their hearts and turn,
So that I should heal them."

Jesus Christ was born under the law (Gal. 4:4) and was known according to the flesh as the Messiah (Rom.9:4-5, II Cor. 5:16). But Paul clearly states, "Even though we once regarded Christ according to the flesh, we regard Him thus no longer." Judaism had proper glory as a religion in the flesh, for the presence of God was behind the veil in the tabernacle, and the Christ came to Israel in the flesh as a Jew. It could have been the crowning success of man in the flesh, but rather, in man, that is, in the flesh, there was no good thing to be found. However, Christians regard Him no longer as Messiah who came to His own, that is, to the Jews. We (believers, of Jew and Gentile both, Eph. 2:14), only regard Him now as, the Son of Man glorified, exalted to the right hand of God. As we said, as for Messiah, Christ came unto His own, but His own people did not receive Him (John 1:11).

John 19:19

"Now Pilate wrote a title and put it on the cross. And the writing was:

"JESUS OF NAZARETH, THE KING OF THE JEWS."

With Messiah fully rejected, and Israel destined to be set aside as a nation in judgment and desolation, Jesus says in John 12:23, "The hour has come that the Son of Man should be glorified. " And therefore, it is to the title of the Son of Man, and the character and work associated with it, we must now give our attention to, in the counsels of God.

Chapter 4:

The Son of Man

The references to the Son of Man title in the Scriptures include these: Seed of the Woman, Seed of Abraham, Second Adam, the Last Adam, the one Man of Rom. 5, the second Man and the heavenly Man of I Cor. 15. This title for Jesus Christ stands distinctly separate from the title of Messiah; therefore, the promises associated with both are equally distinct and separate. And yes, the groups these promises are made to are distinct from each other as well.

Adam, in the beginning in paradise, is a type of the second Adam, who is Jesus Christ, the Son of Man (Rom. 5:14). Then, when man fell in sin, in God's cursing of the serpent afterward, we see the declaration of the Seed of the woman (who is Jesus Christ, the Son of Man from heaven) that would eventually come and crush the power of the serpent. Also, when God confirmed the covenant of promise to Abraham, it was confirmed in his one Seed, who is Christ (Gal. 3:16-18). All this, we will see, points to Christ as the Son of Man, in that title and character. It all predates the existence of Israel and any thought of David or a Messiah from his lineage. It is easy to see that God's counsels and purposes, from the foundation of the world, have their greatest scope and range in Christ, the Son of Man come down from heaven (John 3:13). This can be clearly traced through the scriptures.

The Gospel of the Son of Man

There is also a distinct gospel associated with the mission and work of the Son of Man. We saw previously that Messiah came to Israel with a gospel of healing the masses of the Jews, feeding the thousands, and delivering their oppressed out of Satan's hands. It was a gospel geared to man in the flesh, with many physical blessings, punctuated with miracles, signs and wonders. The gospel of Messiah (Luke 4:18-21) was the preaching of the fulfillment of promises and prophecy; those promises associated with His coming to Israel. But the gospel of the Son of Man is quite different from this;

1 Cor. 15:1-4:

"Moreover, brethren, I declare to you the gospel which I preached to you, which also you received and in which you stand, by which also you are saved, if you hold fast that word which I preached to you—unless you believed in vain.

For I delivered to you first of all that which I also received: that Christ died for our sins according to the Scriptures, and that He was buried, and that He rose again the third day according to the Scriptures,"

This passage easily identifies what is contained in the gospel of the Son of Man, as this whole chapter (1 Cor. 15) is about the Son of Man, the last Adam and the work associated with Him. It is the one gospel preached during the age of grace by which a man may be saved. It is in this gospel, uniquely identified with Paul's mission and ministry, and of which he was not ashamed, that the righteousness of God was contained (Rom. 1:16-17). And of great importance to note, concerning this gospel of the Son of Man, is that it is simply the preaching of Christ crucified (put to death);

1 Cor. 1:22-24

"For Jews request a sign, and Greeks seek after wisdom; but we preach Christ crucified, to the Jews a stumbling block and to the Greeks foolishness, but to those who are called, both Jews and Greeks, Christ the power of God and the wisdom of God."

This gospel of the Son of Man was distinct and different from that of Messiah. This contained suffering, crucifixion, death for our sins and then on to resurrection, ascension, and exaltation. This was not Messiah as come to His own (Israel), but the Son of Man as Savior of the world, glorified to the right hand of the Majesty on high, and as we will eventually see, Redeemer of all creation. The redemptive work of God on man's behalf is the work of the Son of Man, and this is clearly distinguished in the scriptures, so much so, that we constantly see the Lord Himself making this association in the gospels.

Jesus' Own Words Concerning the Work of the Son of Man

Matt. 17:12
"But I say to you that Elijah has come already, and they did not know him but did to him whatever they wished. Likewise the Son of Man is also about to suffer at their hands" (Mark 9:12)

Matt. 17:22
"Now while they were staying in Galilee, Jesus said to them, "The Son of Man is about to be betrayed into the hands of men," (Matt. 26:45, Mark 14:21, Luke 9:44, Luke 22:48)

Matthew 26:2
"You know that after two days is the Passover, and the Son of Man will be delivered up to be crucified."

Mark 10:33
"Behold, we are going up to Jerusalem, and the Son of Man will be betrayed to the chief priests and to the scribes; and they will condemn Him to death and deliver Him to the Gentiles;" (Matt. 20:18, Matt. 20:28)

We can easily see from the above scriptures that Jesus Himself associates betrayal, suffering, crucifixion, and death, with the Son of Man. But He goes further in His testimony as He describes how the Old Testament prophet Jonah is a type prefiguring the redemptive work of the Son of Man, and that after death, on the third day there would be resurrection.

Matthew 12:40
"For as Jonah was three days and three nights in the belly of the great fish, so will the Son of Man be three days and three nights in the heart of the earth." (Matt. 16:4, Luke 11:29-30)

Other times in the gospels the Lord directly references the resurrection of the Son of Man.

Mark 8:31
"And He began to teach them that the Son of Man must suffer many things, and be rejected by the elders and chief priests and scribes, and be killed, and after three days rise again." (Mark 9:31, Luke 9:22, Luke 24:7)

Matthew 17:9
"Now as they came down from the mountain, Jesus commanded them, saying, "Tell the vision to no one until the Son of Man is risen from the dead."

The Son of Man Title in Prophecy

At other times Jesus points out the Biblical truth that there are prophetic scriptures concerning the Son of Man and His suffering. I believe this to be an important understanding, because we shouldn't consider these passages as Messianic prophecies. Many believers and ministers tend to consider any prophetic reference to Christ in the Old Testament as Messianic. In doing so, we fail to distinguish between the two titles, as Christ Himself distinguished between them. Look at what Jesus is saying here;

Luke 18:31

"Then He took the twelve aside and said to them, "Behold, we are going up to Jerusalem, and all things that are written by the prophets concerning the Son of Man will be accomplished."

Mark 14:21

"The Son of Man indeed goes just as it is written of Him, but woe to that man by whom the Son of Man is betrayed! It would have been good for that man if he had never been born."

It is clear from our Lord's own words that the prophets spoke about the Son of Man. Also Jesus is saying that there is a specific work associated with, and to be accomplished by, the Son of Man, as spoken in the prophecies.

The Son of Man title is not the same as Messiah and the work of the Son of Man is not the same as the work of Messiah. If you do not acknowledge this as found in prophecy, you confound certain aspects of the counsels of God in your thinking. If this distinction is not made concerning prophecy, then you make the mistake of thinking that all prophetic reference to Jesus is Messianic. If you do this you make the work of Messiah and that of the Son of Man one and the same. This thinking simply cannot be supported by Scripture, and it is contradicted by the very words of Jesus.

The redemptive work of the Son of Man is certainly a subject found in the writings of the prophets. The Lord Himself has acknowledged this fact here in these verses. Isaiah 53 is prophetic concerning the Son of Man; it is not Messianic and never references the Anointed of Jehovah. Psalm 22 is the Son of Man as well. Psalm 2 is about the Son of God and Messiah, and Psalm 132 is Messianic also. But Psalm 8 is about the Son of Man, and is quoted three separate times by the Spirit of God in Paul's epistles in direct reference to the redemptive work. This work is again spoken of by the Lord;

Matthew 20:28
"…just as the Son of Man did not come to be served, but to serve, and to give His life a ransom for many."

Messiah Stays Forever; the Son of Man Would Go Away

The Lord also speaks of His glorification as the Son of Man while in the presence of His enemies. After His resurrection He would go away to the right hand of God.

Matthew 26:64

"Jesus said to him, "It is as you said. Nevertheless, I say to you, hereafter you will see the Son of Man sitting at the right hand of the Power, and coming on the clouds of heaven."

It is Christ, as the Son of Man, that is now sitting at the right hand of the Power (again, His own words). He sat down there as having finished forever the redemptive work. He is there, now, as the Son of Man glorified. He is not there as Messiah. The Messiah of prophecy, having come to Israel, would remain forever (John 12:34 – this was understood by all the Jews). But the Son of Man, as spoken by Jesus, is always going away (John 8:21). This is an important contrast between the two titles of Christ in the counsels of God, and the carrying out of their distinctive work.

And the Lord, speaking to His enemies at His trial, refers to the Son of Man coming back in judgment to this earth by saying,"...coming on the clouds of heaven." We see in Rev. 1:7, that the Son of Man coming with clouds results in all the tribes of the earth mourning, particularly those who had pierced Him. A kingdom being given to the Son of Man has always been the subject of prophetic scripture (Dan. 7); Jesus specifically references it here in Matthew's gospel;

Matt. 24:30

"And then shall appear the sign of the Son of man in heaven; and then shall all the tribes of the land lament, and they shall see the Son of man coming on the clouds of heaven with power and great glory." (see also Rev. 1:7)

Matt. 25:31

"But when the Son of man comes in his glory, and all the angels with him, then shall he sit down upon his throne of glory,"

There are many other scriptures that speak these same truths and make these same associations that we will eventually look at, especially in Paul's epistles. If there is truth in what I am claiming concerning these principles and associations, and they are the mind of God and His counsels, they will be found in the testimony of the Holy Spirit in the epistles to the church. But here I concentrate on the personal testimony of Jesus Himself. We have His very own words identifying Himself as the Son of Man. And He connects His redemptive work and exaltation to the right hand of God with that character and title. Further examples of these associations are even seen in the parables:

The Son of Man and the Kingdom of Heaven

Matt 13: 36-38,

"Then Jesus sent the multitude away and went into the house. And His disciples came to Him, saying, "Explain to us the parable of the tares of the field." He answered and said to them: "He who sows the good seed is the Son of Man. The field is the world, the good seeds are the sons of the kingdom, but the tares are the sons of the wicked one."

In Jewish thought concerning the coming of Messiah and His kingdom is the expected throwing off and setting aside of Gentile rule and dominion forever. The earthly dominion of Messiah in and with the Jewish people as a consequence of this 'throwing off' of the Gentiles was and is the anticipation of every Israelite rightly held through their belief in the prophetic scriptures. It was into the midst of these beliefs and aspirations Jesus Christ was sent. Yet He and John the Baptist emphatically put forth a unique and different declaration, which was, "the kingdom of heaven was at hand" (Matt. 3:2, 4:17, 10:7, and 13:24-30).

He was and is their Messiah. He came in the midst of a people longing for a Messianic kingdom as they were properly taught to expect by scripture. However a new revelation He gives, involving a mystery, an entirely different kind of kingdom, and all centered on the title and role of the Son of Man (Matt. 13:37). *Please note; the kingdom of heaven is a specific revelation and operation of God distinct to the role of Christ as the Son of Man raised and glorified.* This is of importance for properly understanding the revelation and character of this kingdom and God's counsels concerning it.

One of the obvious characteristics of the parables depicting the kingdom of heaven is a king, landowner, or master of the house having gone away for a period of time. They often concern the events that occur while He is away or the judgments when He returns. For example, ten virgins are waiting for the return of the bridegroom, the parable concerning itself with how they wait (Matt. 25:1-13). Again, the kingdom of heaven is like a man traveling to a far country, and concerns what His servants do in preparation for His return (Matt. 25:14). Then the kingdom, while the Son of Man is away, has this specific experience -- leaven begins to be spread into the three loaves from beginning to end, until it penetrates all (Matt. 13:33). Now all these parables are filled with great insights and spiritual instruction concerning the kingdom, but the specific characteristic of the Son of Man being depicted as "away" is common to them all. My point being, one cannot assign Messianic promises, thoughts of the throne of David, and Israel as twelve tribes restored in the Promised Land to any of Christ's parables depicting the kingdom of heaven. It absolutely does not fit. Any effort to do so requires an intentional twisting and turning of scripture apart from any guidance by the Spirit of God.

It may be important to understand the entire scope of the kingdom of heaven and not to make the mistake in thinking it is simply the church, the body of Christ, on the earth. The understanding of the kingdom revolves around the sovereign work of the Son of Man and His going away for a period of time. But it also includes His return, His judgments, and a millennial reign of the Son of Man over this earth (Matt. 13:41), during which time every enemy is put down, the last one being death in man (1 Cor. 15:24-26). This kingdom also includes the Old Testament saints (Matt. 8:11). Now concerning the body of Christ, the church, it should be clear; the wheat had been separated from the tares, and then removed from the field of the world long before most of these things occur (Matt. 13:30). The parables depicting the kingdom of heaven only show certain aspects and characteristics of it, and often, only certain partial periods of time concerning it. You would have to put them all together to view the entire scope of this kingdom.

The kingdom of heaven is directly related to Jesus as the Son of Man (Matt. 13:37). When this kingdom was spoken of by Jesus or John the

Baptist, it was not yet, but "at hand," (that is, soon, but not present yet – Matt. 4:17). *This kingdom could not come until the redemptive work of the Son of Man was completed and the Son of Man was raised and ascended back to heaven* (John 6:62). It is only through the work of the Son of Man that there are sons of the Kingdom – Matt. 13:38 (these are sons unto the Father – Rom. 8:14-17, Gal. 4:6-7). He is directly responsible for bringing them forth.

It is called the kingdom of heaven because the King has gone away to heaven. The Son of Man is this King, who after the redemptive work and being raised from the dead and glorified, went away to heaven to receive a kingdom. One of the important points not to miss is that the kingdom of heaven is related only to *a raised and glorified Son of Man*. And I reiterate this truth; the glorifying of the Son of Man meant He had to leave, to go away, because, in the counsels of God, this glorification is all the way to the right hand of the Majesty on High. What we discover through the teaching in the remainder of this book is the meaning of all this and the meaning of Jesus' own words here;

Luke 22:69

"Hereafter the Son of Man will sit on the right hand of the power of God."

He is there as the Son of Man now, at this very moment. He is there as a Man. He is there as a glorified Man. He is there as a Man having finished a specific work assigned to Him from God (Matt. 20:28, Luke 18:31, and John 12:27). And He is there as having been on earth and having gone away. All this speaks of the title and role of Jesus as the Son of Man (His divinity remains untouched as the Son of God, regardless of any title or role He takes up). What we will learn and discover is why this "as Man" is so important.

The parable in Matt. 13 depicts certain aspects of the kingdom of heaven as seen from the world's viewpoint, while the King is away in heaven. In a certain physical and spiritual sense He is there hidden from the world (Col. 3:1-3). As I said previously, this definitely doesn't describe Messiah's Kingdom, and these sons are not Israel (at least

THE SON OF MAN

not Israel any longer, Gal. 3:27-28). And all the Jews knew from Moses that when Messiah came He would remain forever, if He was received.

Israel confused about the Son of Man

John 12:34

"The people answered Him, "We have heard from the law that the Christ remains forever; and how can You say, 'The Son of Man must be lifted up'? Who is this Son of Man?"

This certainly doesn't fit the title of Messiah or the makings of the Messianic Kingdom. The Messiah and His coming kingdom over Israel was something understood by every Jew. The Son of Man lifted up and going away, as you can easily see here, is all confusion to them, as it was also to His disciples. That is why Jesus, as the time drew near, constantly spoke to His disciples about the Son of Man suffering many things. But even then they did not understand (Luke 18:31-34). To a great extent, the disciples remained confounded concerning Christ as Messiah and a Messianic Kingdom, even after the resurrection. In Acts 1 we see Jesus, the resurrected Son of Man, about to ascend to the right hand of God (Luke 22:69), and they all are still entertaining thoughts of an immediate kingdom restored to Israel. They held on to these thoughts well past the coming of the Spirit on the day of Pentecost. Not until the calling of Paul and the direct revelations given to him by Christ did these understandings become clear - Eph. 3:3-4). And when His sufferings began, they were shocked, and frightened, and scattered, every man to his own (John 16:32, Matt. 26:31, 56).

John 3:14
"And as Moses lifted up the serpent in the wilderness, even so must the Son of Man be lifted up,"

John 8:28
"Then Jesus said to them, "When you lift up the Son of Man, then you will know that I am He, and that I do nothing of Myself; but as My Father taught Me, I speak these things."

In the gospel of John we find some very unique statements made by Jesus in reference to the Son of Man. In both of the above verses we have the Son of Man being lifted up, which signifies the redemptive work He would do. When this phrase 'lifted up' is used in John 3, it hints at certain spiritual truths in redemption. Moses lifting up the serpent in the wilderness is a type/shadow (I will go into more explanation of types and shadows in the next chapter). The serpent lifted up on the stick is cursed of God; just as Jesus hanging on the tree is cursed in the same way, that being, by God.

The Son of Man Identified with Suffering and Death – the Redemptive Work

Before going to the Types and Shadows chapter, I want to list a few other gospel scriptures where Jesus' own words make the Son of Man title prominent.

Matthew 12:8
"For the Son of Man is Lord even of the Sabbath."

Matthew 18:11
"For the Son of Man has come to save that which was lost."

Matthew 26:45
"Then He came to His disciples and said to them, "Are you still sleeping and resting? Behold, the hour is at hand, and the Son of Man is being betrayed into the hands of sinners."

Mark 9:12
"Then He answered and told them, "Indeed, Elijah is coming first and restores all things. And how is it written concerning the Son of Man, that He must suffer many things and be treated with contempt?"

Mark 9:31
"For He taught His disciples and said to them, "The Son of Man is being betrayed into the hands of men, and they will kill Him. And after He is killed, He will rise the third day."

Luke 9:44
"Let these words sink down into your ears, for the Son of Man is about to be betrayed into the hands of men."

Luke 22:48
"But Jesus said to him, "Judas, are you betraying the Son of Man with a kiss?"

I mentioned previously that John's gospel contained some unique references by the Lord concerning the Son of Man. Here is one that I believe stands out;

John 1:51

"And He said to him, "Most assuredly, I say to you, hereafter you shall see heaven open, and the angels of God ascending and descending upon the Son of Man."

Here the Son of Man is the fulfillment of an Old Testament type/ shadow known as Jacob's ladder. Jesus, in the role of the Son of Man, would become the bridge or ladder of blessing between God and man. Again, it is the redemptive work alone that would bring blessing and grace from God to man and provide the means and nature for man to have a relationship with God. This is what John 3:1-18 is about – an entirely new nature by which a man may have a relationship with God and be able to see and have entrance into the kingdom of God. And from where did these truths come and who brought this heavenly knowledge about this new creation to man? None other than the Son of Man who is in heaven:

The Son of Man and Heavenly Things

John 3:11-13

"Most assuredly, I say to you, We speak what We know and testify what We have seen, and you do not receive Our witness. If I have told you earthly things and you do not believe, how will you believe if I tell you heavenly things? No one has ascended to heaven but He who came down from heaven, that is, the Son of Man who is in heaven."

The Son of Man, as in heaven, could alone have this heavenly knowledge to bring testimony of it to man. He witnesses concerning what He knows and what He has seen, as being the Son of Man there in heaven. This is truly heavenly knowledge and only He who came down from heaven has it to give. Then in the very next verse, John 3:14, He directly links this new nature with the redemptive work of the Son of Man.

There is a deeper understanding to be found here in Jesus' conversation with this man of the Pharisees, named Nicodemus (John 3:1). He, being a ruler of the Jews, should have been able to understand certain things Jesus was willing to speak to him about. He does not receive the earthly things which Jesus shares with him. These things are all Messianic and earthly in nature and calling, promises to Israel concerning the earthly portion of the kingdom of God He is referencing. The heavenly things are about the heavenly portion of the kingdom of God; this is the kingdom of heaven, and the Son of Man come down from heaven who alone could reveal this particular heavenly knowledge (John 3:10-15). Both portions of the kingdom of God, the earthly and the heavenly, require a new creation -- an entirely new nature for man, in order to enter. This new nature speaks of the ability to have a proper relationship with God, more so than just mere entrance in. Regardless, Jesus knew Nicodemus could not understand these heavenly things. And it is sad, *for truly the earthly things were all about to be set aside in the counsels of God, for a long period of time.* Only heavenly things are available presently.

The Son of God, the Messiah, and the Son of Man

Allow me to share this little sequence of events found in John's gospel from chapter 11:1 through 12:36. Here we find the testimony of the Father God given as to who Jesus is and all He was. It also is a testimony of the counsels of God concerning Him as sent into the world and as come unto His own (John 1:10-11). It is a testimony given after the Jews had rejected Jesus, rejecting His words (John 8) and rejecting His works (John 9). This testimony serves to condemn the Jews (John 15:22-24) and the world (John 12:28-31), exposing the true state and condition of man. In raising Lazarus from the dead the Father shows that Jesus is the Son of God (John 11:4). During His entry into Jerusalem He is hailed as the King of Israel, son of David, the Messiah (John 12:13-15, Matt. 21:9). But when the Greeks (Gentiles) come wishing to speak to Him (John 12:21-22), then it is all about the Son of Man being lifted up (John 12:32) and glorified.

The Son of Man in Redemption – the Grain of Wheat that Falls to the Ground and Dies

John 12:23-24

"But Jesus answered them, saying, "The hour has come that the Son of Man should be glorified. Most assuredly, I say to you, unless a grain of wheat falls into the ground and dies, it remains alone; but if it dies, it produces much grain."

I add the 24th verse here to show conclusively how Jesus constantly identifies the title of the Son of Man with His death. This is of importance to see and understand. There isn't good reason to associate any other thoughts and work with the title of the Son of Man. He had a humanity that was certainly different than ours born in Adam, for He was born of God by the Holy Spirit in Mary (Luke 1:35). Nevertheless, His humanity, as seen in the title Son of Man, leads to His death. It is His death that is the redemptive work. His death is the source of all redemptive truths and realities for believers.

God is not just doing something fancy and impressive, this Man being born of a virgin. The incarnation is a special birth that provides two indispensable qualities for the accomplishing of redemption. It provides to Jesus a humanity that is for the suffering of death (Heb. 2:9). It also provides the spotless sacrifice that alone could be offered-up to God (Heb. 9:14). This is why He was sent as the Son of Man from heaven – to suffer death. This is why He was made, for a time, a little lower than the angels.

Also there is the thought of His dependence on another and obedience to another that is associated with the title Son of Man.

His obedience is that He came to do the will of God exclusively, and not His own will. This will of God's, specifically concerning the Son of Man, is His death (Heb. 10:5-10). His dependence on God gives Him the strength to carry out His obedience to the will of God, and not His own, sending Him to His death as Man. It is His death that is central to any redemptive reality and blessing in grace. His death is the reason the Son of Man came down from heaven (John 3:13-15). His death is the crucial point in understanding the will of God in sending the Son of Man (John 12:23, 24, and 27).

The Son of Man Title is Inseparably Linked to His Redemptive Death

When the Son of Man is lifted up, it is His death Jesus is speaking of (John 3:14, 8:28, and 12:32-34). The Son of Man three days and three nights in the heart of the earth is Jesus in the grave. The Son of Man is the one delivered up to be crucified (Matt. 26:2), and also the one condemned to death (Mark 10:33). It is the Son of Man who came for this very reason, to give His life a ransom for many (Matt. 20:28). It should be without controversy that the title of Christ as the Son of Man is inseparably linked to His death. His death is central to the work of redemption; the giving of His life is the ransom and His blood is absolutely the only propitiation before the face of God (Rom. 3:24-25). He put away sin by the sacrifice of Himself (Heb. 9:26) and His being offered up is the means of bearing the sins of many (Heb. 9:28). The only two Christian ordinances we have – water baptism and the Lord's supper, both point to His death. God's redemptive work on behalf of man centers on the death of Jesus Christ, and cannot be separated from the title of the Son of Man.

I make this point in a repetitive way for a reason. I want you to fully understand that His death, and His death alone, is the price paid, the ransom met, the propitiation made to God on man's behalf. This alone defines the redemptive work of God, the redemption of man as a sinner, the righteousness of God contained in the gospel, and the love of God shown in the cross. Redemption is all about His death. Some in the church world point to other things when defining redemption and quickly depart from the truth of Scripture. But the believer can clearly see, by the light of the Spirit, that the basis of God's counsels before the foundation of the world was always a Lamb slain. This is what God's thoughts and purposes centered on (Rev. 13:8).

It simply follows then, that anywhere in Scripture, where it speaks of the redemptive work of God, it is speaking of Jesus as the Son of Man. In the epistles, especially in Paul's letters, we have a much greater degree of development of the doctrines of redemption than anywhere in the gospels. Even though the title of Son of Man is only seen indirectly under the different forms I've previously mentioned, it is still the same redemptive work. It is the same death, and the same sacrifice being offered up that Jesus, in the gospels, links to the title of the Son of Man. Other forms are used, but they all point to redemption, and they all point to the role of Jesus as the Son of Man. For example, after reading the Types and Shadows chapter, we should understand that the Seed of Abraham is truly the Son of Man raised from the dead. And again, the Seed of the women from Genesis, that crushes the power of the serpent, is none other than the Son of Man, who through death destroyed him who had the power of death, that is, the devil (Heb. 2:14).

The Glorified Man of Psalm 8

The Son of Man title originates from Psalm 8, where the first Adam can only serve as a type/shadow of the second Adam, the true Son of Man. The Spirit of God through Paul identifies Psalm 8 as speaking of Jesus, who we see crowned with glory and honor, but not all things yet put under Him (Heb. 2:6-9). Also the term is found in Daniel 7, associated with the Ancient of Days, a kingdom that fills the whole earth, and thrones of judgment. In Rev. 1, Jesus is identified as both the Son of Man and the Ancient of Days (Rev. 1:7, 13-17). You should not be concerned that the term 'Son of Man' is not used in the epistles. In Matthew's gospel, the term 'kingdom of heaven' is used thirty-one (31) times. That is the only place you will find it. Yet it remains a term of great significance and revelation, as does the title 'Son of Man.' The two terms are closely related, as we have already seen.

Then in John 13:31-32,

"When therefore he was gone out, Jesus says, Now is the Son of man glorified, and God is glorified in him. If God be glorified in him, God also shall glorify him in himself, and shall glorify him immediately."

This verse may be a little confusing at first, but it is where we are headed in this book – being able to see clearly the Son of Man in the glory. That is where He is right now, in the glory of God. This was the plan and counsels of God before the foundation of the world -- a Man exalted and brought into the glory (Heb. 2:6-9). And for the believer, that is how we see and know Him now. *Stephen, being full of the Holy Spirit, gazed into heaven and saw the glory of God, and Jesus standing at the right hand of God, and said, "Look! I see the heavens opened and the Son of Man..."*

Chapter 5:

Types and Shadows

would like to make my best attempt at explaining the characteristics and nature of types/shadows used as a teaching tool in Scripture. We find their use by the Holy Spirit in the Word of God to be quite extensive, and so, understanding their elements and substance becomes important. We want to avoid confusion and misunderstandings that easily arise when interpretation is required by the teaching instrument's use. And we should always be careful, as Christian believers, concerning this word 'interpretation' and the situations in which we exercise its use.

Only Use Interpretation When Absolutely Necessary

The understanding of the majority of Scripture is simply a matter of translations, and the use of words inspired by God Himself, their definitions and meanings, and how these words are grouped together in the use of language in the human race. In this statement concerning the study of Scripture, I do not use the word 'interpretation.' It is not needed, is not necessary, and its use is improper in view of the majority of Scripture. You hear many who comment when disagreeing, saying, "That is your interpretation and I see things differently" -- in other words, I have a different interpretation than you on this matter. Often it is not a matter of interpretation at all. The use of it is wholly improper in most situations, where definitions and meanings of words used by the Holy Spirit is all that should be in consideration.

Christians tend to become guilty of abusing the idea of a 'personal privilege of interpretation' as some sort of God given right. It isn't. But this perceived privilege is used to justify, sustain and, if you will, exalt the thoughts of man, and that, against the truth of God. At a certain level this abuse is used to tickle one's own ears, so that we can maintain our own personal excuses, justifying the things we do and the situations we involve ourselves in, as believers. At a different level, this abuse is used to sustain the teachings and doctrinal systems of men, and again, that as against the mind, purpose, and counsels of God. It is a sad thing to see and witness. We stubbornly hold to our own ways and to 'self', while resisting the thoughts of God and the Comforter, the Revealer of all truth (*John 16:13*). We have Scripture that speaks directly to this issue of a 'personal privilege of interpretation.'

2 Pet. 1:19-21

"And so we have the prophetic word confirmed, which you do well to heed as a light that shines in a dark place, until the day dawns and the morning star rises in your hearts; knowing this first, that no prophecy of Scripture is of any private interpretation, for prophecy never came by the will of man, but holy men of God spoke as they were moved by the Holy Spirit."

No prophecy of Scripture should be subjected to a 'personal privilege of interpretation'. And this is referring to the entirety of the Word of God. It is inspired and given by the Spirit of God and its meaning subject to the mind and thoughts of God only. Let God speak from His Word. *Pursue only the thoughts of God, the counsels of God, and the principles of God's ways found in the Scriptures.*

An Example of How Personal Privilege is abused

I can think of a similar example in which a perceived rite or privilege becomes an issue among believers and unbelievers alike; our understandings of the free will of man. These limited thoughts concerning this topic are, all so often, vehemently defended as a right and privilege of all men in absolute and without exception. This perceived right is then held up in the face of God, as limiting and restricting Him, under some dubious reasoning of voluntary acquiescence on His part. Think about such reasoning! The infinitely unlimited and all powerful God is voluntarily limiting and restricting Himself as a favor for fallen man! If such be the case, then God is truly sitting back and hoping that things will somehow go according to His counsels and plans. These counsels, supposedly established before the foundations of the world, yet now, as they play out, are subject to the will of the creature and limiting God to observation and mere wishing that all goes well. God had better have plan two or three ready, or for that matter, an infinite number of plans. If the free will of the creature limits and restricts the free will of the Sovereign in any way, then it becomes ridiculous to think that the Sovereign has a set plan for the future, or that the Sovereign had control of the past. If God is not absolutely sovereign, how can He even be God? By the reasoning of our finite minds we then become guilty of creating a god that is not the One True Living God.

If God be God, there can be only one God. God is God because He is absolute and infinite in all His nature, character and attributes. This means there is no room for even the possibility of another god existing. That is the reasoning in scripture, when it says, concerning the gods men create, that they neither speak nor hear, nor can they answer when men call on them. They cannot move, and perhaps they are sleeping. Why? Because it is not possible that they even exist! If God is God, there is no room for another!

False gods exist in the minds of men, created there by man's reasoning and thoughts. To this point let's consider Greek mythology; a system created by the mind of man which contains multiple gods. Neptune, I believe, is the god of the oceans and seas. He has a limited scope of power and influence, does he not? How can he be considered a god if he is restricted and limited? What happens to Neptune when he is on land? This isn't much different than a comic book character with a super power.

Can a Sovereign God Ever be Limited?

We should be able to see the foolishness of such creations of the mind of man. But what about the thoughts we have in our minds of the One True Living God? Are those thoughts the same as God has revealed about Himself in His Word? Are we guilty in our thinking of trying to limit and restrict who God is in any way? If God is infinite and limitless, how can we be justified in placing limits on Him as the Sovereign God? We need to study God and know Him.

My argument on this matter does not stem from my experience of looking at circumstances I find man in, and trying to explain the nature and character of God by what I see. Nor am I viewing the world and the circumstances of life and then going to the Word of God and twisting and turning it to explain things. That can never be a proper way of receiving the knowledge of God. It is a path that will always be froth with error and supposition. Rather I'm starting with the idea of God, and if there is a God, what would God have to be to be God? And I hope the reader can see and understand the difference in that. In the end, I believe, all mankind will be made to see that the One God is absolutely sovereign, and rest assured, any thoughts different will be proven to be only the foolish notions of man. As far as the number of plans God has, there is, and always will be, only one. For greater understanding on this let us look to Scripture.

God's Word is Sovereign

Isaiah 55:11

"So shall My word be that goes forth from My mouth;
It shall not return to Me void,
But it shall accomplish what I please,
And it shall prosper in the thing for which I sent it."

God's Word never returns to Him void. This remains true regardless of all and any of the doings of men. I must add here for understanding, it is true regardless of the decisions and will of men. His sovereign will always will accomplish His good pleasure. God's sovereign will is unrestricted by man and absolutely independent from man's will. It always fulfills absolutely its purposes and intentions.

Look closely at the above verse; these are God's very own words describing the absolute sovereignty of His own Word. God will not have it any other way. His Word simply reflects His own nature and character as Sovereign.

Therefore it isn't hard to imagine or understand that the plans and counsels of God are of the same character. They are sure and unchanging as well, and will always accomplish all His good pleasure, as He is, once again, sovereign in them. If this wasn't a basic truth concerning how God operates and works, chaos would reign, evil would prevail, and God's Word would be worthless. Prophetic Scripture would be undependable, and we would absolutely have no security for the future. *But He is the Lord God, He changes not... in Him there is no variation or shadow of turning...and we can read in Eph.1:11...who works all things according to the counsel of His will...* This verse alone is a great truth concerning the principles of God in His counsels and ways. He works all things? Yes, He works all things. According to the counsel of His will? Yes, according to His will. That's the definition of a sovereign. That is what a Sovereign God does.

The Free Will of Man was Only Exercised in Paradise

I have one parting thought on this subject of 'the free will of man' and the way it is defended as an absolute truth by so many. *What men point to as free will, and their understanding of it, is as Adam was in paradise.* There man's will was free, when he was in innocence, before the fall. And man exercised his free will in paradise while still there. But things changed, did they not? Right away something was wrong because man hid himself in the bushes and trees from the presence of God. Man is no longer in paradise. Man was forcibly driven out of paradise, away from the presence of God, the cherubim guarding the way of life. Sin had entered into the world, and death was on its coattails (Rom. 5:12).

Was man's will unaffected by all these events? God's Word is clear, that after the fall, man's will became a slave to sin (John 8:34). And sin reigned as a master over all men (Rom. 5:21). Now here is the long and short of my argument. If man's will is a slave, then in no way is it 'free.' If man's will is 'free' as many say it is, then in no way is there any slavery associated with it. There is no middle ground for these two, no percentage between them. It is either a slave, or it is free. As for man and his will after the fall, what is the teaching of Scripture? This is where we are so tempted to look at the world around us and the experiences and circumstances of living, and allow these things to define and interpret the Word of God for us. But I ask again, as for man and his will after the fall, what is the teaching of Scripture?

The Proper Use of Biblical Interpretation

Having chased this rabbit a good bit, let us return to our subject and the point from where we departed. I have voiced my thoughts about the abuse of the perceived right of interpretation by many; so let us look at situations where the use of interpretation is necessary and even demanded in Scripture. There are three obvious instances needing proper interpretation – all parables, all types/shadows, and all symbolic prophetic language. Some prophetic language is quite literal, and should be treated in such a way, requiring some spiritual discernment in knowing the difference. In speaking of *types and shadows*, we will always find certain characteristics concerning this particular teaching tool.

The Characteristics of Types and Shadows

The first characteristic common to all types/shadows is the pairing of two things. This is usually either two experiences, two persons or groups, or two objects. These pairings will have *similarities,* but also important *distinctions and differences in contrast.* Other common elements found is that the types/shadows will always be of a lesser value or a lesser reality in contrast to the actual fulfillment, as well as always preceding and prefiguring the fulfillment in time (foreshadowing). Types are shadows, lacking vivid details and forming inexact images. It is the similarities that form the pairings and establish them as teaching tools, but it is usually the distinctions that do all the teaching. Case in point:

Matt. 12:39-40

"He answered and said to them, "An evil and adulterous generation seeks after a sign, and no sign will be given to it except the sign of the prophet Jonah. For as Jonah was three days and three nights in the belly of the great fish, so will the Son of Man be three days and three nights in the heart of the earth."

Here the Lord uses the experience of the prophet Jonah as a type of the coming experience of the Son of Man in redemption. Jonah was certainly a real person with a particular life experience; however, as the type, his experience is of lesser value and he preceded the Son of Man. The similarities are there - three days and three nights hidden. The distinctions are present as well – Jonah didn't die and he wasn't in the belly of the great fish innocently, or on the behalf of others. Still it is easy to see the foreshadowing of Jonah's experience, and why the Lord used it as a sign.

Here is another type/shadow used by Jesus in John 3, which falls along similar lines as this previous example.

John 3:14

"And as Moses lifted up the serpent in the wilderness, even so must the Son of Man be lifted up,"

The serpent lifted up on a staff by Moses is the object in type/ figure, and the Son of Man lifted up on the cross in crucifixion is the fulfillment of the type. The Son of Man on the cross is of far greater value than the serpent in the wilderness. And the serpent predates the Son of Man lifted up as well. What is being taught by the use of the type is interesting. The serpent lifted up on the staff represents God judging and condemning Israel's sin in the wilderness. The greater reality of the fulfillment is the Son of Man on the cross. Jesus was judged and condemned by God there, for He bore our sins upon the tree (Heb. 9:28) and was made sin for us (II Cor. 5:21). It is judgment and condemnation from God being taught in this particular example.

The book of Hebrews is filled with the use of types/shadows. In Hebrews 8, we have a passage of Scripture that not only teaches spiritual truths by the use of types/shadows, but also points out some of the elements that characterize them.

Heb. 8:4-6

"For if He were on earth, He would not be a priest, since there are priests who offer the gifts according to the law; who serve the copy and shadow of the heavenly things, as Moses was divinely instructed when he was about to make the tabernacle. For He said, "See that you make all things according to the pattern shown you on the mountain." But now He has obtained a more excellent ministry, inasmuch as He is also Mediator of a better covenant, which was established on better promises."

The similarities and contrasts between the shadows and the greater realities as fulfillments are important for believers to see and understand. That which is shadow in this example are two things; the earthly priests (or Aaronic priesthood) and the earthly tabernacle (all its different objects, furniture, veil, tent, courtyard, etc.). As shadows, these have the nature of the lesser value and lesser reality. There are actually two more shadows/types found here; Moses, as a mediator, and the covenant of law which he mediated.

Now, all four types presented to us have specific and distinct fulfillments that are future in time to them. The fulfillments always will have the character of being a greater reality with greater value. They have similarities to the prefiguring types, but also important distinctions that teach believers spiritual truths. Here are the pairings:

Types and Fulfillments:	The Similarities and the Distinctions in Contrast
Earthly priests and a Heavenly Priest	Both of these are priesthoods, but the lesser one is earthly, while the other is heavenly and the more excellent ministry
Earthly tabernacle and Heavenly Things (v.5)	Both of these are tabernacles, but the earthly is only a copy, while the heavenly is far greater in value and nature. The earthly tabernacle serves an earthly people, while the heavenly serves a heavenly calling
Moses, as a mediator and the Mediator of verse 6	Both are mediators of covenants, but the Mediator of verse 6 is far greater in glory and accomplishments
Covenant of Law vs. the Better Covenant and Better Promises	Both are covenants of God, but the Law is a shadow of the good things to come (Heb. 10:1); that which replaced it is a Better Covenant established on Better Promises for Israel (Heb. 8:6-13).

We can see that there is a lot going on in these few verses. The idea that the fulfillments are always of greater worth and reality is seen by the use of the words, 'better covenant' which is established on 'better promises', and 'the more excellent ministry'. In Hebrews 9, the thought that the fulfillments are always of greater value and reality is brought home.

Heb. 9:23-24

"Therefore it was necessary that the copies of the things in the heavens should be purified with these, but the heavenly things themselves with better sacrifices than these. For Christ has not entered the holy places made with hands, which are copies of the true, but into heaven itself, now to appear in the presence of God for us."

Better sacrifices were required to purify the true places made without hands in the heavens. And the blood of Christ is a purifying agent of infinite value and worth, of this there can be no doubt.

One last thought concerning types/shadows. Most of the time types should disappear and cease to exist as to their purpose in God's plan once the fulfillment comes about or is a present reality. This isn't true in 100% of the cases. Yet this is an important understanding for many believers to come to because we like to hang on to things; most often they become things that God no longer acknowledges. A case in point; in Colossians 2 we read,

Col. 2:16-19

"So let no one judge you in food or in drink, or regarding a festival or a new moon or Sabbaths, which are a shadow of things to come, but the substance is of Christ. Let no one cheat you of your reward, taking delight in false humility and worship of angels, intruding into those things which he has not seen, vainly puffed up by his fleshly mind, and not holding fast to the Head..."

All these things are types and shadows, and had their fulfillment, their substance, in the coming of Christ. As believers, we should not hang on to them any longer; they are mere shadows passing away. We should hold fast only to the Head, which is Christ. To see clearly on this matter, Paul says by the Spirit of God, just five verses before;

Col. 2:14

"...having wiped out the handwriting of requirements that was against us, which was contrary to us. And He has taken it out of the way, having nailed it to the cross."

The Law of Moses, the Religion of the Jews, is 'Wiped Out'

The only handwriting of requirements that I have ever heard of in a Biblical setting is the Law of Moses, the religion of the Jews, with all its ordinances, observances, requirements, etc. This was unceremoniously nailed to the cross of Jesus Christ as 'wiped out'. This means it is over and finished, and clearly, as he says, "...out of the way..." This should be understood in pertaining to a believer -- his relationship to the law is finished, abolished, and no more.

There has always been a nagging question in my mind as to when and how Gentiles were ever placed into a relationship with the Law of Moses. I see the law given at Sinai to Israel, but I do not see the Gentiles there. I do not see God ever giving it to the Gentiles. I can see how the law kept Israel separated from the Gentiles. God gives the law to Israel, and this is one of His main reasons in doing so – for the Jews to be set apart. The only way Gentiles have any association with the Law of Moses is through the thoughts and reasoning of men. But the Spirit of God speaks further through Paul in this same chapter;

Col. 2:20-22

"Therefore, if you died with Christ from the basic principles of the world, why, as though living in the world, do you subject yourselves to regulations— "Do not touch, do not taste, do not handle," which all concern things which perish with the using—according to the commandments and doctrines of men?"

Here is what we need to see in this passage, and it certainly is eye-opening for believers. Judaism is identified by the Spirit of God as the basic principles of the world. And the further implication is said, "...as though living in the world..." Christians are not to be of the world, as Christ is not of the world (John 17:16); and when the Spirit says, 'as though living in the world', it is a negative assertion being made. Judaism, in any form or appendage, connects the Christian to this earth and makes him a part of this world. How is this so? Israel, as the people of old, and as the physical descendants of Abraham, always was part and parcel of this world. Divided up, this world is made of Jews and Gentiles. Israel, as a people, has a wall of partition raised up around them, separating them from the Gentile nations (Isaiah 5:1-7); yet still very much part of this unbelieving world. God raised up this wall, giving the Law to Israel, with all its rituals, observances, and services. He effectively separated them from all Gentiles (Eph. 2:11-15, Exodus 19:4-5).

Judaism, the Law of Moses – of the World, of the Earth, and of the Flesh

Let's look at more scriptural evidence concerning Judaism as the basic principles of the world. In the book of Galatians, Paul is combating the influence of Judaism on the Christian faith among the Galatian believers. This is obviously the issue when reading Gal. 3;

Gal. 3:2

"This only I want to learn from you: Did you receive the Spirit by the works of the law, or by the hearing of faith?"

The works of the law is Judaism. That was the problem in Galatia, the addition of Judaism to the Christian faith, or more specifically, an addition to Christ. The Spirit of God would not tolerate this, and the whole book is the expression of the mind of the Spirit against this evil. We see the progression of the thought from verse two,

Gal. 3:3

"Are you so foolish? Having begun in the Spirit, are you now being made perfect by the flesh?"

They began well, in the Spirit by faith in Christ. Adding Judaism to Christ would simply be a work of the flesh. In Gal. 3:10, we see that anyone "of the works of the law" will eventually receive judgment and condemnation from God (under the curse). This is exactly in line with what the Spirit of God says in II Cor. 3:7-9. Judaism, written and engraved on stones was a ministration of death and condemnation. So that, in Gal. 4:3, Judaism is the bondage of the elements of the world, and further, in Gal. 4:9, it is the weak and beggarly elements of worldly bondage. In Gal. 4: 24-25, the covenant from Mt. Sinai, which is the Law of Moses, the religion of the Jews, gives birth to bondage, and Jerusalem and her children (the Jews) are the products of this earthly bondage. And finally, in Gal. 5:1, Judaism is the yoke of bondage not to be entangled with. There is more scriptural testimony on this matter, but what we've mentioned already is overwhelming and conclusive. As a believer, do not add any part of Judaism to

Christ. He alone is sufficient, no rather, infinitely more than enough. Faith in Him alone brings life and righteousness (Gal. 3:21-22).

Isaac a Type of the Son of Man raised-up from among the Dead

Before ending this chapter of types/shadows, I want to share with you one more that is intimately connected to the title and work of Christ, the Son of Man. It is found in Hebrews 11;

Heb. 11:17-19

"By faith Abraham, when he was tested, offered up Isaac, and he who had received the promises offered up his only begotten son, of whom it was said, "In Isaac your seed shall be called, concluding that God was able to raise him up, even from the dead, from which he also received him in a figurative sense."

The covenant of Promise was confirmed in a singular Seed (Gal. 3:16). Now in Abraham's time this singular seed was Isaac his son. If you look closely at Rom. 9:6-9, God speaks clearly, "Through Isaac shall your seed be called." And again He says, "...For this is the word of promise: "At this time I will come and Sarah shall have a son," (notice the phrase, 'word of promise').

But I thought the Seed was Christ? Here is where this beautiful type comes in. In Heb. 11:17-19 the writer quotes the same words of God, "...Through Isaac shall your seed be called..." and here shows that Isaac is a type/prefiguring. But there is presented here a special character to this type for us to properly understand. Because Isaac is offered up, he prefigures Christ offered up by the father (Father) who would not spare his (His) son (Son). This isn't all, the prefiguring goes further. Abraham receives Isaac back from the dead, in type, in resurrection (v.19) *and the greater reality fulfilling the type, is God receiving Christ back from the dead, a risen Christ after His sacrifice was accomplished.*

The promise of the blessing of the nations wasn't given to Abraham and his many seeds. It was made to Abram alone (Gen. 12:3), and confirmed by God in his one Seed (Gen. 22:18). Paul, by the Spirit of God, makes this very clear (Gal. 3:16). Further, it is not that there weren't any promises made to Abraham and his many seeds by God, for certainly there were. For example, an important promise made to the many seeds of Abraham (Israel) in Gen. 12:7 and Gen. 13:14-17 concerns a physical piece of land known as the Promised Land. Here we have this promise given directly to his many seeds. Important for our understanding is to note that the many seeds are physical descendants (after the flesh), and the land is a physical piece of this earth. The Jews' future restoration is very much a physical restoration of prosperity and fruitfulness (Jer. 30:18 – 31:14, Jer. 33:6-14, Joel 2:21-27, Joel 3:17-18). These many seeds after the flesh and the many promises, all physical in character, are associated with Christ as Messiah to Israel, who will be, in the end, the source of all these blessings and restoration (Isaiah 59:20-21, Rom. 11:26-27, Isaiah 61:1-7, Isaiah 9:6-7).

Some Types and Shadows that Prefigure the Church

Let us look at some types that prefigure the church. It can easily be seen, that the physical seed of Abraham is type of the spiritual seed of Abraham. Israel, as physical descendants of Abraham after the flesh, is type of the body of Christ, the children of Abraham by faith (Gal. 3:7, 9, and 29). As with all types, the lesser always precedes the greater. That is why Israel's promises and blessings are earthy; they are descendants after the flesh. Israel is of this world, separated by a wall of partition from the other nations of the world, part of which is their circumcision in the flesh, and their promised land having physical boundaries. This is why Israel is constantly the subject of prophecy – God deals with Israel as part of this world, part of this earth, and the Gentile nations and powers in how they've treated the Jews. In Abraham were both, the type (the physical seed) and the greater reality in fulfillment (the spiritual seed, the believer and church, Gal.3:29).

Yet Abraham himself, identifies with the spiritual seed (the church), for he sojourned in the land of Promise as in a foreign country...for he waited for the city which has foundations, whose builder and *maker is God...and confessed that they were strangers and pilgrims on the earth. For they who say such things declare plainly that they seek a homeland...but now they desire a better, that is, a heavenly country...(*Heb.11:8-16). The fulfillment of all types is always greater and better, as are the promises associated with the fulfillment. As it is said here, "they desired a better...a heavenly country...for He has prepared a city for them." Abraham then is also a type of the believer in a number of ways. First he is a friend and confident of God, entering into His counsels, God not hiding from him what He was about to do. Second he is a pilgrim and stranger on this earth, looking for a better homeland, that is, a heavenly country. Third, in his calling, he is told to leave country and kindred behind, severing all ties to this world. We can learn much from Abraham's life, good and bad, as examples. He is the father of faith.

The First and Last Adams

To finish off our chapter on types and shadows we need to consider the two Adams. In Romans 5, the first Adam is said to be a type of Christ:

Rom. 5:14

"Nevertheless death reigned from Adam to Moses, even over those who had not sinned according to the likeness of the transgression of Adam, who is a type of Him who was to come."

Jesus Christ, as the fulfillment of the first Adam in type, has the title and character of the Son of Man. Adam is the first man, while Christ is presented as the last Adam (I Cor. 15:45). The redemptive work of Christ is the subject and focus of Romans 5 and 6, contrasted with the sin and offence of the first Adam when he fell. Not only does Jesus Himself identify the redemptive work with the Son of Man as we have seen previously in the gospels, but the Spirit of God through Paul does the same. Then we see that all of I Cor. 15 is about the Son of Man as well, with reference to the gospel of suffering, death and resurrection (vs. 1-4). Also there we see the millennial kingdom of the Son of Man (vs. 24-28) over all creation. But clearly the main idea presented in the chapter is how intimately the resurrection and glorification of the Son of Man is associated with the believers' resurrection and glorification. This event in the believers' future, regardless of whether our bodies are corrupting in the grave or we are among those in Christ alive and remaining, is all predicated on and consequent to the glorification of the Son of Man (I Cor. 15:12-23, 35-57, John 12:23).

There are many more truths concerning Christ as the Son of Man found in scripture. We have barely touched on Ephesians 1 and 2, Hebrews 2, 9, 10, Revelation 1-5 and Colossians 1 to name a few. These chapters present both the redemptive work and results of the Son of Man. They show His glorification to the right hand of the Majesty on high with all associated blessing and results. One last thought: it is Adam before the fall that is a type of Christ as the Son of Man. Therefore Eve, as his help-meet, serves as a type as well. This we will take up in later chapters.

Chapter 6:

Messiah Set Aside, the
Son of Man Taken Up

n previous chapters we saw how Jesus came to Israel as their Messiah, with all prophetic promises and physical blessings. This was rejected by the nation and their leaders and they became guilty of nailing Him to a cross. But there remains a lot to think about, and some questions, in considering God's counsels on the subject of Messiah, especially in His first presentation two thousand years ago.

One of the things we should be able to see clearly in all four gospels is Jesus transitioning from the title and role of Messiah to that of the Son of Man. The role of Messiah is one of earthly promises and earthly blessings to Israel. But in prophecy it was more than this; it would be the full restoration and recognition of Israel in the land as the people of God, by the establishing of a Messianic kingdom. This was to happen by Jehovah, the God of Israel, dwelling in the midst of them again (Zeph. 3:14-17, Ez. 48:35). But when Jehovah took on flesh and walked among His own, they did not recognize or receive Him (John 1:1-5, 11, 14, and 12:37-41).

The Transitions between the Two Titles in the Gospels

As for the counsels of God concerning Messiah, this title and role has been put aside by God when Jesus was rejected. I speak about this at length in the 'Israel in the Counsels of God' chapter. In that chapter we learn of all the truths and things associated with the title of Messiah that are set aside at the same time. But what I want to show you here is Jesus, Himself, setting aside this Messianic title, in His own words, and taking up the title and role of the Son of Man.

Luke 9:20-22

"He said to them, "But who do you say that I am?"

Peter answered and said, "The Christ of God."

And He strictly warned and commanded them to tell this to no one, saying, "The Son of Man must suffer many things, and be rejected by the elders and chief priests and scribes, and be killed, and be raised the third day."

Matt. 16:20

"Then He commanded His disciples that they should tell no one that He was Jesus the Christ."

Mark 8:29-33

"He said to them, "But who do you say that I am?"

Peter answered and said to Him, "You are the Christ."

Then He strictly warned them that they should tell no one about Him.

And He began to teach them that the Son of Man must suffer many things, and be rejected by the elders and chief priests and scribes, and be killed, and after three days rise again. He spoke this word openly. Then Peter took Him aside and began to rebuke Him. But when He had turned around and looked at His disciples, He rebuked Peter, saying, "Get behind Me, Satan! For you are not mindful of the things of God, but the things of men."

These are the three different locations in the Synoptic gospels were we can see a noticeable transition taking place. Peter acknowledges Jesus as Messiah, but immediately the Lord commands them to not reveal this to any man. He commands them! This is Jesus setting aside this title and role. Then Jesus immediately begins revealing something different – His sufferings as the Son of Man. In this role and title assumed, He would go down under the power of death. He definitely pairs the role of the Son of Man with His death. And it is this thought that Peter takes issue with, bringing Him aside to rebuke Him. But it is Peter that receives the rebuke. And why? Because he does not understand that this is the working out of the counsels of God – you are not mindful of the things of God! Peter, as well as the other disciples, could still only think and accept the thoughts of natural men. Jesus was the Messiah, as Peter boldly declared. But this wasn't the reason Peter was rebuked. Jesus was revealing that Messiah, in God's counsels, is now set aside – do not reveal Me as Messiah to any man! Peter was rebuked because, at the time, he wanted no part in this Son of Man, and His death in this role.

It is clear from the above scriptures what God's counsels were in this – the setting aside of Messiah and everything associated with that thought. Immediately we see Jesus taking up the title of the Son of Man, and as Man accomplishing the work of redemption. This specifically meant His death on the cross. But there are other passages in the gospels and the book of Acts that speak of this same transition. This we will look to now.

John 1:45-51

"Philip found Nathanael and said to him, "We have found Him of whom Moses in the law, and also the prophets, wrote—Jesus of Nazareth, the son of Joseph."

And Nathanael said to him, "Can anything good come out of Nazareth?"

Philip said to him, "Come and see."

Jesus saw Nathanael coming toward Him, and said of him, "Behold, an Israelite indeed, in whom is no deceit!"

Nathanael said to Him, "How do You know me?"

Jesus answered and said to him, "Before Philip called you, when you were under the fig tree, I saw you."

Nathanael answered and said to Him, "Rabbi, You are the Son of God! You are the King of Israel!"

Jesus answered and said to him, "Because I said to you, 'I saw you under the fig tree,' do you believe? You will see greater things than these." And He said to him, "Most assuredly, I say to you, hereafter you shall see heaven open, and the angels of God ascending and descending upon the Son of Man."

Nathanael was a good Israelite, just with some obvious prejudices about places like Nazareth. Like most Jewish men, he most likely thought that the Messiah could only possibly come from Jerusalem. Jesus saw him as sitting under the fig tree, both literally and symbolically, and reveals this to him. Nathanael's response is all Jewish in content; "Rabbi, You are the Son of God! You are the King of Israel!" This response is all Messianic in nature. Messiah would be Jehovah in their midst, Emmanuel, and King of Israel (Psalm 2).

Heavenly Truths vs. Earthly Things

But Jesus immediately tells him that He would show him things far greater than these truths. Now, pause here for a moment and consider how this could even be possible? To a good Israelite, what could be better than the Messiah of prophecy as Jehovah in the midst of Israel? Jesus answers this question – instead of an earthly Messiah and earthly blessing, it is that which is found in the Son of Man and the reality (not promises in prophecy) of heavenly truths and blessings. We can see that Jesus was ever mindful of the counsels of God, always speaking in line with them. The thought of earthly and heavenly things brings us to our next example.

John 3:9-15

"Nicodemus answered and said to Him, "How can these things be?"

Jesus answered and said to him, "Are you the teacher of Israel, and do not know these things? Most assuredly, I say to you, We speak what We know and testify what We have seen, and you do not receive Our witness. If I have told you earthly things and you do not believe, how will you believe if I tell you heavenly things? No one has ascended to heaven but He who came down from heaven, that is, the Son of Man who is in heaven. And as Moses lifted up the serpent in the wilderness, even so must the Son of Man be lifted up, that whoever believes in Him should not perish but have eternal life."

Again, Jesus is dealing with a decent Jewish man; this time it is a ruler of the Jews and a Pharisee. If a man could have spiritual insight on his own and by his own resources, Nicodemus certainly should have been such a man. Jesus speaks to him first of things he should have understood – earthly things, which are Messianic, Jewish, and prophetic in character and nature. Nicodemus does not understand, nor believe (v. 12). Is it possible for Nicodemus to believe if Jesus tells him heavenly things?

The earthly things concern the nation of Israel, this world, and are known in prophecy; the heavenly things are greater than this, and will exist as realities long before the earthly things come about. The heavenly things are newly revealed by the Son of Man, as the One who came down from heaven, telling us what He saw and heard there (v. 11-13). The heavenly things result consequent to the Son of Man being lifted up on the cross (v. 14), and lifted up apart from the earth and world (John 12:32). Again, this transition in the councils of God is being emphasized by the Lord's own words.

The Son of Man came down from Heaven – the Bread of Life

Next, we look at Jesus' teaching about the Son of Man being the bread of life, come down from heaven; and if we're perceptive, we'll see this transition again.

John 6:27 "Do not labor for the food which perishes, but for the food which endures to everlasting life, which the Son of Man will give you, because God the Father has set His seal on Him."

John 6:32-33 "Then Jesus said to them, "Most assuredly, I say to you, Moses did not give you the bread from heaven, but My Father gives you the true bread from heaven. For the bread of God is He who comes down from heaven and gives life to the world."

John 6:35 "And Jesus said to them, "I am the bread of life. He who comes to Me shall never hunger, and he who believes in Me shall never thirst."

John 6:47-51 "Most assuredly, I say to you, he who believes in Me has everlasting life. I am the bread of life. Your fathers ate the manna in the wilderness, and are dead. This is the bread which comes down from heaven, that one may eat of it and not die. I am the living bread which came down from heaven. If anyone eats of this bread, he will live forever; and the bread that I shall give is My flesh, which I shall give for the life of the world."

John 6:53-58 "Then Jesus said to them, "Most assuredly, I say to you, unless you eat the flesh of the Son of Man and drink His blood, you have no life in you. Whoever eats My flesh and drinks My blood has eternal life, and I will raise him up at the last day. For My flesh is food indeed, and My blood is drink indeed. He who eats My flesh and drinks My blood abides in Me, and I in him. As the living Father sent Me, and I live because of the Father, so he who feeds on Me will live because of Me. This is the bread which came down from heaven—not as your fathers ate the manna, and are dead. He who eats this bread will live forever."

There is a subtle contrast of importance being made by Jesus that I want to try to bring out. The obvious comparison is between the food that perishes (bread and fish), and the spiritual food that results in eternal life that *only the Son of Man has to give.* It is somewhat obvious that the manna Israel had in the wilderness from Moses was not the real spiritual bread and so would also fall into this category of the 'food that perishes.' It still remains, however, that the manna in the wilderness is a type/shadow of the Son of Man, the true bread from heaven. But there is a deeper truth to be found.

By way of review, earlier in John's gospel, at the calling of Nathanael in John 1:43-51, he declares Jesus as the Messiah, the King of Israel. But immediately Jesus moves the understanding for them from Messiah to that of the Son of Man and His redemptive work in type.

In John 3:1-15, when a man of the Pharisees secretly comes to speak with Him, it is mostly about the Son of Man who came down from heaven (v.13). He has the heavenly knowledge (v.11-13) concerning this new created nature that man must have to see and enter God's kingdom (v.3, 5, 7). It would be the redemptive work of the Son of Man, again shown in type (v.14) that has the results through faith of not perishing, but eternal life (v.15). *This is the bread that doesn't perish – the real bread from heaven – given by the Son of Man. Better yet, it is the Son of Man, the bread of (eternal) life.*

The Earthly Messiah and the Food that Perishes

In Matt. 15:21-28 we have our previously discussed passage concerning Christ, distinctively in the role of Messiah, to the house of Israel. Here the Canaanite woman's daughter is delivered of demon-possession. As the Messiah to Israel, Jesus describes her healing as giving *the children's bread* to dogs (v.26). In this same chapter (v.30) He heals the multitude; the lame, blind, mute, maimed, and many others (v.31). This is the children's bread from Messiah. Then in the remainder of the chapter (v.32-38) we see the feeding of the four thousand men, not counting women and children. This also was the promised children's bread from Messiah (Ps. 132:15). Yet, however real and needed these physical blessings were, *this all was the bread that perishes*. And the crowds around Him were pursuing it with passion (John 6:26-27). Yet it was not the real bread from heaven, not the Son of Man as come down from heaven (John 6:32-33).

Eating and Drinking the Flesh and Blood of the Son of Man

As believers, we have eaten the flesh of the Son of Man and drank His blood, to have eternal life (John 6:53-54). The flesh and blood He speaks of is referring to His death. By this eating and drinking, the believer through faith joins to Christ as part and participant in His redemptive work. We go down into death with Him. He then abides in us and we in Him (John 6:56, 15:4-5, 17:21, 23). This is the Son of Man, the true bread from heaven that gives everlasting life. There is a subtle but distinctive difference that Christ Himself makes in John 6, between the roles of Messiah and the Son of Man. The instruction remains the same for all today, *"Do not labor for the food that perishes..."* This is Messianic and earthly. The Son of Man is the true bread from heaven. The heavenly food that is the Son of Man is the only food available today, and the only food we are told to desire. The Son of Man is the only food that is life.

The Son of Man is not Messianic Thought or Prophecy

If you look closely at the gospels, you will notice that Jesus rarely embraces the title of Messiah. It is true that He was the Messiah to Israel. It is also true He admitted the same before the high priest and His accusers during His trial (Matt. 26:63-64); but this was Jesus speaking the truth as to who He was, and certainly wouldn't qualify as embracing the title and role.

Matthew 26:63-64

"But Jesus kept silent. And the high priest answered and said to Him, "I put You under oath by the living God: Tell us if You are the Christ, the Son of God!"

Jesus said to him, "It is as you said. Nevertheless, I say to you, hereafter you will see the Son of Man sitting at the right hand of the Power, and coming on the clouds of heaven."

Jesus had to speak the truth when asked by the high priest of Israel, He could do nothing less. He doesn't say it directly, "I am the Messiah," but simply responds indirectly by saying, "It is as you said." Even here I believe He responded more so because He was asked whether He was the Son of God, not necessarily concerning Messiah. But the counsels of God, and He being obedient to this determined path, are forefront in His heart and mind. Messiah He certainly is, but all these earthly things are now set aside by God. The plan of God, He knows, is revealed in the title of the Son of Man, and all that concerns Him now is the path laid out before Him by God. The counsels of God will bring the Son of Man, as a raised and glorified

Man, to the right hand of God. And it will be the Son of Man sitting there, having completed the redemptive work of the cross.

Luke 22:66-69

"As soon as it was day, the elders of the people, both chief priests and scribes, came together and led Him into their council, saying, "If You are the Christ, tell us."

But He said to them, "If I tell you, you will by no means believe. And if I also ask you, you will by no means answer Me or let Me go. Hereafter the Son of Man will sit on the right hand of the power of God."

The contrasting between the Messiah title and Son of Man is obvious. Jesus doesn't want to even discuss the thoughts of Messiah. The leaders of Israel, as well as all Jewish men, knew the prophecies and promises concerning Messiah. They never sat around discussing how they should put Messiah to death when He came to Israel, in order to fulfill prophecy. They wanted to kill Him because they did not believe He was the Messiah, as well as the Son of God. There is no hesitation on their part concerning the thought of condemning Him to death. The leaders of Israel were not considering they may be making a mistake and inadvertently fulfilling Messianic prophecy. This simply is not Messianic thought. Jesus' thoughts here are only about the counsels of God and the Son of Man. My point here is that, in God's counsels, and in the Lord's thoughts and words, it is the Son of Man who is put to death, not the Messiah. Messiah is set aside, as the Son of God (Jehovah) in the midst of Israel. We have another one of these occurrences in John 10, when Jesus was walking in the temple and they asked;

John 10:24-30

"Then the Jews surrounded Him and said to Him, "How long do You keep us in doubt? If You are the Christ, tell us plainly."

Jesus answered them, "I told you, and you do not believe. The works that I do in My Father's name, they bear witness of Me. But you do not believe, because you are not of My sheep, as I said to you. My sheep hear My voice, and I know them, and they follow Me. And I give them eternal life, and they shall never perish; neither shall anyone snatch them out of My hand. My Father, who has given them to Me, is greater than all; and no one is able to snatch them out of My Father's hand. I and My Father are one."

They ask Him directly if He is the Christ of God, the Messiah. He answers them indirectly by saying He has already told them the answer to their question, but the nation as a whole is blind in unbelief. And this gets to one of the key issues of the matter. If the nation remained in unbelief concerning Jesus as their Messiah, then the title and kingdom would not be forced upon them. The Messiah and the promises would be set aside, as well as Israel. Messiah simply would not work in their state of unbelief. And that state is confirmed by the Lord over and over again in the scriptures (John 5:38, 40, 46-47, 6:36, 8:21, 23-24, 38-47, 12:37-40, 15:22-25, 16:2-3).

The Son of Man is the Good Shepherd

There is a distinct turning away from the thought of Messiah to that of the Son of Man. He still speaks as the Shepherd of His sheep (vs. 26, 27). Back a few verses in John 10:14 He is the good shepherd and in verses 15-18 He lays down His life for the sheep.

John 10:15-18

"As the Father knows Me, even so I know the Father; and I lay down My life for the sheep. And other sheep I have which are not of this fold; them also I must bring, and they will hear My voice; and there will be one flock and one shepherd."

"Therefore My Father loves Me, because I lay down My life that I may take it again. No one takes it from Me, but I lay it down of Myself. I have power to lay it down, and I have power to take it again. This command I have received from My Father."

Just like the Son of Man is the bread of life come down from heaven in chapter 6, the Son of Man is the good Shepherd in chapter 10. It is for the same reason -- he would lay down His life. The good Shepherd would die for His sheep. This is the redemptive work on behalf of the sheep, the work of the Son of Man (not Messiah). The sheep would be those who would benefit from the Son of Man laying down His life (believers). Look closely at verse 17; the Father loves Jesus because He would lay down His life. This should serve to settle for all believers, what truly is the redemptive work – it is His death alone.

There is another reason this shows the Son of Man is the good Shepherd – in verse 16 He says, "And other sheep I have which are not of this fold…" The sheepfold He presently had entered, out of which He gathered only His sheep and no others, was the house of Israel. Having sheep from a different fold that He must gather also, is simply not Messianic (Matt. 15:24). These other sheep would be His from among the Gentiles. They would hear the voice of the Son of Man, who died for them as well. Not only is it distinctly the Son of Man that gives His life for His sheep, but also it is distinctly the same who gathers from a separate fold other than Israel. It is subtle, but it shows important differences between the two roles and titles.

[I will also add this comment in passing, because it is so prominent in this portion of scripture. John 10:1-30 is simply poignant with Jesus' own thoughts and teaching concerning the sovereignty of God. He brings it all out in the open here, as He does not hide it at all. It is certainly worth a second look for all believers.]

I have included the above few paragraphs and comments on John 10:24 because one of my sons happened to point it out to me as a reference to Jesus as Messiah. I do not believe that it detracts at all from anything that I am saying, but only serves to reinforce and support my position. Jesus was Israel's Messiah when presented to them two-thousand years ago. He will still be their Messiah when He presents Himself to the remnant in the future; this will be a second coming of Messiah to Israel. It will all happen exactly according to written prophecy. But that does not mean that presently, in the counsels of God, Messiah isn't set aside. Jesus' own words and actions clearly show this. With the title of Messiah set aside along with all Messianic promises and prophecy, Jesus can only be seen and known presently as the Son of Man.

The Son of Man would go away – to the Right Hand of God

Luke 19:9-12

"And Jesus said to him, "Today salvation has come to this house, because he also is a son of Abraham; for the Son of Man has come to seek and to save that which was lost."

Now as they heard these things, He spoke another parable, because He was near Jerusalem and because they thought the kingdom of God would appear immediately. Therefore He said: "A certain nobleman went into a far country to receive for himself a kingdom and to return."

This is an obvious transition. Zacchaeus is a son of Abraham according to the flesh. In the Jewish mind, if there was to be salvation for the Jew, it would come by an earthly Messiah and an earthly Messianic kingdom. Such a kingdom and salvation would be for the entire nation. They thought, mistakenly, that it would be immediate, for Jesus was heading to Jerusalem, the obvious city of the Messianic King. But Jesus' words do not address Jewish hopes and promises in Messiah. They speak, rather, of the Son of Man – seeking and saving that which is individually lost, and as a nobleman in the parable going far away to receive a kingdom. This is decidedly not Messianic in character. And purposely, Jesus steers away from Messianic thought and talk, and will only speak of what the Son of Man will accomplish with His death.

Jesus was Israel's Messiah and rejected as such. Does that make Messiah then, by default, a promise to the Gentiles? Can Messiah be appropriated by the Gentiles? Where would we have the authority to say or teach such things? Do we see this anywhere in the scriptures? Israel had every advantage and opportunity as a nation. They were blessed and set apart by God, and still blindly rejected their promised Messiah. And the Gentiles, supposedly, in some strange and weird way, will do better? God then, having seen His chosen and separated people refuse Him when He was in their midst, now asks if the Gentiles want the Messiah? Will the land be ours as well? I speak in jest here, but the problem remains. We have to have more spiritual insight than this line of thinking shows. These thoughts only serve to connect the believer to this earth and to this world.

Messiah can no longer be found

The evidence of this transition in scripture continues;

John 8:21

"Then Jesus said to them again, "I am going away, and you will seek Me, and will die in your sin. Where I go you cannot come."

What the Lord is saying is very interesting. He tells the Jews that He is going away – this is the Son of Man glorified to the right hand of God. He says they will seek Him. Well, it couldn't be said that they were seeking Him at that time, for they wanted to kill Him (John 8:37). But He says that they *will seek* Him. So what does He mean? As we've said before; every Jewish man would properly seek the Messiah according to prophecy. You will seek Me -- they still are seeking a Messiah and have been for thousands of years. The problem seems obvious. Even though they legitimately seek for a Messiah after He went away, Messiah cannot be found as long as Messiah is set aside in the counsels of God. You will die in your sin – the blindness and unbelief of the Jews, as it was then and as it is today, only brings death and condemnation to them from God. Where I go you cannot come – as unbelievers this is impossible; their condemnation guarantees this; they cannot come where the Son of Man has gone.

For the believer however, there are some precious thoughts here in His words. We know He went away as the Son of Man raised and glorified to the right hand of God. He is there now, as a glorified Man, as a forerunner in God's presence for us. It was all for us! When He says to the Jews, "Where I go you cannot come," He is not speaking to us. Jesus never says this to His disciples. He never says this to believers. When He speaks to the disciples about His going away, it is so He can prepare a place for us there, where He went (John 14:1-4). And precious promise it is, that when the time is right, He will personally come to get us and take us there. We will forever be in the Father's house, and share in His glory (John 17:23-24). In the meantime, while we wait for Him to come for His body, the church, we have been given another Comforter, who will abide in us forever.

There are similar words and thoughts found in John 7, with the same conclusions drawn from the counsels of God. In verse 26 the question is whether this truly is the Messiah? He never answers them about Messiah at all, but quickly turns His words to His going away.

John 7:33-34

"Then Jesus said to them, "I shall be with you a little while longer, and then I go to Him who sent Me. You will seek Me and not find Me, and where I am you cannot come."

Jesus' words here are even more explicit in revealing the counsels of God concerning Messiah. You will seek Me and not find Me – *Messiah, as set aside, cannot be found.* Further, as unbelievers, they have no part in the Son of Man, and cannot come where He has gone. It is the Son of Man that goes away, and the Son of Man as glorified, who sends the Holy Spirit to all believers (John 7:37-39), a river overflowing out of them.

I previously said that Jesus never seems to embrace the Messiah title in His first coming. Only to the Samaritan women at the well does He freely identify Himself as the Messiah (John 4:25-26). In contrast to this one incidence, which didn't even take place in Judea or around Jerusalem, I see Jesus constantly taking up the title of the Son of Man, and His death with that title. I haven't counted the number of times He speaks of the Son of Man, but I'm sure it is a much larger number than the one concerning Messiah. It gives the reader a general sense of the truth of these things, and the confidence that God's counsels can be known by His children.

The Determined Counsel of God – the Death of the Son of Man

The question comes up as to whether Jesus coming as Messiah to Israel was a legitimate presentation. In many ways it is a similar question as to why God created man and placed him in paradise, when there was a Lamb slain in the counsels of God before the foundation of the world (Rev. 13:8). God certainly knew man would fall and be driven out of paradise, and Jesus certainly knew He would be rejected as Messiah when He came. As God, He was part of these counsels before the creation of the world. We see in Acts, the Spirit of God through Peter testifying as to the reason and purpose for sending the Son of Man from heaven.

Acts 2:22-24

"Men of Israel, hear these words: Jesus of Nazareth, a Man attested by God to you by miracles, wonders, and signs which God did through Him in your midst, as you yourselves also know— Him, being delivered by the determined purpose and foreknowledge of God, you have taken by lawless hands, have crucified, and put to death; whom God raised up, having loosed the pains of death, because it was not possible that He should be held by it."

Jesus always knew that it was the determined counsel and foreknowledge of God that He should die. He came into this world for that purpose. Redemption is the sole basis for any blessing from God for man, even in securing the promises and blessings for Israel in Messiah (Acts 13:34, Rom. 15:8). Jesus knew that only through His death would this be accomplished. But Peter, by the Spirit, even in view of this, does not remove any guilt from the nation of Israel, saying, "...you have taken by lawless hands, have crucified, and put to death..." Jesus also knew Israel would not have Him as Messiah.

The Two Separate Presentations of Messiah to Israel

Luke 22:67-68

"If You are the Christ, tell us."

But He said to them, "If I tell you, you will by no means believe. And if I also ask you, you will by no means answer Me or let Me go."

Matthew 23:38-39

"See! Your house is left to you desolate; for I say to you, you shall see Me no more till you say, 'Blessed is He who comes in the name of the Lord!'"

Jesus knew that in the counsels of God there would be two separate comings of Messiah to Israel. In between these two comings, Israel, as a nation, is set aside and desolate. But do we realize how different these two presentations are in their character and nature? The second coming has all the character of sovereign power, sovereign grace, and sovereign choice. It is simply all God working – He chooses a remnant, He seals a remnant, and He preserves and protects a remnant. He then destroys their enemies and judges the world. He does all this by sovereign work in order that He will be found faithful, while every man is found a liar (Rom. 3:3-4). Every prophetic promise made to Israel in Scripture God will then be faithful to fulfill. He will do so, during the millennium, by sovereign power.

Understanding how God works

In the next three paragraphs I will share some nuggets of spiritual truth that have profound scriptural support, and lay a basis for a better understanding of the remaining chapters. When God works, He does so sovereignly – in power, grace, and choice. The nature of His working, being the Sovereign, means that His work alone is and will remain eternally. His work simply cannot and will not ever fail. It will not be any other way. God working is always for His own glory. *This means that all displays of power, all giving of grace, all God's callings, and every decision and choice He has made are for His very own glory.* A beautiful example of these principles is the believer placed in Christ by the Father. We are His workmanship, created in Christ Jesus (Eph. 2:10), and placed there, for the praise of His glory (Eph. 1:12). Now, if His work alone is eternal and cannot fail, doesn't this truly glorify Him?

When we look at the work of man it doesn't have this character. Man's work always ends in failure, and can have nothing lasting or eternal about it. All men will be judged by their works (Rev. 20:12-13, Rom. 2:5-6). People fail to realize what this really means when standing in the presence of God under judgment – man's works are all his sins. This guarantees condemnation and wrath from a holy and righteous God. Men fool themselves by thinking they will be able to stand before God. They reason that their righteousness is not filthy rags (Is. 64:6), even though in reality man has no resources and is a slave of sin. They actually feel they have true fruits of righteousness to offer to God. However, all unbelievers are no different in state and position than the privileged Jews Jesus was speaking with (John 8:34-47, and 21).

Messiah's first coming to Israel – Mankind's final testing by God

Jesus coming to Israel the first time as Messiah was a testing by God of man in his existing state and condition. This state was in the first Adam by natural birth. Man's condition was a slave to sin as brought in by Adam, and passed upon all mankind (John 8:21, and 34). Jesus came to the tree but found no fruit. Then He condemned it (Matt. 21:19). He says this, "Now is the judgment of this world." At that time God was finished testing man in responsibility, and He pronounces judgment on it all (John 12:31). Jesus, as presented to Israel as their Messiah the first time, was a final testing of responsibility in a very privileged people. This is very different than how Messiah will be presented when He returns. This is the obvious contrast I want you to see between the two presentations.

Was the first presentation of Messiah legitimate? Our finite minds ask questions like this, and our man-made systems of doctrine do not give adequate answers or explanations. One thing I will admit is that I will never know God as He knows Himself (John 10:15). God has reasons and purposes and a will in all that He does. Much of this is finite reasoning of man trying to reach the infinite. However, we can definitely point to what has been revealed in Scripture. Concerning God's general purpose in all things, it is the exaltation of His own

THE SON OF MAN GLORIFIED

glory. More specifically, God did not find fruit from Israel. He then condemned the world by it. As for the counsels of God, He sets aside Messiah and Israel. He then takes up a sovereign work of grace in the raised and glorified Son of Man, sending the Holy Spirit down to gather a primarily Gentile body, the body of Christ (John 7:39).

The Prophecies and Truths concerning the Son of Man are not understood

Luke 18:31-34

Then He took the twelve aside and said to them, "Behold, we are going up to Jerusalem, and all things that are written by the prophets concerning the Son of Man will be accomplished. For He will be delivered to the Gentiles and will be mocked and insulted and spit upon. They will scourge Him and kill Him. And the third day He will rise again."

But they understood none of these things; this saying was hidden from them, and they did not know the things which were spoken.

In the same way that the nation of Israel was confused by what Jesus revealed about the Son of Man (John 12:34), so were His disciples. This passage from Luke reaffirms many of the things we have been saying. There is prophetic scripture that references directly the Son of Man and His death. These prophetic scriptures are not about the Messiah. This transition between the titles of Messiah and the Son of Man was nothing but confusion to those in Israel, including His disciples. Even our Lord's own words were not enough for them to see clearly.

A Final Transition from the Book of Acts

I did promise an example of this transition from the book of Acts. I do explain these thoughts in detail in a later chapter, 'the Real Book of Acts.' The short version I give you here. In response to our Lord's intercession on the cross for Israel, the first seven chapters of Acts becomes Israel's last chance of receiving Jesus as Messiah, at that time. All the testimony by the Holy Spirit and the apostles is only to the House of Israel. The nation would have to repent, acknowledge their guilt, and believe in the name of Jesus. This they failed to do, and with Stephen's death, they reject the testimony of the Spirit of God concerning Jesus (Acts 7:51). Heaven is opened up to Stephen, and he sees the Son of Man in glory at the right hand of God (Acts 7:55-56). From that point on, the book of Acts takes a dramatic turn in the counsels of God.

The purpose of this chapter is to show the reader how, in God's counsels and in the Scriptures, we see this transition from Messiah to the Son of Man. We see this in the Lord's own teachings and words. When we see this we should have the confidence, as believers, to know that we can understand the counsels of God. And not ever again chasing the food that perishes, but may we always feed ourselves on the bread of Life that came down from heaven -- Jesus, the Son of God, as the Son of Man.

Chapter 7:

The Son of Man in the Epistles

n this chapter we will look specifically at the epistles. These are, as previously mentioned, the letters written from the Father and the Son by means of the Comforter to the believer and Body of Christ. We will not find much reference in the epistles to Christ in the role of Messiah. That isn't the proper character of the epistles in any respect, nor as to the counsels of God being carried out presently. What we do find however, are large portions of Scripture that point directly and conclusively to the work of the Last Adam, Jesus Christ, the second Man. It is redemptive work in view, and the epistles bring forth, by the Spirit, a deeper understanding of these truths.

All Mankind comes short of the Glory of God

In the book of Romans we have the righteousness of God revealed in the gospel of Jesus Christ, the power of God unto salvation by faith (Rom. 1:16-17). The epistle presents to the believer a summary of the great foundational truths that form the groundwork of this gospel. We see the heathen without the law and they are guilty (Rom. 1:18, 2:5). Then we see the Jew with the law and they are guilty as well (2:23, 3:20). The former are found lawless, while the latter are transgressors of the law (Rom. 2:12). The conclusion is in Rom. 3:23; *for all have sinned, and come short of the glory of God.*

All mankind, without exception, have come short of a position and proper relationship with the living God. It matters not if one is a Gentile heathen, far away from God, without His law and promises, or if one is of the stock of Israel, with the law, promises, and the oracles of God. All are guilty and cannot possibly enter and live in the presence of God (the glory of God). All are found to be sinners, without means or solution.

All mankind, from the fall of Adam in paradise, come short of the glory of God. Do we have a sense of the full meaning of this truth? As believers, we tend to agree with the first part of Rom. 3:23, that 'all have sinned.' We have an understanding of this; that all men are guilty of committing the acts of sin. What about our understanding of the effects of mankind's relationship with the first man? Do we, as believers, grasp the fullness of the consequences and results of Adam's original disobedience?

We usually find that most unbelievers like to dispute with the first part – the personal sinning that goes on. They refuse to properly see and admit it. The unbeliever may agree that some committing of sins takes place, but usually fails to see or admit responsibility for their actions personally. They then foolishly push any thought from their conscience of standing before God someday and giving account. If they entertain the thought of a judgment for themselves, they have reasoned that it will hopefully go in their favor. They reason that God will look the other way as to their sins, failing to see and understand that God is righteous and holy without measure. When they compare themselves to others, they reason they are better than most, and find solace in this fatal perception. It's as if God has scales of judgment in the skies, and their good outweighs their bad in the balance. What is vitally necessary for the unbeliever is for his conscience to be awakened and quickened, not just to sins, but to a lost condition without strength or resource to change. This lost state is man born in Adam.

Man's Inherited Position and State in Adam, the first man

Believers need to better understand this inherited position in Adam. All mankind has received the presence of sin from the first man (Rom. 5:12). It isn't just that sins will not be in the presence of God, but sin in the flesh will not be tolerated as well. The Adam nature is fallen, sin is reigning in this nature (Rom. 5:14, 17, 21), in the flesh, and man's will is a slave to sin (John 8:34). As believers, we do understand and agree with the first part above – the acts of sin being committed on a universal basis. However, not only are all men guilty of sins, but all mankind inherits from Adam, the head of the human race, a nature of sin. We have this from natural birth and it is present in the flesh.

From Adam onward, there has always been a coming short by all mankind of the glory of God. What I want you to realize and understand, that God's presence and glory is, in a great sense, *the intended destination for man*. And further, it is God's intention and purpose that man can continuously come into His glory and live in His presence. But in man's present state and position (scripturally as in the flesh, of the world, and in Adam), he always falls short of the intended destination. What is implied is that man in his present state, left to his own efforts and means, has a guaranteed outcome; a falling short – certain condemnation (Rom. 3:9, 19). However, of great importance, is the intention and purpose of God in His counsels – man living in the presence of God, in the glory of God. And centerpiece to His counsels is Jesus Christ, the Son of Man. The foundation of all God's counsels is the obedience and work of this one Man.

Both Jew and Gentile guilty and Hopelessly Lost

It is an important truth to realize that both heathen (Gentile) and Jew are in the exact same position before God – hopelessly lost, guilty sinners, and without strength to do anything about it (Rom. 5:6, 8). All are lost, despite all the incredible advantages that Israel was given by God. They never profited by it, did not produce fruit as we have seen previously, and failed to recognize God when He came to them.

Rom. 3:19

"Now we know that whatever the law says, it says to those who are under the law, that every mouth may be stopped, and all the world may become guilty before God."

Israel -- God's Privileged People – is in the Flesh and of the World

Here is the spiritual understanding of importance: Israel, although given all the advantages, was always, in their existence as a people, every bit part of the world as any Gentile nation. Their choosing and being set apart by God was in the flesh and in the world. Israel certainly was separated from the Gentiles around them, but simply by a wall built up by God – their religion being this wall (the law – Judaism). Their separation was all in the flesh and simply amounted to nothing more than the confidences of man in the flesh (Phil. 3:2-8). Israel was a people in the flesh.

What do the Scriptures say about the flesh? Those that are in the flesh cannot please God (Rom. 8:8). In the flesh dwells no good thing (Rom. 7:18).

Rom. 8:9

"But you are not in the flesh but in the Spirit, if indeed the Spirit of God dwells in you. Now if anyone does not have the Spirit of Christ, he is not His."

True believers are in the Spirit, having the seal of the Spirit in them. All unbelievers are in the flesh, according to God's Word. All unbelievers also are part and parcel of the world, and make up what is known in the Scriptures as *'the world.'* In Rom. 3:19 it said that the entire world may become guilty (under judgment) before God; and it is speaking there of Jews and Gentiles. The world is made up, as to its composition, of Jews and Gentiles; believers are not part of the world (John 17:14, 16).

The Law – a Ministration of Death and Condemnation

One more scriptural application as to Israel will be helpful to many. Israel, as a people in the flesh, according to Rom. 8:7-8, possess a fleshly mind that is enmity against God and one that cannot be subject to the law of God -- the very law God gave them. Nor indeed can they be at all subject to it. The law of God through Moses was given to a people in the flesh, a people very much a part of the world. *This was the determined counsel and intention of God.* He had His reasons, none of which led to life and righteousness in Israel (Gal. 3:21, Rom. 10:1-4). That which was written and engraved on stones, by the testimony of the Spirit in II Cor. 3:7, 9, *according to God's purpose, was distinctly a ministration of death and condemnation.*

The Law exposes the Presence of Sin in the Flesh

I believe that those, taught by the Spirit in the scriptures, will understand the intentions of God in this. The law exposes sin. I do not say sins, although certainly the law identifies what transgressions and offences are, as breaking commandments given from God to Israel (Rom. 7:5). The law, in a general overall sense, exposes the presence of sin in man, as inherited from Adam (Rom. 7:7-9, 11-14, 17). Mankind does not inherit sins from Adam, but rather, the presence of sin in the flesh (Rom. 7:17, 20, and 23). It is this presence that has its fruits; sins and death (death, I dare say, cannot be separated from condemnation).

As far as sins are concerned, this is the simple transition to understand: before Israel was given the law, they were lawless, and exactly like the Gentiles committing sins. After they were given the law at Mt. Sinai, they were now transgressors of the law committing offences. *The truth resides in this; when Israel was given the law, they were already sinners.* And the law was powerless to do anything to correct or remedy the existing state of Israel, or that of all mankind in Adam (Rom. 8:3). Besides, what is the clear testimony of New Testament scriptures on the topic of the law? I quote one of many possible scriptures (I Cor. 15:56), "...the strength of sin is the law."

Israel is in the First Adam

Now the above few scriptures draw these simple conclusions: Israel, as a people, as well as all Gentile unbelievers, by nature are in the flesh (Rom. 8:9), of the world (Rom. 3:19), and under condemnation (John 12:31, Eph. 2:3). Israel's separation from the Gentiles by God, a wall built up around them by their law, is very much still a part of the world. Israel, from a scriptural perspective, can be described as still in Adam. All unbelievers for that matter would hold this same state and position before God as being in Adam. The unbelieving world certainly would not be considered to be 'in Christ', the second Adam. The position of all individuals can be described as either in Adam or in the second Adam. The first Adam is the position of being in the flesh. In the Last Adam is the position of being in the Spirit (Rom. 8:9).

The First Adam is a Type of Jesus Christ, the Son of Man

In your studies of God's Word you will find that Rom. 3:21-26 as well as Romans 5, 6, 7, 8, are all speaking of the redemptive work of the second Adam, the Son of Man. The contrasts between the first and second Adams begin in Rom. 5:12-15,

"Therefore, just as through one man sin entered the world, and death through sin, and thus death spread to all men, because all sinned— (For until the law sin was in the world, but sin is not imputed when there is no law. Nevertheless death reigned from Adam to Moses, even over those who had not sinned according to the likeness of the transgression of Adam, who is a type of Him who was to come. But the free gift is not like the offense. For if by the one man's offense many died, much more the grace of God and the gift by the grace of the one Man, Jesus Christ, abounded to many."

My intention for this chapter cannot be the explaining of all the scriptures in the epistles related to the Son of Man, which would be quite extensive. Rather it is showing to the reader that a distinctive relationship clearly exists between the written epistles and Jesus Christ in the title and character of the Son of Man. Here we see that the first Adam is a type of Him, the second Man, who was to come (Rom. 5:14 – Adam is considered a type of the second Adam before man's fall, as he existed in paradise). Also, all the grace of God that abounds to the many is by and through the one Man. The righteousness of God and the believer's justification through the grace of God is secured by this one Man. And Rom. 5:12-21 unfolds the contrasts between the two Adams;

The first Adam, the first man	The second Adam, the Son of Man
Disobedience (Rom. 5:19)	Obedience (Rom. 5:19)
Sin entered the world, death through sin (Rom. 5:12-14) through one man	The free gift, the grace of God (Rom. 5:15) the grace of the one Man
Judgment and associated condemnation (Rom. 5:16, 18)	Justification and the gift of righteousness (Rom. 5:16-18)
Death reigning (Rom. 5:14, 17)	Reigning in life (God's life - Rom. 5:17)
One man's offence (his sin -- Rom. 5:18)	One Man's righteous act (the cross- Rom. 5:18)
Sin reigning as a master in death, the great fruit of sin (Rom. 5:21)	Grace reigning through righteousness unto eternal life (Rom. 5:21)

The explanations of the redemptive work of the Son of Man continue through Romans 6, 7, 8, as well as redemptive realities for those in faith. In chapter 6 it is deliverance from the bondage of sin, and chapter 7 it is deliverance from the law. Chapter 8 is the seal of the Spirit and the Spirit of adoption as sons, heirs of God and joint-heirs with Christ. Also we have the expectation of our hope, and *the revelation of the definite counsel of God*, in the believer being conformed to the image of His Son.

The Son of Man is the First Born from the Dead

I Cor. 15 is a chapter which specifically references the Son of Man. His gospel is found in the first fifteen verses. Further on the chapter speaks of the resurrection of the believer connected directly with Christ, the second Man, who is raised from the dead. Then there is the millennial kingdom of the Son of Man, His reign over all creation (which was given up by the first Adam), the putting all things under

His feet. After that He gives up His kingdom as Man so that the rule of man ends. From this point God is all in all, in all the divine glory, in the new heavens and new earth for all eternity. Once again, we see clearly the similarities and contrasts between the first Adam in type, and the last Adam, the Son of Man.

1 Cor. 15:45-49

"And so it is written, "The first man Adam became a living being." The last Adam became a life-giving spirit. However, the spiritual is not first, but the natural, and afterward the spiritual. The first man was of the earth, made of dust; the second Man is the Lord from heaven. As was the man of dust, so also are those who are made of dust; and as is the heavenly Man, so also are those who are heavenly. And as we have borne the image of the man of dust, we shall also bear the image of the heavenly Man."

Earlier in the chapter Christ becomes the first fruits (vs. 20, 23) because He is now risen from the dead. This is the Son of Man who went down under death and is risen and glorified. We see a group is associated with the risen Son of Man – afterward those who are Christ's at His coming. This is certainly speaking of the believer, but more so, the entire Body of Christ. If Christ was glorified by being raised, as Paul's argument goes, in the same way will the Body of Christ be glorified. This glorification, and the entering into the glory of God, will be by resurrection or change of the believer, as clearly described in verses 50-58. We will all be changed (v. 51); the corruptible through resurrection, or the mortal putting on immortality.

There is now a Man in Glory, and He has many Brethren

In Hebrews 2, Christ, as the Son of Man, was for a time made a little lower than the angels for the purpose of suffering death. In this chapter we see the Son of Man glorified, crowned with glory and honor (v. 9). He is identified by the Spirit as the glorified Man of Psalm 8 (Heb. 2:6-9), which is the primary Old Testament reference to the title of the Son of Man. Again a group is found in Him, the bringing of many sons to glory. This is the entering into the glory of God that all mankind in Adam were guaranteed of falling short of – Heb. 2:10-11.

Hebrews 2:11-12

"For both He who sanctifies and those who are being sanctified are all of one, for which reason He is not ashamed to call them brethren, saying:

"I will declare Your name to My brethren;
In the midst of the assembly I will sing praise to You."

As the glorified Man, Christ has brought us into the same position with His God and His Father that He has. He who sanctifies and those sanctified are one and the same. This is the declared reason He, as the glorified Man, is not ashamed to call them brethren. Then He says, *"I will declare thy name unto my brethren; in the midst of the congregation will I praise thee."* What name? The name of His Father and His God, the One with whom He had found favor, now having put away sin by the sacrifice of Himself.

Christ had felt God's power and wrath against sin. He returns into the enjoyment of the glory, not simply as the eternal Son of God before the world was, but now as the glorified Son of Man. He enters as having finished the work, and now He says, "I will declare thy name unto My brethren." We easily see that when He rose, He said, "Go to my brethren, and say unto them, I ascend unto My Father, and your Father; and to My God and your God." (John 20:17). He is declaring the Father's name to His brethren. He had never really called them this previously -- brethren. He is setting them in the place He had acquired for them. He had completed the needed work, as the Son of Man, and now He brings His disciples into the same relationship He Himself was in with His God. This is in virtue of what He had done as Man; and as we also know, He did not do this for Himself, but for us.

The Son of Man is the Seed of the Woman

Heb. 2:14

"Inasmuch then as the children have partaken of flesh and blood, He Himself likewise shared in the same, that through death He might destroy him who had the power of death, that is, the devil,"

The Son of Man partook of flesh and blood for the reason of death, that He might destroy the power of the devil. The full victory over Satan has been won by Christ. First it was in the wilderness being tempted and then on the cross submitting to death. Satan thought his victory was Christ in the tomb, but on the first day of the week the tomb was empty. Death could not hold Him. As Jesus said, "the prince of this world is judged." (John 12:31). Satan has been totally defeated by the cross of Christ, for death can no longer touch the glorified Son of Man.

He is still around, still doing his work, but he is a defeated devil now. The victory over him has been won by Christ. Satan is just not bound yet. Please note here that this was the fulfillment, in great part, of the promise of the Seed of the woman in the judgment of the serpent in the garden. The Son of Man is the Seed of the woman who would crush the power of the serpent.

In Hebrews 10 we have the viewpoint of the Son of Man as coming from heaven into the world, and a body prepared for Him. He comes, not to do His will, but the will of another, even God. This is so characteristic of the Son of Man. "Your will" is identified specifically in verse 10 as the sacrifice of the cross. Then it says:

Heb. 10:12

"But this Man, after He had offered one sacrifice for sins forever, sat down at the right hand of God..."

After the Son of Man glorified the Father, then the Father glorified the Son of Man. In this verse we have Christ glorified, sitting down at the right hand of His Father's and His God's throne. He is there as a Man, in the glory, representing certain other men. How important is this?

Is there now access to the glory and presence of God where there was only a falling short before? That access is not in the first Adam, not granted to those in him. Those that are there are in the flesh and of the world and earth (the first man was of the earth – I Cor. 15:47). We need the One who has gone up through the heavens, up into the glory, and is seated at the right hand of glory as a forerunner for us. Our access into the glory has been accomplished and is provided for us by this One, the glorified Man (Heb. 10:19-20). Consider these scriptures in the light of this truth:

Heb. 6:19-20

"This hope we have as an anchor of the soul, both sure and steadfast, and which enters the Presence behind the veil, where the forerunner has entered for us, even Jesus, having become High Priest forever according to the order of Melchizedek."

The Son of Man glorified is the forerunner who has entered into the Presence, into the glory of God. *He is a Man in the Presence, in the glory.* This will be the accomplishment of a certain portion of the determined counsels and intentions of God. It is a hope believers have, sure and steadfast. (More teaching on these truths as related to the believer will be discussed in the chapter, 'Many Sons in Glory').

The Son of Man is the One Seed of Abraham

When we turn to Galatians 3 we have the understanding of the Son of Man as the one Seed of Abraham (Gal. 3:16). As we discussed earlier in the Types and Shadows chapter, the covenant of promise was confirmed in Isaac after he was offered up by Abraham. Abraham received him back from the dead as resurrected, only this in type (Heb. 11:17-19). Jesus Christ, as raised from the dead, is the fulfillment of this type. The Son of Man resurrected and glorified is the true Seed of Abraham in whom the covenant of promise was confirmed.

THE SON OF MAN IN THE EPISTLES

This serves to identify Christ, the One Seed of Abraham (Gal. 3:16), as the glorified Son of Man. This accomplishes the specific focus of this chapter, in view of the book of Galatians, which is to show the continuance of the title and role of the Son of Man through the epistles. This does little to address other important subjects entertained by Paul in this epistle which I have difficulty passing by without comment. I will list here what I feel are important thoughts and distinctions that the Spirit of God clearly brings to the forefront in this epistle, and certainly worth the believer's time spent in consideration and study.

The Two Covenants (Gal. 3, 4)

1.) There are two covenants discussed in Galatians 3, 4 that are not the same or even similar, except they are both from God. These chapters contrast and distinguish the two covenants from each other, and in truth, show their incompatibility with each other (Gal. 3:15-18, 4:28-31).

2.) The principle and basis of the covenant of promise is diametrically opposite that of the covenant of law. For the law it is, "the man who does them shall live by them." This places the potential for any blessing from God squarely on the responsibility of man – his decisions, his will, and his works (Gal. 3:12). The principle of the covenant of promise is the character and attributes of God Himself, and that God is faithful to do what He has promised. The individual simply believes what God has spoken (Gal. 3:9).

3.) The covenant of law was given to the nation of Israel. It became the religion of Israel. The two parties involved were God on one side, and angels mediating for Him, and the people of Israel on the other, with Moses mediating for them (Gal. 3:19). The covenant of promise was nothing like this. There is no mention of any mediator, and frankly, that is because there isn't one. Why? There is only one party involved in this covenant. This is the reason why Paul says, "Now a mediator does not mediate for one only, but God is one." In this covenant God stands alone and shoulders every ounce of responsibility (Gal. 3:20). The covenant of promise will never be given to a nation. It is individuals becoming sons of God (Gal. 3:26). 'In Christ' there are no nations (Gal. 3:28).

4.) The covenant of law with Israel is a yoke of bondage (Gal. 5:1-3) that only produces a nation of servants and slaves (Gal. 4:21-25, John 8:31-36). The covenant of promise produces sons of God (Gal. 3:26, 4:5-7), heirs of God (Gal. 3:29, 4:7) and the inheritance He gives (Gal. 3:18, 4:7).

5.) (Gal. 3:12) "Yet the law is not of faith..." This statement should be a red flag going up for any believer. When could there ever be any fulfillment of promise or blessing from God without believing Him? The covenant of promise is by believing God and believing in Jesus Christ, the one Seed of Abraham in whom the covenant was confirmed (Gal. 3:9). The law is not of faith, but rather, is of human responsibility.

6.) By the covenant of law the nation of Israel existed as always under a curse (Gal. 3:10), for as many as are of the works of the law are under the curse. This describes the Jewish people and their religion, and the only expected result and outcome. The curse is nothing special – it simply is death, condemnation, and wrath from God in judgment. There never was a law that could give life or righteousness (Gal. 3:21). This is another red flag. The covenant of promise gives the seal and indwelling Spirit of promise through faith (Gal. 3:2, 5, 14), who is the Spirit of the adoption of sonship (Gal. 4:5-7).

7.) Throughout Galatians 3, 4 the two covenants are compared and contrasted. Here are some of the descriptions and words used.

a.) Works of the law vs. hearing of faith (Gal. 3:2).

b.) Beginning in the Spirit vs. perfection through the flesh (Gal. 3:3).

c.) The sons of Abraham are those of faith, not those of the works of the law (Gal. 3:6-10).

d.) The curse of the law vs. the promise of the Spirit (Gal. 3:13-14), and the promise of an inheritance (Gal. 3:18).

e.) The many seeds after the flesh vs. the one Seed of Abraham (Gal. 3:16-17).

f.) The covenant of promise vs. the covenant of law given 430 years later (Gal. 3:17), which had no power to annul or add anything (Gal. 3:15, 17).

g.) Law gives a curse (Gal. 3:10) – death and condemnation. Promise gives life and righteousness (Gal. 3:21).

h.) Children of bondage (Gal. 4:24-25) vs. children of promise (Gal. 4:28).

i.) Children born according to the flesh (Gal. 4:29) vs. children born according to the Spirit (Gal. 4:29).

j.) Earthly Jerusalem which is itself in bondage (Gal. 4:25) vs. the heavenly Jerusalem that is free (Gal. 4:26), which is the house of the Father (John 14:2, Rev. 3:12), the eternal habitation of all the sons of God.

The covenant of promise involves the blessing of the Gentiles by faith, and the preaching of the gospel of the grace of God through Jesus Christ, the one Seed (Gal. 3:7-9, Rom. 5:15). This covenant of promise was activated after the Seed was raised from the dead (Gal. 3:16-19), and when the covenant of law was set aside for Israel (Gal. 3:23-25).

Promises from God are fulfilled by God in sovereign grace and power; all promises associated with the covenant of promise are solely dependent on the faithfulness of God (Heb. 6:13-18). The covenant of promise has absolutely nothing to do with the responsibility of man. That is why all the promises of God are in Christ as yes and Amen (II Cor. 1:20), because their fulfillment only depends on the sovereign will and power of God. God made promises to Abraham concerning his physical descendants, but those are separate and distinct from this covenant of promise confirmed in Christ, His one Seed. The distinction is clearly seen in Gal. 3:16; "And to seeds," as of many, is speaking of Israel, his descendants after the flesh, and 'as of one, "And to your Seed," who is Christ, is the other. This one Seed again has a group associated with Him, seen in Gal. 3:7, 9, 26, and 29;

7 "Therefore know that only those who are of faith are sons of Abraham."

9 "So then those who are of faith are blessed with believing Abraham."

26 "For you are all sons of God through faith in Christ Jesus."

29 "And if you are Christ's, then you are Abraham's seed, and heirs according to the promise."

Clearly these are believers as the sons of God in Christ Jesus. In Gal. 4:1-7 we have almost the exact teaching concerning the believer as we found in Rom. 8. We are sons of God through redemption in Christ, receiving the adoption of sons, being made heirs of God, and the seal of the Spirit whereby we cry out, "Abba, Father!"

The Son of Man – Head of the Body, and Head of all Creation

If we move on to Colossians, there we learn that the redemptive work of the Son of Man had two great objects of reconciliation; the whole of creation and the Body of Christ.

Col. 1:12-22

12 "...giving thanks to the Father who has qualified us to be partakers of the inheritance of the saints in the light. 13 He has delivered us from the power of darkness and conveyed us into the kingdom of the Son of His love, 14 in whom we have redemption through His blood, the forgiveness of sins."

15 "He is the image of the invisible God, the firstborn over all creation. 16 For by Him all things were created that are in heaven and that are on earth, visible and invisible, whether thrones or dominions or principalities or powers. All things were created through Him and for Him. 17 And He is before all things, and in Him all things consist. 18 And He is the head of the body, the church, who is the beginning, the firstborn from the dead, that in all things He may have the preeminence."

19 "For it pleased the Father that in Him all the fullness should dwell, 20 and by Him to reconcile all things to Himself, by Him, whether things on earth or things in heaven, having made peace through the blood of His cross. 21 And you, who once were alienated and enemies in your mind by wicked works, yet now He has reconciled 22 in the body of His flesh through death, to present you holy, and blameless, and above reproach in His sight—"

As for creation, Christ in His divinity (the image of the invisible God, v. 15, and all the fullness of the Godhead dwelling in Him, v. 19) created all things in heaven and earth, all things visible, as well as all things invisible. They were created by Him and also for Him. He preceded everything, and the continued existence of everything is by His ongoing wisdom and power (v. 15-17). By Christ's shed blood, all things are reconciled back to the Father; things on earth and things in heaven (v. 20). The reconciliation of creation was accomplished by the cross. What He created as God He will take as the risen Son of Man.

This is an important thought. In His divinity, He was the Creator of all things, and has the right to possess all of creation. As the Son of God, He is the appointed heir of all things (Heb. 1:2). But He only takes the inheritance through redemption, and this as Man. The work of the Son of Man in redemption, and His entrance as Man into glory, is key to understanding how there are other men redeemed, and glorified, of which He is not ashamed to call them brethren (Heb. 2:11).

Redemption through the shed blood of Jesus Christ, the Son of Man is provided for the believer (v. 14). And we have been reconciled by Him to the Father (II Cor. 5:17-21), by the work of the cross (v. 21-22). Eventually, we will be presented holy, blameless, and irreproachable to the Father (v. 22). How is this? We are in Christ and He is our life. So now we see that when He takes His inheritance – that which He created as God and has a right to – there will be other men found with Him, as brethren and co-heirs.

The glorified Man has gained preeminence in all things (v. 18). He is the firstborn over all creation (v. 15). Therefore Jesus, the second Adam, is such a greater reality than the first Adam ever was in type/figure. The first Adam is responsible for the defilement of creation, the very creation he was to have dominion over. The second Adam is responsible for the reconciliation of that creation and more, the entire heavens and earth, of simply all things. But the Son of Man is the firstborn from the dead, and is preeminent there as well (v. 18). The glorified Man is both, the Head of creation, and the Head of the body, the church. (This accomplished reconciliation of creation and of the church through the redemptive work of the Son of Man is beautifully brought to light in detail in Rev. 4 and 5.) In Colossians 3 we see more truths associated with Christ in the role of the Son of Man seated at the right hand of God (Luke 22:69).

The Son of Man Presently Hidden at the Right Hand of God

Colossians 3:1-4

"If then you were raised with Christ, seek those things which are above, where Christ is, sitting at the right hand of God. Set your mind on things above, not on things on the earth. For you died, and your life is hidden with Christ in God. When Christ who is our life appears, then you also will appear with Him in glory."

This passage turns the attention of the believer to where it properly should be -- to the heavens. Also it is evident from the passage that Christ is presently hidden there in God. He will stay hidden from the world as long as the work of the Spirit sent down to gather His body is still incomplete, until the fullness of the Gentiles comes in (Rom. 11:25). He is hidden as opposed to the thought of appearing to the world (v. 4), which would be the Son of Man coming in judgment (Rev. 1:7, Dan 7:13, and Matt. 24:30). Regardless, He sits there hidden, in the role of the Son of Man having gone away. When He appears to the world, it will be the Son of Man coming on the clouds of heaven with power and great glory, for judgment and a kingdom.

The last epistle we will look at in this chapter concerning the Son of Man will be Ephesians. In this epistle Christ is presented as the Son of Man glorified throughout. In Eph. 1:19-21, we see the Man, Jesus Christ, raised-up from among the dead by the mighty power of the Father and seated at God's right hand. This is exaltation far above all power and all things. And further we see in Eph. 4:9-10 the reconciliation of the heavens and earth, again of all created things to God through His work. He has preeminence over all things as Head, whether it be creation or the body (Eph. 1:22). This is how the believer is to see Christ, as exalted and glorified. The world does not see Him now, but the time is coming when they will, when He is manifested to the world (Col. 3:4). So now, as for the world, the Man glorified is hidden in God (Col. 3:3, Rev. 12:5). Yet He is not hidden to the believer, to the eye of faith, and we are always taught to be looking there (Col. 3:1-2).

The Son of Man with His Body is exalted above All Things

Ephesians 1 shows the Father's love for individual believers by making us accepted in Christ, in the Beloved (v. 6), again in the position as adopted sons (v. 5) and according to the wisdom of His counsels and purposes (v. 5, 8-9, 11). Believers have been given the Holy Spirit, a guarantee of future things (v. 13-14). But we also know that the Spirit could not have been given until the Son of Man of Psalm 8 had been glorified (this psalm is partially quoted in v. 22). In the second chapter the Spirit, as sent down, is gathering and forming the corporate body of this mystical Man. It is interesting that Christ, as the Head of the body, is so as the glorified Man. This thought is maintained in Eph. 2:19-21, when it says that Jesus Christ Himself is the chief cornerstone, as a stone in the building itself, in which we are stones being built up together as a holy temple in the Lord.

In Ephesians 3 we have the mystery of Christ that was, from the beginning of the ages, hidden in God (Eph. 3:1-12). This mystery is now revealed for it could not be revealed until Christ was glorified (v. 5, 10-11). The mystery revealed is as a dispensation given specifically to Paul (v.2, 8-9). We will have more to say on this important revelation in a later chapter. In Ephesians 4, when Christ is glorified on high, He gives gifts for the growth of the body on earth.

Adam and Eve -- a Type of Christ and the Church

We end our survey of the epistles as related to the Son of Man in Ephesians 5. Here a hidden type (as hidden somewhat in the chapter) is used to describe the association of the glorified Man of Psalm 8 with His body, the church. In Eph. 5:25-32 we start with the exhortation, "Husbands, love your wives...", but the teaching immediately turns to Christ and the church that He loves and has given Himself for. The type/figure is Adam and Eve in paradise, prefiguring Christ in glory and the church as joined to Him, as His body – of His flesh and of His bones (v. 29-30). We can see that Adam and Eve are in the thoughts of the Spirit because Gen. 2:24 is quoted in verse 31. But it is spelled out in verse 32 that Paul is actually talking about Christ and the church.

We know Adam is a type of Christ (Rom. 5:14) before his fall into sin. Eve was made out of Adam, when he was put to sleep, and then afterward she was presented to Adam by God. Adam said then, "This is bone of my bones, and flesh of my flesh" (Eph. 5:30). Adam was to rule over all the works of God's hands. Eve was not a part of the original creation, and she was not lord of it as Adam. But Eve was associated with Adam in all his dominion. Eve was not to be ruled over by Adam, but to be a help-meet and co-heir in the portion that God had given him. The Son of Man, the second Adam, goes down under death (sleep is a figure, see Eph. 5:14, John 11:11-14), and when He wakes up in glory, so to speak, He will present to Himself (for He is God, Eph. 5:27) His bride the church, without spot or wrinkle, holy and without blemish. His bride is the glorified Man's body joined to Him (Eph. 5:30-32), of which He is the Head (Eph. 1:22-23). And so we will find the church to be joined with Christ, the Son of Man, when He takes His rightful inheritance. *(Ephesians 5:32 – This is a great mystery ...concerning Christ and the Church.)*

Chapter 8:

The Gospel of the Glory of Christ

2 Cor. 5:16

"Therefore, from now on, we regard no one according to the flesh. Even though we have known Christ according to the flesh, yet now we know Him thus no longer."

The world knew Christ at one time according to the flesh, when He came to Israel as Messiah (Rom. 9:5). He was rejected at that time, and they would not have Him as their King. The Holy Spirit through the apostle tells believers that we know Christ this way no longer. The title, the idea, and the promises of Messiah have been suspended and put aside by God. They have been that way for a long time. They will stay that way until, in the end, the Israeli remnant says, *"Blessed is He who comes in the name of the Lord!" (Matt. 23:38-39).* We also see in those scriptures that Israel will remain desolate, that they will not have a spiritual recovery and blessing from Jehovah until their Messiah comes to them again.

A Christ in the Flesh is a Messiah to Israel, and on the Earth

The title of Messiah is not the only thought associated with Christ coming according to the flesh. There are the various aspects of His humanity -- born of a woman, born under the law, and the Son of Man sent from heaven. Also we understand that divinity took on flesh. The Son was sent to reveal what God in human flesh would look like, the words He would speak, the works He would do. But Christ coming to Israel according to the flesh [Rom. 9:5] certainly centers on the prophecies of the Messiah, and the many Messianic promises to this specific nation. Knowing Christ according to the flesh is as Messiah in Israel on this earth (II Cor.5:16). Man can no longer know Him this way, and He presently cannot be found as such. This all has been set aside.

A Christ in Glory is the Son of Man Raised and Glorified

But how is it that we know Christ, if we, as believers, know Him no longer according to the flesh? We only know Him now by and through His redemptive work as the Son of Man. We only know Him as a Man raised up from the dead (John 20:17). And more specifically, we know Him as He is now – Jesus Christ, *the Son of Man glorified (Heb. 10:12).*

John 12:23-24

"But Jesus answered them, saying, "The hour has come that the Son of Man should be glorified. Most assuredly, I say to you, unless a grain of wheat falls into the ground and dies, it remains alone; but if it dies, it produces much grain."

Jesus Christ fully glorified God by His obedience to the cross and in completing the redemptive work. He did this while He was on the earth. He is the single grain of wheat that falls into the ground and dies. This again is a symbolic picture of the redemptive work of the Son of Man, a work that He finishes alone, going down under death, and forsaken by God. This is so that in His glory He would not be alone, but the work producing much grain – many sons in the glory with Him, as His brethren – Rom. 8:29-30.

Jesus Christ, the Son of God

What we will find, if we are attentive to the scriptures, is that the Son of God was sent from heaven. Jesus Christ, in eternity past, was the only begotten Son, dwelling in the bosom of the Father (John 1:18). It was the only begotten of the Father that was sent to this earth to dwell among men as the Word became flesh (John 1:14). When Jesus speaks of being sent and about the one who sent Him, He is referring to the Son being sent by the Father (John 10:36). This is true in the overwhelming majority of incidences in which He speaks of this (John 5:23, 36-38, 6:29, 38-40, 7:16-18, 28-29, 8:16-18, 42). This is the divinity of Christ, whereby He could say to the Jews, "Most assuredly...before Abraham was, I AM." (John 8:58).

The Son of God enters into the Counsels of God

We also find that the Son of Man came down from heaven (John 3:13). How are we to understand this? He is always the Son of God. But the Beloved Son has to enter into the counsels of God by taking up a title. He has to accomplish a specific work associated with that particular title, whether it involves Messiah or the Son of Man. It becomes clear, that the eternal Son took up the title of the Son of Man before He was sent and left heaven. How else would we be able to understand Jesus saying, "What then if you should see the Son of Man ascend where He was before," if He hadn't taken up the title there? (John 6:62). And how could He be the Son of Man who is in heaven and then be speaking to Nicodemus? (John 3:13). When He says, "We speak what we know and testify what We have seen," it is from the viewpoint of the Son being in heaven, having taken up the Son of Man title. The 'We' that is testifying to Nicodemus is the Son of God as the Son of Man. As for God's counsels and the taking up this title, there was a Lamb slain before the foundation of the world (Rev. 13:8). The Lamb slain is the Son of Man -- the Lamb of God who takes away the sin of the world (John 1:29).

The Obedience of Christ – Two Distinct Works

We will consider now the obedience of Christ. It can be seen as two distinct exercises, two distinct workings. The Son of God shows obedience to the Father. But also we will see the Son of God in the role of the Son of Man, showing obedience to God. It is a unique and special obedience producing a work that alone is the foundation of all the counsels of God. I speak of the redemptive work – His death. This isn't the only reason the Son of God was sent from heaven, but it is the only reason why the Son of Man came down (John 3:14, 12:23-24, and 34).

The performance and fulfillment of God's will in redemption as the specific reason the Son of Man came from heaven (John 3:13-14, 6:53) is the emphasis of a portion of scripture found in Hebrews. This entire passage in Hebrews 10:1-12 is specifically about sacrifices and death, and the will of God concerning this in God's counsels.

Hebrews 10:4-12

"For it is not possible that the blood of bulls and goats could take away sins.

Therefore, when He came into the world, He said:

"Sacrifice and offering You did not desire,
But a body You have prepared for Me.
In burnt offerings and sacrifices for sin
You had no pleasure.
Then I said, 'Behold, I have come—
In the volume of the book it is written of Me—
To do Your will, O God.'"

"Previously saying, "Sacrifice and offering, burnt offerings, and offerings for sin You did not desire, nor had pleasure in them" (which are offered according to the law), then He said, "Behold, I have come to do Your will, O God." He takes away the first that He may establish the second. By that will we have been sanctified through the offering of the body of Jesus Christ once for all."

"And every priest stands ministering daily and offering repeatedly the same sacrifices, which can never take away sins. But this Man, after He had offered one sacrifice for sins forever, sat down at the right hand of God,"

The Obedience of Jesus Christ, as the Son of Man – the eternal Sacrifice

There are many things here that are useful in identifying the Son of God taking up the title of the Son of Man, and coming to this earth. He says God prepared a body for Him. Also the phrase, 'when He came into the world,' is prominent. But verse 12 is unmistakable in its identification of the Son of Man in that it says, 'But this Man, after He had offered one sacrifice for sins forever...' The sacrifice for sins, the redemptive work, takes center stage as the performance of the will of God and fulfillment of all God's purpose through this Man's coming and mission (John 12:27-28). It is the commandment given by God to the Son, as the Son of Man to obey (John 14:31).

The will of God spoken of in the above passage has a very narrow focus that is important to see. This will is the desire of God for a sacrifice, one that would please God in finally addressing sin and putting it away (Heb. 9:26). God found no pleasure in all the sacrifices and offerings that came before, which were offered according to the law (Heb. 10:1). These previous sacrifices were mere shadows, having no substance, and no effective power or result. Not only did God desire a sacrifice to deal with sin, but also one He could take pleasure in. A sacrifice was needed that would fully glorify Him. It would have to be a perfect sacrifice, for God is holy and righteous. Sin would have to be dealt with in light of God's own eternal nature. If this sacrifice was perfect, it would be eternal, never to be repeated, a finished work that would put an end to all that preceded it. The will of God spoken about in this passage is this sacrifice – the death of the Son of Man. His obedience to do this will is the obedience of Jesus Christ, the Son of Man (Heb. 10:10).

Jesus Christ fully glorified God by His suffering, crucifixion, and death. This is not the glorifying of the Son of Man. Instead it was the absolute glorifying of God by His obedience specifically to the cross and His drinking the cup of wrath from God (Luke 22:42-44).

The Obedience of the Son of God – Revealing the Father

There is another distinct obedience that Scripture points to concerning Jesus. It is the obedience of the Son to the Father. All the words He spoke were given to Him by the Father (John 14:10, 24, John 3:11-13, John 7:16, 8:26, 38, 40, 12:49-50). Also all the works He did were as He saw the Father doing (John 14:10-11, John 5:19-20, 36, John 8:28-29, 9:4, 35-37, 10:32, 37-38). These examples and scriptures show the Son's obedience to and dependence on His Father (John 5:30, 6:38), and are the proof that He came from the Father (John 17:8, 8:42). The Son of God willingly assumes the role of servant to His Father. He never shows any independence from the Father, in order to perfectly reveal the Father and bring glory to Him.

John 17:1-5

"Jesus spoke these words, lifted up His eyes to heaven, and said: "Father, the hour has come. Glorify Your Son, that Your Son also may glorify You, as You have given Him authority over all flesh, that He should give eternal life to as many as You have given Him. And this is eternal life, that they may know You, the only true God, and Jesus Christ whom You have sent. I have glorified You on the earth. I have finished the work which You have given Me to do. And now, O Father, glorify Me together with Yourself, with the glory which I had with You before the world was."

The Son had glorified the Father on the earth by finishing the specific work of revealing the Father. This was the reason the Son was sent by the Father. He revealed the Father by speaking the Father's words and doing the Father's works (John 5:19-20). The Son alone could do all this because He alone knew the Father (John 10:15, Luke 10:22). This is the divinity of the Son, taking on human flesh, so to bring a greater revelation of God into the world. He does not ever do His own will, but always the will of His Father, thus revealing the Father (John 5:30, 6:38).

We know the above passage is about the Son of God, because only the Father and the Son had life in each other, and could give it to whomever they desired (John 5:21, 26, 6:44, 10:28-29). But also the passage speaks of the glory He had with the Father before the world began – this was as the Son of God, in eternity past. He speaks of re-entering this previous glory. Important note – the truth concerning all the counsels of God, from this point forward, is that the Son of God re-enters the glory now, eternally, as the Son of Man. When the Son came from heaven, a body was prepared for Him, and He took up the title of the Son of Man forever – Jesus Christ, Son of God, as the Son of Man.

When Jesus was speaking in the above passage, the work of the Son perfectly revealing the Father was already finished – "I have glorified You on the earth, I have finished the work which You have given Me to do." This is not the same thing He was speaking of earlier when He said, "Now the Son of Man is glorified, and God is glorified in Him." This is the Son of Man glorifying God (John 13:31-32), not the Son glorifying the Father (John 17:4). And the work of the Son of Man was still ahead of Him, waiting to be accomplished. It is the Man who glorifies God, by the appeasing and propitiating of God, through the sacrifice of Himself. It is the Son who glorifies the Father, by revealing Him.

The Life of Christ – the Father always with the Son and in the Son

In His walk on this earth, He was the Son of God with the Father abiding in Him. This is an important point of doctrine. He walked as God in human flesh – the Son of God. In His walk He never was separated from His Father. The Father always lived and abided in Him (John 10:38). He revealed the Father as the only one who has ever seen the Father (John 6:46) or known Him (John 10:15). This is not walking as the Son of Man. There is a distinct difference between these two forms of obedience. One is done by God – the Son, voluntarily taking on the role of servant to the Father -- so to perfectly reveal the Father, as only the Son had the experience and ability to do. The other obedience is done by Man, and that accomplished by the Man alone (Heb. 10:12).

John 14:6-11

"Jesus said to him, "I am the way, the truth, and the life. No one comes to the Father except through Me.

"If you had known Me, you would have known My Father also; and from now on you know Him and have seen Him."

Philip said to Him, "Lord, show us the Father, and it is sufficient for us."

Jesus said to him, "Have I been with you so long, and yet you have not known Me, Philip? He who has seen Me has seen the Father; so how can you say, 'Show us the Father'? Do you not believe that I am in the Father, and the Father in Me? The words that I speak to you I do not speak on My own authority; but the Father who dwells in Me does the works. Believe Me that I am in the Father and the Father in Me, or else believe Me for the sake of the works themselves."

Only the Son had the Father dwelling in Him to perfectly reflect the image of the Father to the disciples (John 12:45). Only God could reveal God. You have seen the Father, if you have seen Me; you know the Father, if you know Me. From now on you know Him and have seen Him. It is the Son who reveals and declares to the disciples the Father's name (John 17:6, 26). And it is the Son who gives the disciples the Father's very words as given to Him (John 17:8) – proof that the Father sent the Son and that Jesus is, in fact, the only begotten Son of God (John 1:18).

The Son of Man glorifies God by the Cross – a Work He does alone

However, when Jesus speaks of the Son of Man glorifying God (John 13:31-32), it is not at all a reference to the Son revealing the Father. It is not a reference to the Son's obedience to only speak the Father's words and only do the works He saw the Father doing. It is not a reference to His walk on this earth as the Son – the Word become flesh. That which was the means of absolutely glorifying God was the work the Son of Man accomplished on His own, apart and forsaken by God. This was what He does on the cross alone. His experience on the cross is as Man – the wrath of God poured out on Him, the power of Satan present, the sins of men borne, and the hatred of the world against Him. He is made sin in the flesh on the cross by God. It was all accomplished in isolation, all on His own. The three hours on the cross was the propitiation – the debt fully paid to God for an eternal redemption for those who believe (Rom. 3:24-25). It alone perfectly establishes the righteousness of God (Rom. 3:26). How is this? By the cross and His death, His blood being shed, God has perfectly and eternally dealt with the sins of man, as well as sin in the flesh. It is the means by which God remains just, in and of Himself, and yet becomes the justifier of men (Rom. 3:26). The cross was the absolute glorifying of God by the Son of Man.

As the Son of Man in the counsels of God, He came from heaven to do the will of God -- the redemptive work. As Man there was anguish in His soul, for He possessed a complete human nature. Without attempting to get too deep in thoughts and doctrine that easily become unprofitable, we can understand that the humanity of Christ was not from the first Adam and in a sense quite special. That which was born in Mary was conceived by the Holy Spirit and born of God. I Cor. 15:47 also tells us, *"The first man was of the earth, made of dust; the second Man is from heaven."* As the Scriptures declare, the Son of Man had a body prepared for Him (Heb. 10:5-7).

This explains His humanity which was paramount to the redemptive work of the Son of Man. It is not as easy to explain the anguish He felt in His soul, in view of impending events soon to take place in Jerusalem. We could point to His humanity and that He was the Son of Man. But He was first and foremost the Son of God, who was eternally in the bosom of the Father God. The impending events – His suffering, crucifixion, and death – would be accomplished as forsaken by His Father. This would be the first time ever in all eternity.

John 12:27

"Now My soul is troubled, and what shall I say? 'Father, save Me from this hour'? But for this purpose I came to this hour."

Notice Jesus says, "...save Me from this hour?" The work of the Son of Man was for a certain point in time – the three hours on the cross. This is when the Son of Man is lifted up (John 12:32). His walk on the earth was as the Son of God. This is different. This was not redemptive. There was obedience by the Son to the Father's will, but this is not propitiation. It is not substitutionary, and it is not the display of the righteousness of God. His obedience as the Son is blessed and perfect, certainly glorifying the Father. We marvel at what it shows and reveals, but we cannot make it something it is not. This obedience is not the work of the Son of Man in redemption. It is not the work of the Son of Man in the counsels of God.

John 13:31-32

"So, when he had gone out, Jesus said, "Now the Son of Man is glorified, and God is glorified in Him. If God is glorified in Him, God will also glorify Him in Himself, and glorify Him immediately."

This is the glorifying of God by the Son of Man. It is by His death we have redemption and propitiation. The Son of Man glorifying God is the foundational work by which all the counsels of God will be brought forth and fulfilled. The Son of God revealing the Father, however perfectly this revelation was, is not the working out of the counsels of God. These verses in John 13 strictly involve God's counsels for two reasons. First, it is the title of the Son of Man spoken of, and the redemptive work of this Man referred to. Second, it is God specifically being glorified by this work, and not said to be the glorifying of the Father. It is God who had to be propitiated. It is God who had to be satisfied by what was done in judging sin in the flesh of man (II Cor. 5:21). It is God's righteousness that is fully brought out by His own holy and righteous judgment of Christ on the cross. This simply is not a revelation of the Father by the Son of God, but rather God's very own counsels being established in Jesus Christ, the Son of Man.

What I am attempting to say in the above paragraph is that in Scripture, the Holy Spirit has different and distinct uses for the word Father apart from the word God. Christ was made to be sin by God, so that we might become the righteousness of God in Him. The

Holy Spirit never uses the term 'the righteousness of the Father' in Scripture. The blood of Christ is the propitiation before God, to demonstrate God's righteousness. It is not said that the Father remains just and becomes the justifier of the one who has faith in Jesus (Rom. 3:23-26). The name of the Father is connected to the Son of God being sent, and what the Son reveals of Him. The name of the Father is always associated with the many sons, in blessing, grace, and the relationship of sonship. These are the ones the Father has made accepted in the Beloved Son (Eph. 1:5-6). Yet Christ's title of the Son of Man is connected with glorifying God through the redemptive work He accomplishes. The Son of Man is associated with God judging sin, and He remaining holy and righteous while doing so.

As a reminder to the reader, none of this is Messianic in its character and nature. Even though the two titles, Messiah and the Son of Man, are both in the counsels of God, this glorifying of God is obviously only associated with the Son of Man. And we can readily see from these verses that God's counsels concerning the Son of Man do not end with Him in the grave. It says that God will glorify Him, and do so immediately. This is what this book is mostly about – what relationship and association the believer has, in the counsels of God, with the Son of Man in glory.

The Counsels of God – Messiah, Israel, Prophecy, the Earth, and Time, all presently set aside

Messiah, as a title and work, has been set aside for the present time in the counsels of God. Israel as well, has been set aside. Their house will remain desolate until... And just an added thought would be the idea that prophecy, the earth, and time are set aside in the counsels of God as well. It is simply that, in God's counsels, these five things are inseparably linked together. Nevertheless, for this purpose, the Son of Man came to this hour, that is, to give His life and die.

Here are a few more scriptures concerning the obedience of Jesus as both the Son of God and the Son of Man.

John 6:37-40

"All that the Father gives Me will come to Me, and the one who comes to Me I will by no means cast out. For I have come down from heaven, not to do My own will, but the will of Him who sent Me. This is the will of the Father who sent Me, that of all He has given Me I should lose nothing, but should raise it up at the last day. And this is the will of Him who sent Me, that everyone who sees the Son and believes in Him may have everlasting life; and I will raise him up at the last day."

As we can see, this is the Son of God sent into the world to reveal the Father – therefore He says, "This is the will of the Father..." Also of note in this passage is the understanding that eternal life exists in the Father and in the Son (John 5:26), and that they give this life to whomever they will. Eternal life existing in the Son now has a connection to the title and work of the Son of Man. The Son is the bread of life come down from heaven (John 6:32-33, 35-40); but now it only comes to man by eating the flesh and drink the blood of the Son of Man (John 6:53-58).

John 5:19-21

"Then Jesus answered and said to them, "Most assuredly, I say to you, the Son can do nothing of Himself, but what He sees the Father do; for whatever He does, the Son also does in like manner. For the Father loves the Son, and shows Him all things that He Himself does; and He will show Him greater works than these, that you may marvel. For as the Father raises the dead and gives life to them, even so the Son gives life to whom He will."

Here we can easily see how the Son of God always takes the position of servant to the Father; He always is obedient to the will of the Father so as to fully show only the Father to the world.

The Son of God as the Son of Man

John 5:22

"For the Father judges no one, but has committed all judgment to the Son,"

John 5:26-27

"For as the Father has life in Himself, so He has granted the Son to have life in Himself, and has given Him authority to execute judgment also, because He is the Son of Man."

These two passages together show another connection between the Son and the Son of Man. In the first statement, all judgment is committed to the Son of God. Now this means absolutely all judgment, even the great white throne at the end of the millennial reign of the Son of Man. The second statement links the exercise of this judgment by the Son of God to His title and role as the Son of Man. It is the position of all human individuals in relation to the redemptive work of the Son of Man that is the basis of all His judgment. The Son has authority to execute judgment because he is the Son of Man.

John 12:49-50

"For I have not spoken on My own authority; but the Father who sent Me gave Me a command, what I should say and what I should speak. And I know that His command is everlasting life. Therefore, whatever I speak, just as the Father has told Me, so I speak."

The obedience of the Son to speak only the words given to Him by the Father is viewed by Him as a command from the Father to be obeyed. This obedience was perfect; yet we can only view it as divinity within divinity, the Father abiding in the Son and the Son in the Father (John 14:10-11). "And he who sees Me sees Him who sent Me." This is the Son speaking, and in a great sense, referring to His own divinity (John 12:45).

John 14:30-31

"I will no longer talk much with you, for the ruler of this world is coming, and he has nothing in Me. But that the world may know that I love the Father, and as the Father gave Me commandment, so I do. Arise, let us go from here."

Here, I believe, the redemptive work is in view for the ruler of this world is coming. The commandment and the obedience are to the cross by the Son of Man, or at least, the Son of God, as the Son of Man. I've endeavored to distinguish between the two areas of obedience of Christ. What I hope the reader sees and understands is that the work of the Son of Man, those three hours on the cross, was a very unique display of obedience by Man; that those three hours have no equal. As the Son of God in the role of the Son of Man on the cross, He was without the Father for the first and last time, in all eternity. By this specific work, all God's counsels for man will be accomplished. It is the foundation of all blessing for man.

The Son of Man is glorified by God

Having a better understanding of how God was fully glorified, we now turn to the glorifying of the Son of Man by God. This is the second part of the portion from John 13 that we considered earlier in this chapter, and so we'll look at it again.

John 13:31-32

"So when he had gone out, Jesus said, "Now the Son of Man is glorified, and God is glorified in Him. If God is glorified in Him, God will also glorify Him in Himself, and glorify Him immediately."

We have seen that God was glorified completely by Him, and so God will glorify the Son of Man, in Himself. How? The Son of Man glorified God, by obedience in suffering, crucifixion, and death. And we will see that God glorifies Him by resurrection, ascension, and exaltation. This glorifying is easily seen in many scriptures, but is succinctly brought out in Ephesians 1;

Eph. 1:19-21

"...according to the working of His mighty power which He worked in Christ when He raised Him from the dead and seated Him at His right hand in the heavenly places, far above all principality and power and might and dominion, and every name that is named, not only in this age but also in that which is to come."

It is the Father's mighty power working towards Christ in raising Him and exalting Him. This is how God, in turn, glorified the Son of Man. And this has to be Jesus Christ as the Son of Man (not the title and character of Messiah), who obediently chose to go down into death, bearing sins and being made sin. And it is the Father, by His mighty power, that brings Christ up out of death and into glory. This is what the above verses are clearly teaching.

The Resurrected Son of Man and the Glorified Body

In the above passage Christ is distinctly depicted in the title and character of the Son of Man, only now it is Man after resurrection and placed in God's glory (the entire book of Ephesians shows Christ from this viewpoint). There are three understandings that show this truth about the above passage. First, as we mentioned previously, it is the Son of Man that went down into death, and therefore, He is the same Man that is raised. He is the object of the Father's mighty power working in resurrection. Second, He is raised in a glorified human body that He sits down in at the right hand of God. In I Cor. 15, we see an entire chapter that speaks of spiritual truths associated with the Son of Man. Chief among these truths is how the resurrection of the Son of Man is the genesis of the resurrection of all believers -- those who are Christ's (I Cor. 15:23). In this chapter in Corinthians we see a description of the glorified human body the Son of Man has now, as 'Christ the first fruits' from the dead (v.20, 23);

1 Cor. 15:42-43

"So also is the resurrection of the dead. The body is sown in corruption, it is raised in incorruption. It is sown in dishonor, it is raised in glory. It is sown in weakness, it is raised in power."

The Son of Man – the Glorified Man of Psalm 8

Then there is this third understanding. All of Psalm 8 is about the Son of Man. You might read that psalm and think it is about Adam, and in a limited sense it is. But remember, Adam is only a type of the last Adam, the Son of Man, who is Jesus Christ. Paul, by the Spirit of God, partially quotes this very psalm in three different places in his epistles, identifying Christ as the glorified Man of Psalm 8. In the above passage from Ephesians (1:22) we have Ps. 8:6 partially quoted, "And He put all things under His feet..." Christ, raised from the dead and exalted, is the Man of this prophetic psalm. This same verse is quoted again in I Cor. 15:27, the Son of Man chapter on resurrection. But even further, a passage from Ps. 8 is found in the second chapter of Hebrews where it becomes crystal clear that Jesus Christ is this glorified Man.

Heb. 2:6-9

"But one testified in a certain place, saying:

"What is man that You are mindful of him,
Or the son of man that You take care of him?
You have made him a little lower than the angels;
You have crowned him with glory and honor,
And set him over the works of Your hands.
You have put all things in subjection under his feet.

For in that He put all in subjection under him, He left nothing that is not put under him. But now we do not yet see all things put under him. But we see Jesus, who was made a little lower than the angels, for the suffering of death crowned with glory and honor, that He, by the grace of God, might taste death for everyone."

But we see Jesus...crowned with glory and honor. This is how we see Him presently. Even though we had known Christ according to the flesh, *yet now we know Him thus no longer.* How do we now know Christ? In His own words, 'Now the Son of Man is glorified.'

The Son of Man Glorified – no longer lower than the Angels

Before leaving this passage in Hebrews 2, there is an important understanding about the glorifying of Christ that has consequences for the believer. In verse 9 it says Jesus was (past tense) made a little lower than the angels. This was for a certain period of time (that which we commonly call His humiliation) and for a specific reason in the counsels of God – *for the suffering of death.* But we have already noticed that after He is raised, in His exaltation as the Son of Man, the Father has placed Him at His right hand in the heavenly places, *far above all principality and power and might and dominion (Eph. 1:20-21).* He is no longer a little lower than the angels. He is far above them now. And important for our understanding is that Jesus was lower then, as the Son of Man in his humiliation, but exalted higher now, *as the Son of Man glorified.*

The Son of Man title in the counsels of God is something wonderful for the believer to behold. From the point in time that Jesus was nailed and lifted up on the cross, He would be inseparably linked to that title and counsels. He is the Son of Man for the suffering of death. As Man, He bears our sins on the tree. As Man, He endures the full wrath of God against sin. He goes down under death, the power of Satan. As Man, He is raised from the dead. His resurrected body is as a Man glorified. He ascends up into the heavens as a Man, far above all principalities and power. As a Man He sits down at the right hand of God. It is not difficult for the believer to see the importance of these truths in God's counsels towards us.

Jesus being lifted up as the Son of Man on the cross, and the three hours until His death, is the foundation of all the work contained in the counsels of God. His death is the means by which many sons are brought into the glory. Further, it is the basis for securing all Messianic promises to Israel – the sure mercies of David (Isaiah 55:3, Acts 13:34). We will even be made to know that the new heavens and new earth, wherein dwells righteousness, are founded on the work of this Man.

Without getting into a technical theological discussion, I trust the believer can see how it is Christ, in this title of the Son of Man, who was made perfect through sufferings (Heb. 2:10). Also He learned obedience (Heb. 5:8), He is the firstborn from among the dead (Col. 1:18, Rev. 1:5, I Cor. 15:20, 23), and He came into the world having a body prepared for Him so to do the will of God (Heb. 10:5-7). There are many more scriptures that could be referenced concerning Christ in His role as the Son of Man. Philippians 2 succinctly tells the story of the Second Adam from start to finish,

Phil. 2:5-11

"Let this mind be in you which was also in Christ Jesus, who, being in the form of God, did not consider it robbery to be equal with God, but made Himself of no reputation, taking the form of a bondservant, and coming in the likeness of men. And being found in appearance as a man, He humbled Himself and became obedient to the point of death, even the death of the cross. Therefore God also has highly exalted Him and given Him the name which is above every name, that at the name of Jesus every knee should bow, of those in heaven, and of those on earth, and of those under the earth, and that every tongue should confess that Jesus Christ is Lord, to the glory of God the Father."

This is the Son of Man in His humiliation, and then exalted by God. The end of verse 11 indicates that this all is for the glory of God. At this present time the Son of Man is in the glory of God, sitting on the right hand of the Father's throne (Rev. 3:21). As believers we have to see and comprehend that Christ, in the title and role of the Son of Man does all these things. And after completing the work of redemption, the one-time sacrifice that is forever, *He sits at the right hand of God as the Son of Man.* The importance of this understanding is crucial. And as Jesus identified His suffering and death with the title of the Son of Man, so also He identifies for us the title and character in which He sits at the right hand of the Father.

Matthew 26:64
"Jesus said to him, "It is as you said. Nevertheless, I say to you, hereafter you will see the Son of Man sitting at the right hand of the Power, and coming on the clouds of heaven."

Luke 22:69
"Hereafter the Son of Man will sit on the right hand of the power of God."

He indicated such in John 13:32, *"...God will also glorify Him (the Son of Man) in Himself (in God).* The following is a similar thought with a slight difference. I am repeating this teaching from earlier in the chapter for the reader because of its importance, and because it is simply exciting.

John 17:4-5

"I have glorified You on the earth. I have finished the work which You have given Me to do. And now, O Father, glorify Me together with Yourself, with the glory which I had with You before the world was."

The Son of God re-enters His Glory, as a Man

The glory He had with the Father before the world existed is His glory as the Son of God. This is a glory related to His person, to who He is eternally. But the significant understanding here is, that He re-enters this glory now, as the glorified Man – as the Son of Man glorified – and this according to the counsels of God, not according to His person.

This is the story of the Son of Man. This is the gospel of the glory of Jesus Christ. This is how we, as believers, know Him now. We know Him in resurrection power. We know Him as the King of the kingdom of heaven, ascended up on high. We know Him as the exalted Man sitting down on the right hand of the throne of His Father. We know Him as glorified in the very glory of God. We know Him as crowned with glory and honor. We know Him as the firstborn among many brethren. So appropriately, we find in II Corinthians;

2 Cor. 4:3-4

"But even if our gospel is veiled, it is veiled to those who are perishing, whose minds the god of this age has blinded, who do not believe, lest the light of the gospel of the glory of Christ, who is the image of God, should shine on them."

This is the gospel of the glory of Christ, the gospel of the glorifying of the Son of Man. This is the gospel preached by Paul, knowing Christ no longer after the flesh, but a Christ only now found in the glory at the right hand of God. There is no longer a veil over the glory of God. There always was in the Old Testament tabernacle and over Moses' face (II Cor. 3:7, 13). In Christ however, the veil is taken away. I have to repeat this point – Jesus Christ is in the glory at the right hand of God. He is there as the Son of Man raised and glorified. He is there as Man, which teaches us that He is not there for Himself. He is there absolutely and completely on our behalf (the believer). It is the means, in the counsels of God, by which God brings man into His presence eternally, into the glory. It is that a Man has made the way, and this Man is there now as a Forerunner for us.

The Glorified Son of Man – the Forerunner for the Believer into the Presence of God

Hebrews 6:19-20

"This hope we have as an anchor of the soul, both sure and steadfast, and which enters the Presence behind the veil, where the forerunner has entered for us, even Jesus, having become High Priest forever according to the order of Melchizedek."

The believer's hope goes in there, behind the veil, because the Forerunner is already there ahead of us. Our hope, as the Spirit implies, is absolute, sure, and steadfast, resting on the fact that the Son of Man is there already. And it was all for us. God's love, before the foundation of the world, in His very counsels, was set on the believer, with all intention and purpose on His part to bring this to pass (Eph. 1:3-4). This line of thought is what believers need to grasp.

Allow me to make a distinction here for better understanding of this passage. It speaks of this as our hope. If we are spiritually taught, we know that any hope which is seen is not hope; for why does one still hope for what he sees? But if we hope for what we do not see, then we eagerly wait for it with perseverance (Rom. 8:24-25). With this thought, we understand that the above passage from Hebrews isn't referring to the believer in prayer; it is not our coming boldly to the throne of grace to obtain help in time of need, which is for our walk on this earth. What is the true hope? It is that all believers in Christ will be brought into the very presence of God. This isn't in our prayers now, but physically into the Father's house and the Father's glory. This is what we truly wait for, in our walk on the earth, with perseverance. We see more in another place in Hebrews;

Hebrews 9:24

"For the Christ is not entered into holy places made with hand, figures of the true, but into heaven itself, now to appear before the face of God for us."

It is for us, the believer. It was always for us. It was not in any way for Himself. The sins were not His own, they did not belong to Him. But for man to come into the Presence, into the glory, God would have to deal with the sins of man and sin in the flesh of man. The first Adam brought the human race into sin and it was proven, man had no way out. God would have to make a way for man. In dealing with the sins, God would have to fully judge them all if He was to remain just (Rom. 3:26). This He does through the death of Jesus Christ. This is how the righteousness of God is demonstrated in the cross (Rom. 3:25), and how it is contained in the gospel (Rom. 1:16-17). And again in Hebrews we see this;

Hebrews 1:3

"…who being the brightness of His glory and the express image of His person, and upholding all things by the word of His power, when He had by Himself purged our sins, sat down at the right hand of the Majesty on high,"

Christ bore our sins and died, by which God has judged and condemned it all. Christ has purged our sins and left them down in death. He could not still have them and sit down in the presence of God. That would not be possible. He sits down as having completed the work. (Compare Heb. 10:11 with Heb. 10:12 -- earthly priests always standing to this Man sat down, having finished the work for ever). He sits down there as Man, the righteousness of God and brought into the glory. God's righteousness has been displayed in putting the Man who bore the believer's sins at His right hand in glory. For the believer then, Christ is our righteousness before the face of God. This is where the gospel in its fullness begins. And until He sat down at God's right hand, the Holy Spirit was not sent down (John 7:38-39).

By the Son of Man, the Believer will enter the Presence and Glory of God

Jesus did this all as the Son of Man, so that He could share this glory with us (John 17:22). He certainly had this glory as God before time began (John 17:5). But He did not hold on to it as something to be grasped, and lowered Himself in taking on flesh and coming into this world (Heb. 10:5-9, Phil. 2:6-8). But He re-enters it here, raised and exalted, as the glorified Man (Eph. 1:20-21). We were the ones always falling short of the presence of God, the glory of God. But God, in His counsels before time began, purposed to make a way, and Jesus, as the Son of Man came from heaven to fulfill this plan, to do the will of God, and accomplish the work. Here we have this understanding;

2 Timothy 1:9-10

"...who has saved us and called us with a holy calling, not according to our works, but according to His own purpose and grace which was given to us in Christ Jesus before time began, but has now been revealed by the appearing of our Savior Jesus Christ, who has abolished death and brought life and immortality to light through the gospel,"

We are in Christ by God's grace and purpose, before time even began. This simply is an incredible and exciting thought. This is the gospel of the glory of Christ. And believers are intimately associated with it, for we are forever in Christ.

The Believer will be conformed into His Image and Perfection

2 Corinthians 4:6-7

"For it is the God who commanded light to shine out of darkness, who has shone in our hearts to give the light of the knowledge of the glory of God in the face of Jesus Christ. But we have this treasure in earthen vessels, that the excellence of the power may be of God and not of us."

All the glory that God possesses, and all God is in essence, shines forth in the face of Jesus. For believers there is no veil over this glory. All believers, with unveiled faces, beholding the glory of the Lord, are being transformed into the (very) same image from glory to glory (emphasis added by author – 2 Cor. 3:18).

The only perfection placed before the believer is conformity to Christ in glory. He is the believer's life, for Christ lives in us (Gal. 2:20) and He is in the glory. The perfection of the glorified Son of Man in heaven is what the believer looks at and stares at, knowing we will be conformed to His image when the time comes. It will be then and only then that we will be made perfect – holy and without blame before the Father (Eph. 1:4). This is the holiness of God required of man to enter into His presence; presently Christ, in glory, is the full expression of man being brought into the glory of God.

The believer's calling in Christ is a heavenly one (Heb. 3:1). It is so, because that is where Christ is, the object of this calling. It is not a Christ on the earth or in His humiliation, but the Son of Man perfect in glory, in the heavens. We have no other calling at all except to a risen and glorified Christ. There is no other kind of model of holiness for the saint other than the image of Christ seated at the right hand of God. What God puts before all believers to look at is exactly this. The glorified Man is the image we will be conformed into. It is the only Christ there is (for we know Christ after the flesh no longer), and so, the only proper object of our calling.

2 Thessalonians 2:13-14

"But we are bound to give thanks to God always for you, brethren beloved by the Lord, because God from the beginning chose you for salvation through sanctification by the Spirit and belief in the truth, to which He called you by our gospel, for the obtaining of the glory of our Lord Jesus Christ."

While we walk on this earth, we are to be like Him as much as possible. Beholding Him in glory, we are changed. When we look at and dwell on Christ now, we become every day more and more like Him. It is our contemplation of the Lord in glory that has a sanctifying power in our lives (I John 3:2-3). And how does this happen? "Sanctify them by Your truth. Your word is truth," (John 17:17). God's word is the only means He employs to change the believer from glory to glory. For the believer the veil has been taken away and we behold the full glory of God in the face of Jesus Christ, the glorified Man. This is the gospel of the glory.

Chapter 9:

Many sons in the Glory

Ephesians 1:19-21;

"...and what is the exceeding greatness of His power toward us who believe, according to the working of His mighty power which He worked in Christ when He raised Him from the dead and seated Him at His right hand in the heavenly places, far above all principality and power and might and dominion, and every name that is named, not only in this age but also in that which is to come."

The Son of Man has been raised up and has entered into the glory, the very glory of God. The above verses make this clear. However if we look closely we can see that the focus of this passage is not the Father's glorification of Christ, although that certainly took place. Rather it is the Father's exceedingly great power towards the believer, and our understanding of that power and knowing this work and its results. The truths surrounding redemption are little known by believers today. When the believer looks for Christ and sees the cross, we should know that He is not there. When we look for Him in the tomb, He is not there as well. Is He in Galilee walking around with His disciples? He is not. We know Christ no longer according to the flesh if we are looking with the eye of faith (II Cor. 5:16). We should always walk by faith and not by sight (2 Cor. 5:7).

In the counsels of God there is a Man in Glory

God has exalted a Man into glory; the Son of Man has been glorified, and is now sitting at the right hand of God. How important is this? It is the means by which many others will be brought into the glory.

Heb. 2:10

"For it was fitting for Him, for whom are all things and by whom are all things, in bringing many sons to glory, to make the captain of their salvation perfect through sufferings."

John 17:22

"And the glory which You gave Me I have given them, that they may be one just as We are one."

Many sons into the Glory – Heirs of God, Co-Heirs with Christ

It is through Jesus Christ that many sons are brought to glory. He is the firstborn (Rom. 8:29, Col. 1:18) and the forerunner (Heb. 6:20), gone before us into the presence of God. But the incredible truth of scripture is that it is all for us and on our behalf (Heb. 9:24), and all because of the redemptive work of Jesus Christ, the Son of Man. If He is the firstborn from the dead, then there will be many others raised in Him. If He is the forerunner into the glory behind the veil, it means that many more will follow Him there. If He is the Beginning of the creation of God (Rev. 3:14), it is because there are many new creations in Him and by His work (2 Cor. 5:17, Gal. 6:15). Jesus Christ, the Son of Man, is the One who brings many sons to glory. And we will be brought there because the believer has been made an heir of God and equal heirs with Christ.

Romans 8:16-18

"The Spirit Himself bears witness with our spirit that we are children of God, and if children, then heirs—heirs of God and joint heirs with Christ, if indeed we suffer with Him, that we may also be glorified together

For I consider that the sufferings of this present time are not worthy to be compared with the glory which shall be revealed in us."

The Believer brought into the same position as the Glorified Son of Man

For the believer, nothing can compare to the glory that God will place us in. We will be in it as the Body of Christ and the Bride of Christ (Eph. 5:27). Every individual believer will be there as a son in the house of the Father (Matt. 13:43). We also see that there is an inheritance to be given by the Father to all those in relationship with Him as sons – this is Christ and His brethren (John 20:17). This passage in Galatians confirms the same.

Galatians 4:7

"Therefore you are no longer a slave but a son, and if a son, then an heir of God through Christ."

Through Christ all believers have been made heirs of God the Father. It is the Father's love set on us and His very own counsels choosing us in Christ before time began (2 Tim. 1:9) that has given us this inheritance. The following two verses show this truth.

Colossians 1:12

"...giving thanks to the Father who has qualified us to be partakers of the inheritance of the saints in the light."

The idea here is that the believer has been made fit by God to be a partaker of the inheritance. The Father has qualified us by enabling us in Christ. The believer has been brought into the very same position with the Father that Christ has, as the glorified Son of Man. He is our God and our Father (John 20:17). And we have been made accepted by the Father in Christ (Eph. 1:6). Also in Ephesians we read:

Ephesians 1:11 "...in whom also we have obtained an inheritance, being predestined according to the purpose of Him who works all things according to the counsel of His will,"

In Him means the believer is in Christ. But it was the Father's purpose and counsel of will that placed us there in Christ. There we have obtained an inheritance, the very same one that Christ will be given, for we are Christ and we are, as believers, in Him eternally. We see something else in Ephesians.

Every true Believer is sealed with the Holy Spirit – the guarantee of Sonship and Inheritance

Ephesians 1:13-14

"In Him you also trusted, after you heard the word of truth, the gospel of your salvation; in whom also, having believed, you were sealed with the Holy Spirit of promise, who is the guarantee of our inheritance until the redemption of the purchased possession, to the praise of His glory."

Every true believer has been sealed with the Holy Spirit. This is the Father's stamp of authenticity on the many sons. This seal identifies those that are His. The Holy Spirit dwells inside every true believer. For us this seal is the guarantee of the inheritance. The presence of the Holy Spirit in us is the down payment of all future glory. We also have Christ in us, dwelling in our hearts by faith (Eph. 3:17, John 14:20). Christ in us, the ever present hope of glory (Col. 1:27). And we further know that all scriptural hope is sure and steadfast (Heb. 6:19).

It is a wonderful thought and meditation that the Father has so blessed the believer in Christ. Co-heir with Christ of the Father is a privileged position. We wouldn't be able to believe such a thought if it wasn't the declared counsel of God. But it is all true. We must remember that in all things Jesus Christ holds the preeminence (Col. 1:18). He is the Head of creation as having created it all (Col. 1:16). He is the Head of the Body, the church, and this as the Son of Man -- the firstborn from the dead, redeeming us through His death, His blood being shed (Col. 1:14, 18). These two things have been reconciled back to God by the Son of Man: all of creation and all believers (Col. 1:20-22).

But the reconciling does not place these two things in the same position. Creation -- all things that were created -- is the original right of possession of the Creator. We see that all things were created through Him and for Him (Col. 1:16, Heb. 1:2). But when man was given dominion over the works of His hand, the first Adam only brought defilement and cursing upon it. The second Adam comes in and through His death brings all things defiled back to God in reconciliation (Col. 1:20). All things are described in greater detail by the following scriptures in Colossians;

Colossians 1:16

"For by Him all things were created that are in heaven and that are on earth, visible and invisible, whether thrones or dominions or principalities or powers. All things were created through Him and for Him."

Colossians 1:20

"...and by Him to reconcile all things to Himself, by Him, whether things on earth or things in heaven, having made peace through the blood of His cross."

When the Son of Man reconciled all things, it was all things in heaven and earth. It was all things visible and invisible, thrones, dominions, etc. This is the inheritance of the Son of Man. This is what we are co-heirs of, all things, all of creation reconciled. We do not yet see all things put under His feet as a physical reality, but His work as the Son of Man gave Him the title to it. We are in Christ, a part of Him, His Body and co-heirs with Him of all these things. The distinction between the two things reconciled in the first chapter of Colossians is that all of creation is the inheritance, while believers are the heirs of it with Christ. We see a similar train of thought in Ephesians;

Ephesians 1:9-11

"...having made known to us the mystery of His will, according to His good pleasure which He purposed in Himself, that in the dispensation of the fullness of the times He might gather together in one all things in Christ, both which are in heaven and which are on earth—in Him. In Him also

we have obtained an inheritance, being predestined according to the purpose of Him who works all things according to the counsel of His will,"

In this portion of Scripture we have everything we have been discussing. There are the counsels and purpose of God, all things in heaven and earth gathered into the Headship of Christ, and an inheritance given to those in Christ according to God's counsels. In Him we have obtained an inheritance. Simply, all this is in Christ and for all those placed by God in Him.

The Holy Spirit gathers the body of the Glorified Man

1 Corinthians 12:12

"For as the body is one and has many members, but all the members of that one body, being many, are one body, so also is Christ."

We have shown previously the importance of believers seeing with the eye of faith Christ at the right hand of God, as the glorified Son of Man. It has always been the intention of God, in His counsels before the foundation of the world, to gather a body to be associated and united to this glorified Man. When Christ sat down at the right hand of the Father, the Holy Spirit was sent from heaven to this earth to accomplish the gathering of the body, and the sealing of the believer. This is what is taking place now.

All mankind existed in failure in responsibility before God in the first Adam; all falling short of the glory. But God had His own counsels concerning the believer before time began. The revelation and accomplishment of these counsels had to wait until the Son of Man laid the foundation for it, finishing the work of redemption. All our failure in responsibility we have accumulated in our relationship with the first Adam, Christ has met. He bore our sins and was made sin for us on the cross, and yet, glorified God in the midst of it.

The Believer's association with Christ, the Son of Man

In the first chapter of Ephesians we see these very counsels of God revealed. We see God's thought and purpose, to have the believer with Christ and like Christ, His own Son in glory. These are truths now that we possess. The believer is associated with the second Adam in glory, and so, we will eventually be made like Him. We are not there yet, in the glory, but He is there, in His resurrected and glorified body. He is at the right hand of God as the forerunner and the first born from the dead. *Beloved, now are we the sons of God; and it does not yet appear what we will be, but we know that when He appears, we will be like Him, for we will see Him as He is (I John 3:2).*

Allow me to further show this association with Christ in Scripture. The believer was crucified with Christ (Gal. 2:20, Rom. 6:6). We died with Him (Rom. 6:8, Col. 2:20, 3:3). And then we were buried with Him (Rom. 6:4, Col. 2:12). After that, the believer was raised from the dead with Christ (Col. 2:12, Col. 3:1, Eph. 1:19-20, 2:5) by the exceeding greatness of the Father's power. The life we have is not ourselves, but Christ living in us (Gal. 2:20, Col. 3:3-4). But, as I've mentioned before, this was not the end of God's counsels towards us. When Christ was seated at God's right hand, exalted above all principality and power, the Father, at the same time, exalted His body, the church, with Him. We are the fullness of Christ, all things put under the feet (Eph. 1:20-23). These things are already accomplished in title.

In Christ the believer has title to these blessings and truths now

Romans 8:29-30

"Because whom he has foreknown, he has also predestinated to be conformed to the image of his Son, so that he should be the firstborn among many brethren.

But whom he has predestinated, these also he has called; and whom he has called, these also he has justified; but whom he has justified, these also he has glorified."

The language here is in the past tense as already accomplished from the Father foreknowing all the way to the believer's body being glorified. It is already finished as to God's mind and purpose, and in Christ we have been given the title to it all. Only one portion of the above passage is yet future for the believer – to be conformed to the image of the Son. And this is a hope that is sure and steadfast as we see earlier in this same chapter:

Romans 8:23-25

"Not only that, but we also who have the firstfruits of the Spirit, even we ourselves groan within ourselves, eagerly waiting for the adoption, the redemption of our body. For we were saved in this hope, but hope that is seen is not hope; for why does one still hope for what he sees? But if we hope for what we do not see, we eagerly wait for it with perseverance."

The believer has received salvation now, but all our hopes remain to be fulfilled as a finalizing of our redemption. We were saved (past tense) in this hope (future). We have the title to it already, in a certain sense; we are in Christ and have been sealed with the Holy Spirit.

2 Corinthians 5:4-5

"For we who are in this tent groan, being burdened, not because we want to be unclothed, but further clothed, that mortality may be swallowed up by life. Now He who has prepared us for this very thing is God, who also has given us the Spirit as a guarantee."

2 Corinthians 1:21-22

"Now He who establishes us with you in Christ and has anointed us is God, who also has sealed us and given us the Spirit in our hearts as a deposit."

The Holy Spirit, as given to us by God, is the deposit and guarantee of the future redemption of our bodies. There is a future event in God that will fulfill and finalize our salvation, by which we will be brought to the house of the Father and into the very presence of the invisible God, into the glory. But how could this happen in these earthly tents and with most of the other bodies corrupted in the grave? It would be impossible. No, the corruptible must put on incorruption, and the mortal put on immortality. As we said previously, this event, for the body of Christ, will be resurrection or change.

Our present bodies – Our last connection to this Earth

Hopefully we can see then, that our last and final connection to this earth and to the first Adam, is our physical bodies. Therein still resides the sin nature passed on from him to all mankind. When sin entered in, death came in as well, as the very fruit of it (Rom. 5:12). Sin in the flesh is what makes the body mortal, subject to death. But the future event I speak of, for all true believers from the entire time of the church on the earth, is the changing of our bodies by the sovereign power and grace of God. Mortal puts on immortality, corruption puts on incorruption, and the power of death that Satan holds is defeated on our behalf (Heb. 2:14-15, I Cor. 15:53-56). How is this? Well, certainly God has the power to do as He pleases. This event is the removal of sin from the flesh, from the physical bodies of believers. Is this not a necessity? The believer, brought into the very presence of God must have sin removed from the flesh. This is what is meant by the Father predestining us to be conformed to the image of His Son (Rom. 8:29). This is the glorification of the bodies of all believers.

Our physical bodies are our only connection to this earth, as believers. We are partakers of the heavenly calling in Christ, but again in title and purpose, and not yet a completed physical reality. Every member that ever was in the body of Christ still has their physical body on this earth, whether in the grave or still alive. That is why the scriptural doctrines concerning the church always place it on the earth (clearly seen in Eph. 4:4-16).

But you say there are believers in heaven. This is a blessed truth, for to be absent from the body is to be present with the Lord (2 Cor. 5:8). But this is not the believers hope and constant expectation, nor God's counsels for the church. We do not want to be unclothed, but further clothed, that mortality may be swallowed up by life (2 Cor. 5:4). This is our proper hope. This is God's designs for the believer, to be conformed into the image of His Son. Our bodies have to be glorified. They must be made fit to be brought into the heavens, and into the glory of God.

It is my hope that you will grab hold of these truths and never allow them to fade from having a presence in your thoughts and faith. We are, as believers, always and in everything, associated with Christ. We are His body, a part of Him; flesh of His flesh, bone of His bone (Eph. 5:30), and fellow brethren with Him in the house of His Father. We are as Christ. Christ is our life. When the Father looks at any believer, He sees them in Christ, clothed with the righteousness of God, and accepted in the Beloved (Eph. 1:6). When Christ was raised from the dead, we were raised with Him in the same power and purposes of the Father (Eph. 1:19-20, Eph. 2:5). When the Father thinks of the inheritance He will give to His Son, every believer is in His thoughts, according to the counsel of His will, as equal heirs having obtained the inheritance, to the praise of His glory (Eph. 1:11). The only part of Christ we do not share in is His divinity. With these understandings, other truths from God's word await illumination by the Spirit.

The Church eternally existing in the Heavens – the manifold wisdom of God

Ephesians 2:7

"...that he might display in the coming ages the surpassing riches of his grace in kindness towards us in Christ Jesus."

Ephesians 3:9-11

"...and to make all see what is the fellowship of the mystery, which from the beginning of the ages has been hidden in God who created all things through Jesus Christ; to the intent that now the manifold wisdom of God might be made known by the church to the principalities and powers in the heavenly places, according to the eternal purpose which He accomplished in Christ Jesus our Lord,"

His manifold wisdom is now displayed by the existence of the church, the centerpiece of His mystery hidden, but now revealed. It is into these things that angels want to look (I Pet. 1:11-13). They stand in amazement of God's revealed counsels towards us, and how God's holiness and righteousness was glorified by bringing man into His glory. It is in man that the angels learn what God does in His ways and counsels, for the simple reason that in these counsels the Word of God became flesh, became man—that He who created angels does not take up angels, but takes up man (Heb. 2:16). This taking up of man was when he was a sinner, in order to display in him the glory of God. It was all the work of Jesus Christ, the Son of Man. He has truly brought many sons into the glory. And the Father has placed us in Him. In the ages to come the Father will show towards the believer His surpassing riches of grace.

John 17:24,

"Father, I desire that they also whom You gave Me may be with Me where I am, that they may behold My glory which You have given Me; for You loved Me before the foundation of the world."

Chapter 10:

The Revelation of the Father

Exodus 6:3

"I appeared to Abraham, to Isaac, and to Jacob, as God Almighty, but by My name Jehovah I was not known to them."

In the Old Testament God revealed Himself to the forefathers by the name of the Almighty One who could protect and deliver by His awesome power – El Shaddai. To Israel He is Jehovah. To this nation He is the One who never began and will never end, the self-existing God, who will always be faithful to keep His promises. When God gave Abraham victory over his enemies, the priest Melchizedek reveals God as the Most High God, possessor of heaven and earth (Gen. 14:18-24). The name, Most High God, as well as the exercise of Melchizedek's priesthood, points to and speaks of millennial glory. It will be God literally repossessing the heavens and earth. His government of the earth will be centered with physical Israel (Deut. 32:8-9), and millennial blessings after the defeat of Israel's enemies. These are the names of God as revealed then, and the extent of the Old Testament revelation of whom and what God is.

Missing from this is the New Testament revelation of the Father. The Son of God was sent for the express purpose of revealing Him.

Matthew 11:27,

"All things have been delivered to me by my Father, and no one knows the Son but the Father, nor does anyone know the Father, but the Son, and he to whom the Son may be pleased to reveal him."

In speaking of the Son Jesus is referencing the Son of God, not the Son of Man. No one can know the Son as the Father does, and no one can know the Father as the Son (Luke 10:22, John 1:18). It is just not possible. Only divinity can truly know divinity, and this is the sense of what He is saying. But again, what is revealed and declared by God is the believer's to know and understand. In the case of the Father being revealed, it is for the believer's intimate relationship in love -- this relationship ultimately as sons of the Father, not just a dry understanding of knowledge. But there is no doubt that without the Son coming into this world, there would have been no revelation of the Father.

Both Titles – Messiah and the Son of Man – are part of the counsels of God

The titles of Messiah and the Son of Man are the subject of this book. By the comparisons and contrasts made, we may gain understandings into the counsels of God, and with this, a sound means of rightly dividing scripture. There is an important understanding to grasp before speaking more of the revelation of the Father. When we speak of Messiah, it is a title and a role that Jesus took up according to promises and prophecy. Messiah was presented to Israel. He was not received, but rejected, and the title and role was set aside by God. This was done by God's determined counsel, and so, we must acknowledge the sovereignty and purpose of God in this.

Messiah is a title taken up and set aside, only to be taken up at a future time when Israel is recognized again by God. It will be a time of God's choosing, where God will be found faithful to fulfill His promises to Israel according to the revelation of His name, Jehovah. This understanding of the title and role of Messiah make it an understanding of and in the counsels of God.

A few more thoughts can be brought out concerning the title of Messiah and God's counsels. This title is specifically related to Israel, the earth, and prophecy. The counsels of God concern the gathering of all things – things in heaven, and things on earth – into Christ (Eph. 1:10). This entire plan, all the work God does in the gatherings, is into Christ as the Son of Man glorified. This is the title He took up before leaving heaven. This is the title in which the foundational work for the carrying out of all God's counsels was done.

The title of Messiah is only a portion of the overall scope and reach of the authority and headship of the Son of Man. All things gathered on the earth during the millennium is the earthly kingdom of the Son of Man over the entire world. Messiah reigning over Israel is only a portion of this overall earthly reign of the Son of Man. Messiah for Israel, according to prophecy, simply sets Israel at that time as the center of Christ's earthly glory, and as the most exalted nation on the face of the earth.

The title and role of the Son of Man is the basis of all the counsels of God. As we have shown, this title is associated with the redemptive work for man, taken up by Jesus for the specific reason of suffering death. This work is the foundation of those counsels. This Man, having perfectly finished the work, enters as Man into the glory of God. This title was shown as embraced by Jesus, particularly after the title of Messiah was set aside. But in contrast to the title of Messiah, this title, having been taken up, and the work perfectly completed, will never be laid aside by Him in all eternity. And it is my hope that the reader may see, with me, the grand scope and reach of these thoughts, in contrast and comparison to that of Messiah. The title of Son of Man is understood as taken up by Jesus, and this of the determined counsels of God.

Jesus Christ, the eternally Beloved Son

When we consider Jesus as the Son of God, it is not according to the counsels of God. He is not the Son of God because a distinct work of God is to be accomplished. This is not a title and role taken up. Jesus is the Son of God, known to believers as the second person of the

Godhead. This is who He is, who He was in eternity past, and who He always will be. As the Son, in His divinity, and in eternity past, He shared the infinite glory of God (John 17:5). This is Jesus, the Son of God. In the beginning was the Word; the Word was with God and the Word was God (John 1:1).

John 1:14

"And the Word became flesh and dwelt among us, and we beheld His glory, the glory as of the only begotten of the Father, full of grace and truth."

John 1:18

"No one has seen God at any time. The only begotten Son, who is in the bosom of the Father, He has declared Him."

Here is the divinity of Jesus as the Word from eternity past. We also see clearly these two distinct beings -- the Father and the Son. The revelation progresses by telling us that the Word, the Son, was sent and became flesh, taking on human form, coming in the likeness of men (Phil. 2:6-7).

What is prominent, and even a point of faith in the gospels, is the thought that the Son was sent into this world by the Father. The Father, in the fullness of grace, sends the Son. The Son shows forth the Father perfectly, and glorifies Him (John 17:4). We are to understand, by the Spirit and the Word, that all that the Father had given to Jesus was the gift of the Father to the Son on the earth (John 17:1-8 -- this is not Jehovah establishing the Messiah). The Father had sent Him in sovereign grace, and He had come from the Father. The last part of the above passages in John 1 is that the Son was sent for the reason of declaring or revealing the Father (Luke 10:22).

No one knew the Father with perfect knowledge, except the Son who was eternally in the bosom of the Father. The Son of God was sent to reveal God, to reveal the Father.

John 6:46

"Not that anyone has seen the Father, except He who is from God; He has seen the Father."

John 10:15

"As the Father knows Me, even so I know the Father; and I lay down My life for the sheep."

John 5:23

"...that all should honor the Son just as they honor the Father. He who does not honor the Son does not honor the Father who sent Him."

The Father seeks true worshipers

It is clear that the Son was sent into the world by the Father to bring a greater revelation on the topic of God – to reveal the Father. And what was revealed? Many things, if we are taught by the Word and the Spirit. For instance, the Father is seeking true worshipers. All else, as far as worship in the flesh, and according to the beggarly elements of the world, He will put aside and bring to an end (John 4:21). Those that worship Him *must* worship in spirit and truth (John 4:23-24). There would be no compromising on this. The more we think about it, the easier it is to see from this passage in John 4, that worship of the Father and worship in spirit is not associated with this world or earth. Basically Judaism is set aside by God. A further point made concerns the timing of this change by God; He says, "But the hour is coming, and now is..."

The Father's love displayed for His sons

Another truth the Son revealed is the Father's love for His Son and sons. The Father has brought the believer into the same position and relationship as the Son. This is the sense of what Jesus is saying after His resurrection (John 20:17). As we have previously discussed, He is the firstborn among many other brethren. In Christ, all believers have been made sons of the Father. An amazing truth of the Father is that He loves us with the same love He has for the Son (John 15:9-10, 14:21-23, and 16:27).

John 17:23

"I in them, and You in Me; that they may be made perfect in one, and that the world may know that You have sent Me, and have loved them as You have loved Me."

This is hard to fathom, but it is what the Son reveals about the Father. The invisible God, whose form no one has ever seen at any time, who dwells in unapproachable light, loves us with the same love that He has for His Son, Jesus Christ. It is the same love as for the Son who was eternally in the bosom of the Father (John 1:18). (A connection to note; we are sons of the Father because the title of the Son of Man was taken up by the Son of God, and the work of the Son of Man was finished, creating many brethren through Him and with Him according to the counsels of God.)

John 14:7

"If you had known Me, you would have known My Father also; and from now on you know Him and have seen Him."

The testimony of the Revelation of the Father – the Words and Works of the Son

This is how the Father was revealed. The Son of God, the only one who has seen and knows Him, was sent to reveal Him. The Son, being sent, was nevertheless always in the Father and the Father always in Him (John 14:10). Again, this is divinity we are speaking of. The testimony that confirms this truth is the words He spoke. They were the words from God He always spoke, as given to the Son on earth by the Father (John 17:7-8). They were words spoken by One who possessed the Spirit without measure, in contrast to the prophets of old (John 3:33-35, 14:24). The works were those of the Father given to the Son on earth to do (John 10:25, 37-38). All this was from the Father and serves to reveal Him.

John 14:8-11

"Philip said to Him, "Lord, show us the Father, and it is sufficient for us."

Jesus said to him, "Have I been with you so long, and yet you have not known Me, Philip? He who has seen Me has seen the Father; so how can you say, 'Show us the Father'? Do you not believe that I am in the Father, and the Father in Me? The words that I speak to you I do not speak on My own authority; but the Father who dwells in Me does the works. Believe Me that I am in the Father and the Father in Me, or else believe Me for the sake of the works themselves."

If you are looking at the Son come into this world, you are looking at the Father. If you know the Son, you know the Father. If you love the Son who took on flesh, then you love the Father (John 15:10, 16:27). If the believer struggles with this abstractness in faith, then your belief may be helped by the testimony of His words and works, as the Son being sent by the Father. It is this testimony that Israel rejects. It proved they did not know the Father at all (John 15:21-24), and in fact, having seen the Father, they hated Him (John 15:24).

When it came to the Jews receiving this revelation of the Father, things didn't go very well. Was it mainly a problem with Jesus being the Son of God, sent to reveal the Father? Or was it their previous revelation they held close, that Jehovah is one God? What about Israel's state and condition as being in Adam, in the flesh, and part of this unbelieving world? Did their actual position in Adam afford them enough spiritual sight to see God, recognize God, and receive Him? Or were they dull in understanding and blind in spiritual sight? I believe the answer is that all of this is correct, and Israel, highly privileged as they were, simply could not see and understand. But we must examine what the scriptures say on these points and questions.

Rejection of the Son is rejection of the One who sent Him

John 5:16-18

"For this reason the Jews persecuted Jesus, and sought to kill Him, because He had done these things on the Sabbath. But Jesus answered them, "My Father has been working until now, and I have been working."

Therefore the Jews sought all the more to kill Him, because He not only broke the Sabbath, but also said that God was His Father, making Himself equal with God."

In this entire chapter Jesus, the Son of God, was speaking of the Father, revealing Him to the Jewish people. By the testimony of the Spirit through John we see two reasons why the Jews persecuted Jesus and wanted to kill Him. One reason was for breaking the law. The other reason was for claiming that God was His Father – making Himself God, that is, the Son of God. They could not acknowledge Jesus as the Son of God. By rejecting Him as the Son they were rejecting the Father. If the One the Father had sent was rejected, then the Father was rejected. If the One that the Father had sent was hated, then the Father was hated as well.

The Lord is One; and Israel's difficulty

John 15:22-24

"If I had not come and spoken to them, they would have no sin, but now they have no excuse for their sin. He who hates Me hates My Father also. If I had not done among them the works which no one else did, they would have no sin; but now they have seen and also hated both Me and My Father."

1 John 2:23

"Whoever denies the Son does not have the Father either; he who acknowledges the Son has the Father also."

You have to reason that Israel's revelation and truth that God is One may have been a great hindrance to them receiving the Son of God coming to them, speaking of the Father. This previous truth was meant to guard the nation against turning to Gentile idolatry, keeping the Jews separated and undefiled as a people. The first commandment, which the following statement prefaced, shows to Israel that Jehovah was the one true living God, that everything else is just stone or wood. But would the Jews be able to understand the only begotten Son eternally in the bosom of the Father, now sent to them to progress the revelation of God?

Deuteronomy 6:4

"Hear, O Israel: The LORD our God, the LORD is one!"

It is often true that previous revelations, though certainly having their proper place, may hinder the individual or group from receiving and understanding more. In the New Testament, and certainly with the sending of the Son from the Father, we are given the fullness of the revelation of God – the Trinity. I believe Israel has difficulty with this because Jehovah is One God. When Jesus admits to the elders of Israel at His trial that He is the Son of God as they say, it is immediately judged blasphemous and worthy of death (Mark 14:61-64, Luke 22:66-71).

Israel – in Adam, in the Flesh, and part of the World

As for Israel's position in Adam, as in the flesh and part and parcel of this world, this is well documented in the scriptures. I often use M&Ms sitting on a table-top as an illustration of Israel and their relationship to the rest of the world. If I separate all the green M&Ms over to one side (for the green ones truly have my favor) and place a little toy fence around them, leaving all the other M&Ms where they are -- this is what God did in choosing and separating the Jews. They are all still M&Ms, and they all remain on the table-top. The green ones are simply chosen and separated with a toy fence around them! Israel received privilege as favored by God. Their law, their religion, is the little toy wall separating them from the other M&Ms -- the Gentiles. But what is obvious is that the wall never had the ability to change the green M&Ms into anything different. Now the green M&Ms are chosen and separated, this is true; but they remain M&Ms on the table-top, no different than the Gentiles.

This simple illustration can easily be verified from the testimony of Scripture;

Romans 3:19

"Now we know that whatever the law says, it says to those who are under the law, that every mouth may be stopped, and all the world may become guilty before God."

The Jews are those under the law. If the Jew is condemned, and they are God's privileged and separated people, the cream of the crop of humanity, then the conclusions are easily arrived at — every mouth is stopped and the entire world is guilty before God. All are guilty, all face judgment. Every mouth does not exclude anyone.

The entire world is judged by God

John 12:31

"Now is the judgment of this world; now the ruler of this world will be cast out."

Has the entire world been judged by God? It certainly has, and this, in the time of Christ. The ruler of the world deceived and blinded the Jews into hating and despising the Son that the Father sent to them. They plotted and planned His murder and death. The Gentile part of the world had their involvement with Pilate and the Roman soldiers, for this was not a Jewish stoning, but a Roman crucifixion. But God has judged and condemned the whole world. How was this? Simply, all mankind, in their position in Adam and in the flesh, has failed in responsibility. Man in his works, in his responsibility, is man in his sins. This is not fruit before God, and it is universal to all mankind.

God's last test of Mankind

In the end God sent His Son, saying, "They will respect my Son." But the world said, "Come, let us kill Him and seize His inheritance," (Matt. 21:37-38). This was the last test! God was finished testing, the whole world proven lost and ruined. It was *the fullness of time* (Gal. 4:4) and *the end of the ages* (Heb. 9:26) when God sent the Son. Why? The sending of the Son was the final testing, and with His rejection God had seen enough, and the whole world was set in judgment.

John 12:37-40

"But although He had done so many signs before them, they did not believe in Him, that the word of Isaiah the prophet might be fulfilled, which he spoke:

"Lord, who has believed our report?
And to whom has the arm of the Lord been revealed?"

Therefore they could not believe, because Isaiah said again:

"He has blinded their eyes and hardened their hearts,
Lest they should see with their eyes,
Lest they should understand with their hearts and turn,
So that I should heal them."

Israel's eyes were blinded, their hearts were hardened. They could not see with their eyes, they could not understand with their hearts. Simply put, they could not believe. It was impossible for them to believe. We cannot accuse the Holy Spirit of playing loosely with words. Here is how the Spirit shows this through Paul:

Romans 3:9-12

"What then? Are we better than they? Not at all. For we have previously charged both Jews and Greeks that they are all under sin.

As it is written:

"There is none righteous, no, not one;
There is none who understands;
There is none who seeks after God.
They have all turned aside;
They have together become unprofitable;
There is none who does good, no, not one."

The Question: Are we better than they?

In a previous chapter I was speaking about the rejection of Jesus as Messiah to Israel, and humorously asked some questions concerning the Gentiles. Is the promise of a Messiah now a promise God gives to the Gentiles by default, in view of the outright rejection of Him by His privileged people? In the above passage the Holy Spirit presents a question for the believer to answer. If you answer this question honestly, without simply parroting Paul's answer, it will show where you stand in your understanding of one of the great principles of God found in His ways and counsels.

If we consider the facts of the results of the gospel being preached from Pentecost through today, what do we see? The circumstances show the overwhelming percentage of those saved are Gentile. In view of the results, does this prove the Gentiles are smarter and better than Israel? This brings out another important thought – why wouldn't we answer the question based upon the results? It is the scientific method and contemporary thinking – draw your conclusions based on the gathering of data and what the facts of the case present. If what we think and believe is based on what we see as obvious results, then we conclude yes, we are better and smarter than Israel. Why wouldn't we have such thoughts, and such conclusions? Israel rejected God when He came to them, we did not! The results speak for themselves!

Believers would never voice these thoughts. It would be viewed as rude and arrogant, and we do not want others to have this impression of us. However, our unwillingness to speak doesn't mean that these thoughts and conclusions do not remain in the back of our minds. To be frank, these are the proper conclusions of any Christian who holds any degree of Arminian thought and doctrine. Arminianism maintains and guards the works, the choices, and the will of man, to one degree or another. It does so to the detriment of the sovereignty, power, and glory of God. In this example, the Arminian doctrine is that unbelieving man actually seeks after God and chooses God in accepting the gospel. Then we must agree, in Arminian thought, this choice by an unbeliever has to involve the gathering of information and data, and some use of the intelligence of the mind in reasoning and proper decision making. At the very least the Arminian must be willing to admit that those who believe made a 'better' decision. Are we better than they? How do you explain the nation of Israel rejecting God, when He was among them in the flesh? Was this simply a 'poor' decision and an unusual coincidence that the nation as a whole was guilty? Those who have Arminian doctrine can only answer Paul's question with a 'yes.' They have no explanation in their doctrine that allows them to honestly answer 'no.' In Arminianism, the responsibility of the will of man and all his choices remains with man.

I can't tell you how far off scripturally this line of thinking is and how far away it is from God's thoughts and sound doctrine. Yet we would have to say that over 85% of Christianity today could not draw any different conclusions, and have no other logical explanation for the results that we readily observe. Sadly it is not simply the results observed in the world around us. The evil is the leaven we hold as doctrine and teaching that can only, and logically, end in such conclusions.

The Leaven spreads and saturates throughout

What am I saying? What am I doing? If I am a teacher of the Word of God and I see evil growing and ripening in Christianity today, should I remain silent? Or do I have a responsibility to sound a warning? "The kingdom of heaven is like leaven, which a woman took and hid in three measures of meal till it was all leavened." (Matt. 13:33). These are our Lord's very own words. Every believer should take them to heart. Man cannot stop the evil leaven from penetrating. At the end there is total saturation of the evil doctrine. It may be hidden and subtle, but certainly it is there in Christianity. The unique thing about this is the leaven itself will blind the church world to its own presence. If believers recognize the evil, the leaven will erroneously have them thinking we can stop it, we can prevent it, and with God's help we will remedy the entire situation.

But God isn't helping. He says this is what will be in the Christian world. The evil will grow and ripen. Rest assured, in the end He will fully judge it. But does He help us with a remedy now? He does not. What does He want the believer to do? The scriptural instruction is to fully recognize evil, turn from it, and have no part in it (2 Tim. 3:5, 1 Pet. 3:11, Rom. 12:9).

What is the leaven? What is the evil doctrine? It is the insidious pretense of man exalting himself. When man does this in the world he builds a tower of Babel. When man did this in Israel, he took the law and exalted himself in pride and self-righteousness. In the early church the Judaizers made their additions to the simplicity of Christ. What were these additions? They were the Jewish works of the law. It wasn't long before all the Christian faith was Judaized. The history of the church on the earth is the testimony to this. God eventually worked in sovereign grace in the Reformation, shining light on the authority of God's Word and justification. But in Protestantism, man in responsibility nationalizes the church, and the tares are welcomed in. In the history of Christendom man has always been building on the earth. He thinks he builds with gold, silver, and precious stones. He does not. In exalting himself he has built with wood, hay, and straw. It all will be tested by the fire of God and it will not remain (I Cor. 3:9-15). Arminian doctrine represents the last form this leaven takes in subtly exalting man in the presence of God.

The last church judged in Revelation 3 depicts the ending condition of Protestantism – in reality it is the arm of Protestantism known as Evangelical Christianity. One thing I find remarkable about the character of the Laodiceans is how the evil has brought them to see themselves as diametrically opposite from how the Lord actually sees them and judges them. "I am rich, have become wealthy, and have need of nothing..." You do not know that you are wretched, miserable, poor, blind, and naked (Rev. 3:17). The leaven is blinding, corrupt, and deceiving.

What then? Are we better than they? This is the question the Holy Spirit asks. Does your faith and doctrine, even in view of the world and circumstances, allow you to truthfully answer along with the apostle – 'No, not at all.' This is the spiritual answer with understanding. But if the leaven is working in you, you will not be able to answer truthfully.

None Seeks after God

The previously quoted portion of Scripture from Romans 3 is the Spirit's description of the world. It is both Jews and Gentiles, all under sin. How can there be any unbelievers in the world seeking after God, if there is none who seeks after God? How can anyone be judged as basically good when there is none who does good, no, not one. Now let us look further at the words of Jesus contained in John 8. They reveal of how God views the Jews and the world.

John 8:19

"Then they said to Him, "Where is Your Father?"

Jesus answered, "You know neither Me nor My Father. If you had known Me, you would have known My Father also."

John 8:21

"Then Jesus said to them again, "I am going away, and you will seek Me, and will die in your sin. Where I go you cannot come."

John 8:34

"Jesus answered them, "Most assuredly, I say to you, whoever commits sin is a slave of sin."

John 8:38

"I speak what I have seen with My Father, and you do what you have seen with your father."

John 8:42-43

"Jesus said to them, "If God were your Father, you would love Me, for I proceeded forth and came from God; nor have I come of Myself, but He sent Me. Why do you not understand My speech? Because you are not able to listen to My word."

John 8:47

"He who is of God hears God's words; therefore you do not hear, because you are not of God."

Israel's Hopeless State in Adam

His statements are quite emphatic. He says they do not know Him, nor the Father, and you can sense the hopelessness of any possibility of this reality changing. He tells them He is going away and they will die in their sin. Again their condition is hopeless. It is not the Son being hopeless, or feeling hopeless. He is speaking with authority and with words directly addressing their condition. "You will die in your sin," are words of condemnation, for the Jew first, and then in general, for the entire world in Adam. [It is the same truth the Spirit of God teaches through Paul in the first three chapters of Romans, up to the concluding statement in Rom. 3:23; "...for all have sinned and fall short of the glory of God."] He says, "Where I go you cannot come," once again declaring an impossibility and hopelessness as to their position.

In Adam they are slaves to sin with no freedom or possibility to do anything else. They are obeying their father and doing his work, but their father, unfortunately, is the prince of this world. This is in total agreement, once again, with what the Spirit teaches through Paul in Ephesians.

Ephesians 2:1-3

"And you He made alive, who were dead in trespasses and sins, in which you once walked according to the course of this world, according to the prince of the power of the air, the spirit who now works in the sons of disobedience, among whom also we all once conducted ourselves in the lusts of our flesh, fulfilling the desires of the flesh and of the mind, and were by nature children of wrath, just as the others."

When he says, '...among whom also we all once conducted ourselves...,' it is Jews and Gentiles alike, the whole world dead in sins and following after the course of the world and its prince. In John 8 quoted above, Jesus says, "...you are not able to listen to my words." As slaves of sin, they have no ability to hear God's words. They are not of God, but of Adam. They possess what he has given them, sin reigning in the flesh to serve and obey. By Adam and positioned in him, the whole world will die in their sin. You were dead in trespasses and sins. This is the 'judgment of the world.' And it is sealed up and declared complete with the coming of Christ. Israel, as part of the world and in this position, could not hear or receive the revelation of the Father as given by the Son.

The World Condemned

"Now is the judgment of the world...," is a solemn statement by Jesus in John 12:31. We need to fully understand it. It is the end of the world. It is judgment and condemnation to all in it. The world was proven by God as defiled and ruined in Adam.

John 17:9-16

"I pray for them. I do not pray for the world but for those whom You have given Me, for they are Yours. And all Mine are Yours, and Yours are Mine, and I am glorified in them. Now I am no longer in the world, but these are in the world, and I come to You. Holy Father, keep through Your name those whom You have given Me, that they may be one as We are. While I was with them in the world, I kept them in Your name. Those whom You gave Me I have kept; and none of them is lost except the son of perdition, that the Scripture might be fulfilled. But now I come to You, and these things I speak in the world, that they may have My joy fulfilled in themselves. I have given them Your word; and the world has hated them because they are not of the world, just as I am not of the world. I do not pray that You should take them out of the world, but that You should keep them from the evil. They are not of the world, just as I am not of the world."

What if I were to tell you that Jesus does not pray for the world? That He never prays for the world? Would that be considered blasphemous? Jesus never prays for the world, but prays for those given to Him by the Father out of the world. These are those given by the sovereign choice of God (John 15:16, 19, 6:70, 13:18, 5:21, 17:2-3, 6, II Thess. 2:13, and Rev. 17:14). As we have seen in John 12:31, God has judged and condemned the world already. Jesus will not pray for it.

Another truth is found here. The world, as ruined and judged, having hated Him and ready to put Him to death, is no longer fit for the Lord to stay in. He would soon be the raised and glorified Son of Man. He is not of this world, and it is especially evident when the Son of Man is lifted up from the earth (John 12:32). He would have to leave and go back to the Father, away from this world. As the glorified Son of Man, He could no longer stay here. Have you ever noticed that He never shows Himself to the world after His resurrection? This will wait until His return and physical judgment of the world (Col. 3:4).

After He was raised from the dead, in the glorified body, He no longer had any connection whatsoever with this world. I've said elsewhere in this book that the believer's only remaining connection with this world and this earth is our physical bodies. When this physical change is finalized for the believer, the end of our salvation, it will be by God's sovereign power we are conformed into the very image of Christ (Rom. 8:29). When our bodies are glorified, then the world will not be fit for us to remain in as well. He will come for us and take us (John 14:1-3), so that where He is, we may be also (John 17:24).

The Father and the Son possess Life

There is one more truth revealed about the Father and the Son that we should look at. All that is revealed about the Father in the New Testament cannot possibly be discussed in this chapter, nor is it my purpose. What I wanted to establish is that the Son of God was sent to reveal the Father, and what connection the Son has with the title of the Son of Man.

John 5:24-26

"Most assuredly, I say to you, he who hears My word and believes in Him who sent Me has everlasting life, and shall not come into judgment, but has passed from death into life. Most assuredly, I say to you, the hour is coming, and now is, when the dead will hear the voice of the Son of God; and those who hear will live. For as the Father has life in Himself, so He has granted the Son to have life in Himself."

The Father has life in and of Himself. The Son of God has life as well. This is eternal life given to those who hear the words of the Son and believe in the Father who sent Him. The entire world is dead in Adam, dead in trespasses and sins (Eph. 2:1). Jesus tells us that the hour is coming, and now is, when some of those that are dead will hear the voice of the Son speaking to them, and they will live (quickened). This is the way eternal life comes to a man;

John 5:21

"For as the Father raises the dead and gives life to them, even so the Son gives life to whom He will."

John 10:27-28

"My sheep hear My voice, and I know them, and they follow Me. And I give them eternal life, and they shall never perish; neither shall anyone snatch them out of My hand."

John 17:2-3

"...as You have given Him authority over all flesh, that He should give eternal life to as many as You have given Him. And this is eternal life, that they may know You, the only true God, and Jesus Christ whom You have sent."

Each one of the above three verses speaks about eternal life. Each one has an appeal for understanding of the sovereignty of the divine Son involved in the giving of this life. Once the life is given, they shall never perish, as kept by the divine power of the Son. It is impossible for anyone to snatch them from His hand. The Father is involved in this as well, for eternal life is given by the Son to as many as the Father has given to Him, as well as Himself giving life to the dead (John 17:6, 9-12). Eternal life given by the Father or the Son is now connected to the title and work of the Son of Man in the counsels of God.

The Son of God as the Son of Man gives Eternal Life

John 6:27-29

"Do not labor for the food which perishes, but for the food which endures to everlasting life, which the Son of Man will give you, because God the Father has set His seal on Him."

Then they said to Him, "What shall we do, that we may work the works of God?"

Jesus answered and said to them, "This is the work of God, that you believe in Him whom He sent."

John 6:47-51

"Most assuredly, I say to you, he who believes in Me has everlasting life. I am the bread of life. Your fathers ate the manna in the wilderness, and are dead. This is the bread which comes down from heaven, that one may eat of it and not die. I am the living bread which came down from heaven. If anyone eats of this bread, he will live forever; and the bread that I shall give is My flesh, which I shall give for the life of the world."

John 6:53-54

"Then Jesus said to them, "Most assuredly, I say to you, unless you eat the flesh of the Son of Man and drink His blood, you have no life in you. Whoever eats My flesh and drinks My blood has eternal life, and I will raise him up at the last day."

Here the title of the Son of Man has association with the Son of God and eternal life. Both were sent by God and came down from heaven. Eternal life that is in the Son, is given to man through the work of the Son of Man – His death. As believers we partake in the death of the Son of Man so that we may have life. We eat His flesh and drink His blood. This directly refers to His death, and our dying with Him. Eternal life as given by the Son is now the resurrected life of the Son of Man. It is only on the other side of death, that we have the life He gives, as the true bread of life.

The Son of God as the Son of Man has been given all Judgment

John 5:22

"For the Father judges no one, but has committed all judgment to the Son,"

John 5:26-27

"For as the Father has life in Himself, so He has granted the Son to have life in Himself, and has given Him authority to execute judgment also, because He is the Son of Man."

The Son, having been given all judgment to execute, does so only having taken up the title of the Son of Man. We can see that the giving of eternal life to certain ones, and then the judgment of all that remains, is through the Son of God as the Son of Man. The association of the Son of Man title with the Beloved Son is clear in God's counsels – both eternal life and judgment are dependent on His death.

The Counsels of God – the Heavenly and Earthly Glory of Christ

The counsels of God are of great importance for understanding. It is all the work of God that brings glory to His name eternally (Eph. 1:9-10). This work centers in Christ – there is a bringing together of all things in the heavens under His dominion; the heavenly glory of Christ. The Son of Man glorified has already entered into the heavens. Now the Spirit has been sent to the earth to gather His body. He will not take up His power and reign until His body is joined to Him in His heavenly glory. He will take us, all believers in Christ, into the heavens. That is the establishing of the heavenly glory of Christ, to the eternal glory of God.

All things on earth are brought together under the dominion of Christ as well, as the Son of Man and a millennial kingdom over all the nations on the earth (Dan. 7:13-14, 2:34-35, Matt. 25:31). A subset of this is the earthly kingdom of Messiah over a restored Israel. It will be the focus of the government of God on the earth (Deut. 32:8-9), and the center point of the earthly calling of the remnant. The Gentile nations that remain on the earth will be gathered to and blessed by the earthly calling in Israel. The glory of the Son of Man will fill the earth. This is the establishing of the earthly glory of Christ, to the eternal glory of God.

The two titles – Messiah and the Son of Man – are critical to distinguish in God's counsels. All the work of God is contained and associated with them. The Son of God takes up these two titles, but the Messiah title is set aside for a time. The Son of God as the Son of Man is a glorified Man forever. The scope and reach of the title of the Son of Man in God's counsels goes far beyond that of Messiah. It reaches into all the heavens and all the earth, all of creation. Finally, it is the Son of God sent, who takes up these titles in the counsels of God, but also the Son, who alone can reveal the Father.

[If you want to study more of what Jesus reveals of the Father, read the gospel of John, paying attention to the name Father, and what the Son sent by Him has to say. Then study the first two chapters of Ephesians, and insert the Father's name every place in every sentence where it refers to Him. These will be eye-opening experiences for the believer. An index attachment of these chapters has been provided in the back of this book with some notes.]

Chapter 11:

The Promise of the Comforter

John 14:16-17

"And I will pray the Father, and He will give you another Comforter, that He may abide with you forever, even the Spirit of truth, whom the world cannot receive, because it neither sees Him nor knows Him; but you know Him, for He dwells with you and will be in you."

This is the promise of the coming of the Comforter to the believer. The Holy Spirit is sent by the Father at the request of Jesus Christ. It becomes clear in the revelation of Scripture that this sending is related exclusively to the Son of Man raised and glorified. There is an inseparable link and dependence of the ministry of the Holy Spirit to the redemptive work and exalting of the Man, Jesus Christ. The presence of the Holy Spirit on earth, in this specific role and character as Helper, was consequent to the Father glorifying the Son of Man (John 13:31-32).

The Holy Spirit given after the Son of Man was glorified

John 7:39

"But this He spoke concerning the Spirit, whom those believing in Him would receive; for the Holy Spirit was not yet given, because Jesus was not yet glorified."

This confirms the relationship we have just mentioned and adds to the significance of Christ taking up the title and role of the Son of Man. It barely needs mentioning that Christ as the Messiah to Israel has no association with the sending of the Holy Spirit. The Holy Spirit would be for those who believed in Christ. They would be given the Holy Spirit after He was glorified.

This is the great teaching being presented. The Holy Ghost was sent down to live in believers, consequent to the glorifying of the Son of Man. This would be in place of having an earthly Messiah according to the promises of God. Rejected as the Anointed One and all associated with that in prophecy set aside (John 7:25-27), Jesus takes His place as Man, according to the eternal counsels of God. His exaltation and sitting down at God's right hand speaks of the redemptive work finished (Heb. 10:10-12). This work was done in such a way that it forever established the righteousness of God (Rom. 3:24-26), and perfectly glorified the Father, who then glorifies Jesus with Himself (John 13:31-32). Therefore having fully established all God's glory through the cross, and taking this position in the glory, Jesus sends down the Holy Ghost.

The Spirit is the witness of the Son of Man in glory, and the gospel of the glory into which He has gone. He is witness to the fullness of the redemptive work of Christ and gives testimony of this Man sitting down at the right hand of the Father (Heb. 1:3, 10:12).

The Testimony of the Apostles – as Eye-Witnesses of what they saw

But this is not the testimony that the twelve would bear (John 15:27). Certainly their testimony would be under the guidance of the Spirit sent down from on high, but it would not be a revelation of His present glory. Their testimony, empowered by the Spirit, was of what they were eye-witnesses to. They saw His walk on this earth in humiliation, not His exaltation in heavenly glory. He walked as the Son of God clothed in flesh, and always, in His humanity, careful to reveal the Father. This He did in the midst of evil and hatred against Him. In perfect grace, He had to continuously adapt Himself in circumstances -- events resulting in His rejection by the very world He had created, and came to save. He also bore in grace with the weaknesses and infirmities of those He kept (John 17:12). Their testimony was noticeable to the world as of those who had been with Jesus (Acts 4:13), as Jesus said of the twelve, you have been with Me from the beginning (John 15:27).

The Testimony of the Holy Spirit – of the Man Exalted in Glory

But the Holy Spirit would also bring testimony as witness of the present glory of the Son of Man. This testimony is different from that of the eye-witnesses to His humiliation. His personal glory accomplished, He is now out of this world of heartache and resistance, and in a perfect place, accepting and honoring Him, as the Man exalted on high. It is His glory that is revealed and who better to do it, but the Holy Spirit who witnessed all this, and now has been sent to reveal it (John 15:26).

I believe that the eye-witness testimony of the apostles, empowered by the Spirit, is the emphasis of the first seven chapters of the book of Acts. Then before Stephen is murdered by unbelieving Israel, he gives a special testimony by the Spirit of the Son of Man in glory at the right hand of God (Acts 7:55-56). *This is the beginning of the testimony of the Spirit to the present glory of Christ, the Man in glory.* It marks a distinct closing of the Messianic door to the house of

Israel, and the opening of the door to the Gentiles. God now would build a new house, by the Holy Spirit sent to gather the body of this Man exalted in glory (Eph. 2:11-22). This gathering is primarily out of the Gentiles and can be attributed to the testimony of the Spirit to the revealed glory of Christ. Also playing a large part in the gathering of the Gentiles was the calling in sovereign grace of a chosen instrument – an eye-witness to this glory, who would preach as his own gospel, the gospel of the glory of Christ. This story is told in detail in a later chapter in this book (The Real Book of Acts).

The believer's possession of the Holy Spirit is the essence of Christianity. It is not merely something entirely new and not of Israel, but the full disclosure of the abundance of grace given to us in the revelation of Christ glorified. We will certainly have our part and participation in that glory, but the believer knows that it is our proper position now, and the redemptive work completed gives us the right to be there. We wait for the return of Jesus for us before we will enter into it, our bodies being transformed into the likeness of His glorious body. This is an abundance of grace shown to us by the Father, clearly demonstrating God's fullness of love toward the believer (Rom. 5:8). And the revelation of this very love is the testimony of the Spirit given to us (Rom. 5:5).

The Operations of the Spirit in the Gospel of John

Being here in John 7 affords us the opportunity to observe the three operations or workings of the Holy Spirit revealed in this gospel. In chapter 3 we are born of the Spirit, as quickened by God. In chapter 4 the Spirit is a fountain in the believer springing up unto everlasting life. In chapter 7 the new man, the new creation in Christ, enters into the knowledge and enjoyment of things unseen, heavenly, and eternal. It is the testimony of the Spirit that reveals the truths of Christ in glory. These are truths that are associated with the believer and fill our hearts to overflowing. The overflow becomes a testimony to others being drawn of God. Once we are satisfied and filled, the overflow goes out to other thirsty souls (John 7:37-38).

There are many other truths worth looking at concerning the ministry of the Comforter. We can understand from John 14 above that He was with the disciples when Jesus was still with them. But what is distinct about His being sent after Christ sat down at the right hand of God was that He would now dwell in them, the believer being the temple of the living God (2 Cor. 6:16-18). When sent, the Spirit will abide in us forever.

The Believer has the Spirit of God within...eternally

And so, we should understand that when the saint is conformed into the image of Christ, our bodies glorified in resurrection, the Holy Spirit will not leave us. Presently, much of the believer's spiritual energy by the Spirit is expended in our resistance of sin in the flesh (Gal. 5:17) or against the wiles of the devil and his minions (Eph. 6:11-12). This is while we still walk on this earth. When the church is removed from this world these things will simply not exist in us or against us any longer. We will be brought into the glory, and the Spirit, still abiding in the believer, will be the power and capacity to fully know and enjoy the width and length and depth and height – of the glory and presence of the Father (Eph. 3:18). Is this not what the Holy Spirit is revealing through Paul in Ephesians?

Ephesians 3:10-12

"...to the intent that now the manifold wisdom of God might be made known by the church to the principalities and powers in the heavenly places, according to the eternal purpose which He accomplished in Christ Jesus our Lord, in whom we have boldness and access with confidence through faith in Him."

The multi-faceted wisdom of God concerning His eternal purpose for forming the church and exalting it in Christ is presently and clearly displayed to the principalities and authorities in the heavens. And what is the outcome? It is that through the confidence of faith in Christ, this body has a bold entrance and eternal access to the presence and glory of the Father. If you will receive it, by the Spirit of God and through His word, we may understand that God's intentions are for this body, the church, to be His very own habitation and dwelling place throughout the eternal ages to come. These understandings are associated with the mystery of God, *and this mystery is presently revealed by the Holy Spirit* (Eph. 3:2-5).

The Spirit of Truth – so the Believer May Know Spiritual Truth

We also see in John 14 above that the Holy Spirit is the Spirit of truth. Again in John 15:26, He is the Spirit of truth who proceeds from the Father. And in John 16:13 it is, "However, when He, the Spirit of truth has come, He will guide you into all truth..." We have discussed this in the first chapter of this book, so I just add a few thoughts on this. It is by the Spirit of God that the believer understands and apprehends the truth of God. By the Spirit of truth we know and are enlightened concerning the mind and counsels of God.

1 Corinthians 2:9-12

"Eye has not seen, nor ear heard,
Nor have entered into the heart of man
The things which God has prepared for those who love Him."

But God has revealed them to us <u>through His Spirit.</u> For the Spirit searches all things, yes, the deep things of God. For what man knows the things of a man except the spirit of the man which is in him? Even so no one knows the things of God except the Spirit of God. Now we have received, not the spirit of the world, but the Spirit who is from God, <u>that we might know</u> the things that have been freely given to us by God."

In this passage we have three distinct workings of the Spirit on our behalf. First, we see these things are revealed by the Spirit (v. 10-12 above). Second, they are communicated by words the Spirit taught (v. 13). Third, the power of the Spirit allows us to spiritually discern (v.14). All three are the operation of the ministry of the Comforter in the believer.

It is always God's intention for believers to understand what He reveals. All enlightenment we receive of God's revelation must come through His Spirit. This is the emphasis of the above passage. We would be in the dark without the ministry of the Comforter. It is often said and implied that the simple mentality of a fisherman is all you need to understand God's word. This is a human thought and reasoning of the carnal mind. The truth is, whether you have a simple mentality or an advanced well-educated one, without the working of the Spirit in the believer, you will know nothing of the truth of God. The teaching of the Spirit and the understanding of God's Word that the Spirit makes known to us, is contrasted with the spirit of the world (v. 12) and the knowledge the wise of this world possess.

The Truth of God is not Worldly Wisdom and Thinking

1 Corinthians 1:20-24

"Where is the wise? Where is the scribe? Where is the disputer of this age? Has not God made foolish the wisdom of this world? For since, in the wisdom of God, the world through wisdom did not know God, it pleased God through the foolishness of the message preached to save those who believe. For Jews request a sign, and Greeks seek after wisdom; but we preach Christ crucified, to the Jews a stumbling block and to the Greeks foolishness, but to those who are called, both Jews and Greeks, Christ the power of God and the wisdom of God."

The whole unbelieving world is represented here. It includes the specially chosen Jews, and the worldly thinking Gentile Greeks. But the wisdom of God cannot be comprehended by these two groups. They do not have the Spirit of God. God's wisdom and counsels are either foolishness or a stumbling block to them. The entire world, both Jews and Gentiles alike, is in the flesh and without the Spirit (Rom. 8:8-9). The world cannot receive Him. The world cannot see Him or know Him (John 14:17). And the conclusion is this:

1 Corinthians 2:14

"But the natural man does not receive the things of the Spirit of God, for they are foolishness to him; nor can he know them, because they are spiritually discerned."

There is a stark contrast made between the wisdom of God and that of the world. There is quite a difference between what the believer can and may understand and what the unbelieving world can fathom. As I said previously, the saint has been placed by God into a privileged position, invited into the counsels of God. By the Comforter, we are to understand all that God freely gives to us in grace in Christ. It has been provided for us by the redemptive work of the Son of Man (1 Cor. 2:12). By the Comforter, the heavenly glory of the Son of Man is revealed to us, and all the believer's association and union with Him in His glory (Eph. 3:4-5). And further, by the teaching of the Spirit, we know that the Son of Man will not take His inheritance until His co-heirs are united to Him, as His body, in glory. How else then, when He is manifested to the world in glory, will we be manifested in glory with Him (Col. 3:4)?

John 15:26-27

"But when the Comforter comes, whom I shall send to you from the Father, the Spirit of truth who proceeds from the Father, He will testify of Me. And you also will bear witness, because you have been with Me from the beginning."

The testimony of a risen Christ by the apostles, empowered by the Spirit, began at Pentecost. This testimony found in the beginning portions of the book of Acts was strictly to the nation of Israel. The content of their preaching, and what they testify to, is very Jewish in character. It is Israel's last chance for realizing Messianic promises for the nation at that time. But the leaders of Israel put a definite end to this testimony, beheading James, stoning Stephen, threatening Peter and John, and organizing a state wide persecution of all those who call on the name of Jesus (Acts 8:1, 9:1-2). Certainly we see the dual testimony of the Spirit and the apostles, rejected by the nation. The nation is guilty of always resisting the Holy Spirit (Acts 7:51).

The Spirit is the Seal of the Adoption of Sonship

There was also a testimony of the Comforter to the believer. The Spirit proceeding from the Father is the seal of the Spirit of adoption for sonship in the Father's house and family (Rom. 8:15-16, Gal. 4:5-

7). It is the Spirit that cries out in our hearts, "Abba, Father!" By the Comforter, the believer realizes and understands his relationship to the Father as a son. This is the nature of the promise found in John 14:17 concerning the Comforter being sent from the Father. The indwelling Comforter would reveal to the believer our position of sonship along with His Son, in the Father's presence. It is also by the Comforter that we commune and have fellowship with the Father, on a personal and individual level (John 14:21-23). Further, the Spirit given to the sons brings the clear and complete revelation of the Father spoken about by Jesus before He left:

John 16:25

"These things I have spoken to you in figurative language; but the time is coming when I will no longer speak to you in figurative language, but I will tell you plainly about the Father."

He is referring to the time when the Comforter would be given to the believer, as a son, to clearly reveal the Father. The revelation of the Father is by the Son of God sent to the earth to reveal Him – John 1:18. This revelation was flatly rejected by Israel. They would not receive it (Jesus speaking to the Jews in all of John 8 makes this point). Jesus speaks intimately of the Father, not to Israel, but to chosen ones of the Father in John 14-17. But it would be later that the Comforter makes things clear, as the Spirit of truth and the Spirit of adoption.

The Spirit Reveals Our Present Association with Christ in Glory

The Comforter, as sent by Jesus (John 16:7), would reveal Christ to the believer, as well as the things of Christ. This also the Lord points to as a time coming after He had left them:

John 16:12-15

"I still have many things to say to you, but you cannot bear them now. However, when He, the Spirit of truth, has come, He will guide you into all truth; for He will not speak on His own authority, but whatever He

hears He will speak; and He will tell you things to come. He will glorify Me, for He will take of what is Mine and declare it to you. All things that the Father has are Mine. Therefore I said that He will take of Mine and declare it to you."

The Comforter bears testimony to the believer of the glorified Christ. It is this; *"Now the Son of Man is glorified, and God is glorified in Him. If God is glorified in Him, God will also glorify Him in Himself..."* All things that the Father has are Christ's. The things the Father has given Him, is the Father's own glory (John 17:24). The glory of God now is in the face of the Son of Man; *the light of the knowledge of the glory of God in the face of Jesus* Christ (II Cor. 4:6). This knowledge the Spirit reveals. The Comforter reveals the present position and glory of Jesus Christ to us. He glorifies Christ and declares these things to the believer. By the Spirit we behold the glory of the Lord as in a mirror, and by the ministry of the Spirit through the Word, we are changed from glory to glory (2 Cor. 3:18).

The epistles are the written communications of the Father and the Son, given through the Comforter to the church. Why them? Two important understandings I believe will bring this out. First, the Comforter could not come until Christ sat down at the right hand of the Majesty on high. It would be a specific point in time after Christ was raised from the dead, ascended on high, and exalted to God's right hand. The Spirit could not come until then. That's important, and Jesus makes it a point of emphasis (John 16:7). Secondly, the ministry and work of the Comforter is based on a promise of Christ to individual New Testament believers. That promise is one that is unique to the believer. There is nothing in the Old Testament or with Israel that compares with this. Why? Israel, regardless of all the distinctions separating them from the Gentiles, still were a people very much in Adam, in the world, and in the flesh. You are in the flesh if you have not the Spirit of God.

The Comforter was sent to the earth after the work of redemption was completed. He gathers and forms the body of Christ, joining the members to the Head. Those joined to the Lord are one spirit with Him (1 Cor. 6:17). Christ is in glory. Our union to Christ by the Spirit is a union to a Christ in glory. Early in John 14, Jesus only talks of He being in the Father and the Father in Him (John 14:9-11) – this refers to the present moment in which He was speaking. But later in the chapter He again refers to the time when the Comforter would be given.

John 14:20

"At that day you will know that I am in My Father, and you in Me, and I in you."

Our union with Christ is that we are in Him and He is in us, and we know this by the Spirit given to us. We also see that the assembly of God is built up on the earth -- a unified house as the habitation of God in the Spirit (Eph. 2:22, I Cor. 3:4-16). All of these things depend on the presence of the Comforter on the earth, and are founded on the completed work of Christ on the cross.

The Sending of the Holy Spirit is the Coming of a Divine Personage to this Earth

My intention was not to teach all that the Holy Spirit does for us as believers. It was simply to show the connection between the Son of Man and the coming of the Comforter. When Christ was born in Bethlehem, it was the coming of a divine person to this earth. Even though Christ created everything, and there were Old Testament appearances, His incarnation was God among Israel in the flesh. The God who made the world was now present in the world. This was a distinct personal coming of a divine person

The coming of the Spirit at Pentecost was the coming of a divine person to this earth as well. It is unique and very different than the Holy Spirit inspiring Old Testament prophets. This is not merely the Spirit speaking words, in times past, pointing to what would be accomplished in the counsels of God. It is the Comforter being sent as a result of the work already completed, Christ having sat down (Heb. 10:11-12). The Holy Spirit is the power of the Christian life and faith (Rom. 8:2). He is also the guarantee of all our sure and steadfast hopes in Christ (Eph. 1:13-14, 2 Cor. 1:22, 5:5, Rom. 8:11, 23-25). I hope you realize all these things as part of the ministry of the Spirit.

Jesus did not leave us comfortless. Where we are now as believers, is a place between the Holy Spirit being sent down and the complete results in glory.

2 Corinthians 5:4-5

"For we who are in this tent groan, being burdened, not because we want to be unclothed, but further clothed, that mortality may be swallowed up by life. Now He who has prepared us for this very thing is God, who also has given us the Spirit as a guarantee."

The Father's counsels are to bring the body of Christ into glory. He has prepared us for this very thing. The Father has predestined us to be conformed to the image of His Son, that there would be many brethren in His glory (Rom. 8:29). Jesus Christ has been taken into the glory, as the Son of Man, the forerunner there ahead of us. It is for this very purpose we have been given the presence of the Spirit within – to be associated and united with Christ in heavenly glory. All of the truths about the present glory of Christ are made known to us by the Spirit.

Chapter 12:

The Earthly Calling

Genesis 13:14-17

*"And the L*ORD *said to Abram, after Lot had separated from him: "Lift your eyes now and look from the place where you are—northward, southward, eastward, and westward; for all the land which you see I give to you and your descendants forever. And I will make your descendants as the dust of the earth; so that if a man could number the dust of the earth, then your descendants also could be numbered. Arise, walk in the land through its length and its width, for I give it to you."*

Genesis 15:18

*"On the same day the L*ORD *made a covenant with Abram, saying:*

"To your descendants I have given this land, from the river of Egypt to the great river, the River Euphrates"

Genesis 17:8

"Also I give to you and your descendants after you the land in which you are a stranger, all the land of Canaan, as an everlasting possession; and I will be their God."

The Sovereignty of God in Choosing Israel

The land was given in promise from God to Abraham for his descendants after the flesh. It would not be through Ishmael, but Isaac, as God chose (Gen. 17:18-19). The physical line in the second generation would be traced through Jacob, not his twin brother Esau, and again the sovereign choice of God is in view (Rom. 9:10-13). From Jacob came the twelve brothers and the heads of the twelve tribes of the nation of Israel. The one brother among them that they hated and despised, in turn, through compassion for them, becomes their savior. Joseph is an amazing type of Christ in many ways. But God also spoke to Abraham about his descendants being captive in Egypt.

Gen 15:13-14

"Then He said to Abram: "Know certainly that your descendants will be strangers in a land that is not theirs, and will serve them, and they will afflict them four hundred years. And also the nation whom they serve I will judge; afterward they shall come out with great possessions."

The nation of Israel descended from Abram. It is obvious that Almighty God promised the land to this particular nation. It is these initial promises to Abraham concerning Israel that establishes the earthly calling of that nation. They are tied to the earth and tied to the land as a people by the very promises of God. And God promised, "...to your descendants forever."

The Character and Nature of Biblical Prophecy

When we study the overall content of Biblical prophecy, it overwhelmingly centers upon Israel and God's dealings with that nation. Also the character of prophecy can be described as God's dealings with the earth and His government of it. This government was exercised when God was present on the earth in Israel, His glory in the tabernacle and later in Solomon's temple. Afterward God works only in providence from heaven. God removed Himself from the earth because of the many sins and apostasy of the Jews. God sent them, or what was left of them, into captivity.

God Sets Up All Civil Authority

God now exercises His influence from heaven in providence or by indirect judgments. He remains responsible for the setting-up of all civil authority, in the hands of the Gentiles. God's oversight of all civil power is taught in Daniel (Dan. 4:17, 25, 32-37), and confirmed by Jesus (John 19:11) and Paul (Rom. 13:1-5). Through time and prophecy, God has acknowledged Israel as His people, and then as not His people. There is a time in the end, when He takes them back up and again acknowledges them as His people to fulfill the promises He made to Abraham and David. At this present time they are not His people and He is not their God (Hosea 1:9), but their house remains desolate, as the Lord says, until they say again, "Blessed is He who comes in the name of the Lord!"

Jehovah's Inheritance – Israel Restored in the Land

In the midst of all this, we can see that God has promised that the physical descendants of Abraham would be established forever in the Promised Land. We clearly understand that this has never occurred, as in 'forever'. Yes, there have been periods of time when Israel was in the land, but never there by themselves and never inhabiting the entire expanse of it as given by God. Regardless, forever means forever, and that simply has not happened either. I have no doubt that in the end it will be exactly as God has promised. God is not a man that He should lie, and the unbelief of Israel cannot negate the faithfulness of God. God is faithful to all His promises, in and of Himself (Rom. 3:1-4). Israel will be forever restored and established in their land, twelve tribes and all, by Jehovah, their God. Once restored, they will be His inheritance.

Deuteronomy 32:9,
"For Jehovah's portion is his people; Jacob the lot of his inheritance."

1 Kings 8:53,
"For thou hast separated them from among all peoples of the earth, to be thine inheritance, as thou spoke through Moses thy servant, when thou brought our fathers out of Egypt, O Lord Jehovah."

Isaiah 19:25,
"…whom Jehovah of hosts will bless, saying, Blessed be Egypt my people, and Assyria the work of my hands, and Israel mine inheritance!"

Israel's Inheritance in the End – to possess the Land and be a Blessing

Israel's inheritance is to be in possession of the land, and in the end, restored and prospering in it under the hand of Jehovah.

Ezekiel 48:29,
"This is the land which ye shall divide by lot unto the tribes of Israel for inheritance, and these are their portions, says the Lord Jehovah."

Ezekiel 47:13
"Thus says the Lord Jehovah: This shall be the border whereby ye shall allot the land as inheritance according to the twelve tribes of Israel: Joseph shall have two portions."

Deuteronomy 15:4,
"…save when there shall be no one in need among you; for Jehovah will greatly bless thee in the land that Jehovah thy God gives thee for an inheritance to possess it,"

So we easily see that all these prophecies and promises connect Israel as a people to this earth and to the Promised Land. All of prophecy never contradicts this thought. Now other promises were added and given by God over time concerning Israel, yet these additions never altered the basic premise. For example, God made promises to Israel about choosing Jerusalem as His holy city and Mt. Zion as Jehovah's habitation.

Jerusalem – the Capital City of God on the Earth

Zechariah 8:3,
"Thus says the LORD: 'I will return to Zion, And dwell in the midst of Jerusalem. Jerusalem shall be called the City of Truth, The Mountain of the LORD of hosts, The Holy Mountain.'"

Zechariah 2:10
"Sing and rejoice, O daughter of Zion! For behold, I am coming and I will dwell in your midst," says the LORD."

Joel 3:17,
"So you shall know that I am the LORD your God, Dwelling in Zion My holy mountain. Then Jerusalem shall be holy, and no aliens shall ever pass through her again."

Isaiah 8:18,
"Here am I and the children whom the LORD has given me! We are for signs and wonders in Israel, from the LORD of hosts, Who dwells in Mount Zion."

The amount of prophecy related to these promises is too numerous to print here (some other passages from Psalms for your studying – Ps. 9:11, 14:7, 48:1, 87:2, 99:2, 102:16, 21, 110:2, 125:1, 128:5, 132:13, 134:3, 135:21, 146:10). God also made promises to David about his physical descendants, an eternal throne, Judah, and a Messiah for all of Israel from his lineage. This doesn't change anything of the original promises. It simply gives a fuller picture of what God will do, and how God will work for them in the end. What God does and how God works for Israel brings an understanding of what is contained in the counsels of God concerning the earthly glory of Christ. For example;

1 Kings 2:33,
"Their blood shall therefore return upon the head of Joab and upon the head of his descendants forever. But upon David and his descendants, upon his house and his throne, there shall be peace forever from the LORD."

1 Kings 2:45,
"But King Solomon shall be blessed, and the throne of David shall be established before the LORD forever."

Isaiah 9:7,
"Of the increase of His government and peace There will be no end, Upon the throne of David and over His kingdom, To order it and establish it with judgment and justice From that time forward, even forever. The zeal of the LORD of hosts will perform this."

The last reference above is the kingdom of the Messiah in Israel, established as the throne of David reigning forever on this earth. Again the numbers of scripture in prophecy that confirm these thoughts are too many to list. They just add to the body of prophecy, which I remind the reader again, always has the character of God's dealings with Israel and God's government of this earth. The content of Biblical prophecy connects Israel, as a people and nation, to the earth.

A remnant of Israel under grace and in the Body of Christ

That does not mean that individually some cannot come in under grace, as many as the Lord may call. Certainly in the past, from the day of Pentecost on, some of Israel were saved, and came under grace and into the body of Christ. But those have always been considered a remnant. This specifically is discussed in Romans; the calling in grace of at least two different remnants of Israel -- two remnants separated in time.

Rom. 11:1-7

"I say then, has God cast away His people? Certainly not! For I also am an Israelite, of the seed of Abraham, of the tribe of Benjamin. God has not cast away His people whom He foreknew. Or do you not know what the Scripture says of Elijah, how he pleads with God against Israel, saying, "Lord, they have killed Your prophets and torn down Your altars, and I alone am left, and they seek my life"? But what does the divine response say to him? "I have reserved for Myself seven thousand men who have not bowed the knee to Baal." Even so then, at this present time there is a remnant according to the election of grace. And if by grace, then it is no longer of works; otherwise grace is no longer grace. But if it is of works, it is no longer grace; otherwise work is no longer work.

What then? Israel has not obtained what it seeks; but the elect have obtained it, and the rest were blinded."

The Holy Spirit indicates that at the time Paul was writing, there was a remnant out of Israel according to the election of grace. Paul himself was part of this remnant that was now under grace and part of the church. But it certainly is individual, for the nation of Israel as a whole failed to obtain the election of grace.

We can address some important spiritual points. It should be obvious to anyone that after the day of Pentecost, those initially saved were all of Jewish descent. This continued on through the stoning of Stephen and the calling of Paul. In this period of time the individuals saved, all being formerly of the Jewish nation, formed a remnant according to the election of grace. In a sense they were a Jewish remnant, a type prefiguring the 144,000 in the end waiting for their Messiah (Rev. 7). They certainly formed a remnant in the midst of Israel in the beginning chapters of the book of Acts. They were a remnant in comparison to the nation of Israel, not in comparison to the overall numbers that were saved at the time. This latter part would quickly become true after Jerusalem was destroyed and God turned to the Gentiles (Acts 28:28).

The teaching and doctrine of the Body of Christ was first revealed to Paul and through Paul, a dispensation of grace was given to him for the Gentiles, to reveal the mystery of Christ (Eph. 3:1-6). These important truths concerning the existence of the church and its relationship to the glorified Son of Man had to wait until Paul's epistles. In his writings alone do we find the church, the corporate Body of Christ.

In the Body of Christ there is no Jew or Gentile

In Ephesians we are taught that there no longer exists a wall of partition between Jew and Gentile – that is, in the Body of Christ (Eph. 2:11-16). Therefore, as concerning this remnant, if any individual through grace came out of Israel and into the Body of Christ (for example, Paul), then that person is in a place where there is no Jew or Gentile (Gal. 3:27-28, Col. 3:10-11). Formerly Jews, now they have lost their connection with that nation and their nationality. Further, as being in Christ, they no longer have a connection to this earth. They are not part of this world, and they have no hope in the earthly calling of Israel. They are now part of the heavenly calling in Christ, and they are no longer the proper subject of prophecy. Now we must remark that their new position in Christ is far superior and blessed than anything they thought they had previously in Israel. But many have a hard time letting go.

The composition of the body of Christ, according to scripture, will always be a remnant out of Israel in the midst of a mass of Gentile believers. This was true in the time of Paul and will be similar to this until the church is removed from the earth. The Holy Spirit has been sent down from heaven to gather together His Body, His Bride, and will continue to do so until *the fullness of the Gentiles* comes into the Body of Christ -- Rom. 11:25.

Israel Restored on the Earth in the Land

As far as Israel and their earthly calling, let us consider prophecies concerning their restoration in the land and earthly physical blessings.

Amos 9:13-15

"Behold, the days are coming," says the Lord,
"When the plowman shall overtake the reaper,
And the treader of grapes him who sows seed;
The mountains shall drip with sweet wine,
And all the hills shall flow with it.
I will bring back the captives of My people Israel;
They shall build the waste cities and inhabit them;
They shall plant vineyards and drink wine from them;
They shall also make gardens and eat fruit from them.
I will plant them in their land,
And no longer shall they be pulled up
From the land I have given them,"
Says the Lord your God."

Jeremiah 31:12

"Therefore they shall come and sing in the height of Zion, Streaming to the goodness of the LORD— For wheat and new wine and oil, For the young

*of the flock and the herd; Their souls shall be like a well-watered garden,
And they shall sorrow no more at all."*

Isaiah 27:6

*"Those who come He shall cause to take root in Jacob;
Israel shall blossom and bud,
And fill the face of the world with fruit."*

Israel --the Earthly Glory of Christ

We have seen many things concerning God's promises establishing the earthly calling of Israel. God has pledged to the physical descendants of Abraham possession of a mass of land, and a restoration in that land with prosperity and physical blessings. A Deliverer is promised, coming out of Zion defeating all their enemies (Zeph. 3:14-20) and purging ungodliness from Jacob (Rom. 11:26-27, Ps. 110:2). This Deliverer will be the Messiah of prophecy, reigning on the throne of David over the twelve tribes of a united Israel. All this describes the earthly glory of Jesus Christ. Israel, the earthly calling, will be the center of His earthly glory.

How will these promises be fulfilled in the end? In a general way the answer is simple. These promises will be fulfilled by the working of God in His sovereignty and faithfulness, and that, exactly according to the prophecies. It will be a work of God on the earth, and for the earth, as the curse on creation will be lifted at that time. Certainly we see how the prophecies concentrate end time events in the Promised Land and around Mt. Zion and Jerusalem (Zeph. 3:16-17). But in the end it will be a remnant of Israel (Is. 10:20-23, Zeph. 3:12-13). They will be sealed with an earthly seal (Rev. 7:1-8), preserved by God in the world (Rev. 12:6, 14), redeemed as the first fruits from the earth and among men, and walking with their Messiah on Mt. Zion (Rev. 14:1-4). Certainly there are many more events that will occur at the close, but they all relate to an earthly bound Israel and God's government of this world.

There are two perspectives I want to share with the reader that help considerably in gaining an overall understanding of God's purposes and counsels towards Israel. Both perspectives have a relationship with Israel and the earth. The first concerns God's government of the earth and His saying to Israel in Hosea;

Hosea 1:9

"Call his name Lo-Ammi, For you are not My people, And I will not be your God."

Jehovah governed the Earth from the midst of Israel

God's presence was on the earth and He governed the earth while dwelling among Israel. This started at Mt. Sinai and the tabernacle, through David's tabernacle on Mt. Zion, and then Solomon's temple. The glory of God indicated the presence of God, which was always behind the veil. In the first eleven chapters of Ezekiel the prophet sees the glory of God and the cherubim leave the temple, leave Jerusalem, and leave the earth. God could no longer tolerate the sins, idolatry, and apostasy of Israel. He could no longer live among the people and He declares, 'Lo-Ammi' to the prophets. Until that point in time the presence and glory of God, and the throne of God, was on the earth for the purpose of governing from Israel. *The conclusion is that the acknowledgment of Israel by God as His earthly people corresponds to God's presence on the earth for government.* The two go hand in hand.

The Times of the Gentiles

The glory of God is the presence of God. What did God's presence on earth mean? It meant that God ruled the earth from the midst of Israel. What did the glory of God leaving the earth with the cherubim mean? It meant God no longer acknowledged Israel as His people and He as their God – Lo-Ammi was declared by God (Hosea 1:9). Then what happened? *The times of the Gentiles began* (Luke 21:24), and the four beasts of Daniel come forth upon the face of the earth -- for civil government, and to rule the world (Dan. 7:1-8). The fourth beast was in the time of Jesus Christ as the Roman Empire. *The times of the Gentiles* started with Nebuchadnezzar and Babylon and continue on until the end with the two beasts of Revelation thirteen. The first beast of that chapter is the fourth beast of Daniel 7, a revised Roman Empire, raised-up again, coming out of the bottomless pit (Rev. 11:7, 17:8). Until the end Israel remains Lo-Ammi; not acknowledged by God. Until the end there is no direct government of God on this earth and in this world. Until then, the times of the Gentiles continue.

Earlier in the chapter we saw that Abraham was told by God that his physical descendants would be captive in Egypt (Gen. 15:13-14). When God delivered them, He brought them into the wilderness to be before Him at Mt. Sinai. There He gave Israel the law *after* they agreed to obey all the Lord Jehovah asked them to do (Ex. 19:8). This was before Moses went up the mountain to receive the tablets of stone. Israel made a golden calf and worshiped it before Moses made it down the mountain with the tablets. We see Israel's failure from the very beginning of their history as a nation. The tablets of stone never made it into the camp. The law was broken in more ways than just Moses throwing the tablets down at the base of the mountain. The tabernacle was moved outside and away from the camp of Israel, so Moses could speak with God away from the people. This was all related to Israel's failure in being responsible from the very outset. In spite of all their failures, God will remain faithful to keep all His promises to Abraham and David in the end. Inevitably Israel will possess the land by the sovereign hand of God. This is a certainty.

Micah 7:20

"You will give truth to Jacob
And mercy to Abraham,
Which You have sworn to our fathers
From days of old."

Interesting enough, we find a prophecy in Jeremiah 30 concerning Israel being brought back and restored in the land in the last days (vs. 18-22). This ends with the Lord saying to Israel, *'You shall be My people, And I will be your God.'* As I said earlier in the chapter, there is coming a time when Israel will once again be acknowledged by God as His earthly people (also seen in prophecies in Ez. 37:23, 27, 34:30-31, Jer. 31:33). Messiah will again be among them, as their

Deliverer (Ez. 34:23-24, 37:21-28, Jer. 33:14-17). It will be a time when the presence and glory of God will be re-established on the earth for the government of this world. It will be in an earthly Jerusalem and again Jehovah will live among Israel as His earthly inheritance. Israel will be established in the land under a new covenant that Jehovah makes with them.

In the End, Israel will have a New Covenant with Jehovah

Jeremiah 31:31-33

"Behold, the days are coming, says the Lord, when I will make a new covenant with the house of Israel and with the house of Judah— not according to the covenant that I made with their fathers in the day that I took them by the hand to lead them out of the land of Egypt, My covenant which they broke, though I was a husband to them, says the Lord. But this is the covenant that I will make with the house of Israel after those days, says the Lord: I will put My law in their minds, and write it on their hearts; and I will be their God, and they shall be My people."

This new covenant is what Israel will walk in under the reign of Messiah during the millennium. Jehovah will write His Law, not on tablets of stone, but on their hearts, so they will obey it. Please note that this is not at all the position that the New Testament believer or Body of Christ has with God. This is an earthly covenant for God's earthly people Israel. At this time they are still an earthly people, having not experienced a resurrection and glorification. Throughout the millennium, they will be maintained in their natural bodies by the sovereign power of God. This new covenant is the Law of God as it was with Moses. At this future time, by His sovereign work, the law will be written on their hearts by the finger of God, just as He did in the tablets of stone at Sinai. This is all still very earthy in character and nature. In the last part of the prophecy, Jehovah will again acknowledge Israel as His earthly people. The government of God will be re-established on the earth.

When the glory left Solomon's temple early in Ezekiel, God brought Nebuchadnezzar to destroy Jerusalem, the temple, and to take Judah captive to Babylon. God sets up Nebuchadnezzar as king in the first of four Gentile world monarchies (the four beasts of Daniel 7). When God presented Messiah to Israel at first, it was during the beginnings of the fourth beast, the Roman Empire. In making the connections, we can see that as long as Israel is not acknowledged by God, the Gentiles rule. And God exercises providential control over the earth from the heavens. The general outcome of prophecy in the end has God taking back direct control of the government of the earth, as the only real God of the earth (Rev. 11:4). Of course the ruling Gentiles put up a fight, as does the dragon, but their time has run out. But this all leads to a better understanding of some general principles that help to paint a more accurate picture of the plans and counsels of God, in the earthly calling of Israel.

Israel's History shows an External Redemption in the Flesh

God lives on the earth among Israel only after they are externally redeemed in type, God delivering them from slavery in Egypt and out from under Pharaoh's oppression. He brings them through the Red Sea, Moses stretching out his staff and saying, "behold the salvation of the Lord." Israel's whole external state and condition was changed. And we know that God did not live on the earth prior to living in the midst of Israel. He did not dwell with Adam. He did not live with Abraham. He lives among Israel after Sinai, but they have no access to Him, as He stays behind the veil. His presence is about the government of the earth from Israel. He gives them His law, but it is external as well. There is no internal spiritual redemption of man at all, no actual atonement, just types and shadows, all in the flesh.

Israel's religion is for man in the Flesh. God was testing mankind in Adam

The law, which is Israel's religion, was given to man in the flesh, as we have discussed previously. It was a testing by God of man in the flesh and in the first Adam. These were the circumstances in which God originally gave the law to Israel. These circumstances did not change the entire time Israel had the law and practiced it, from Mt. Sinai through the coming of Messiah. This entire time was the testing by God of man in Adam. God wanted to see and prove whether man could produce righteousness as a fruit before God, and therefore receive life. But the religion of Israel could not produce righteousness and could not give life (Gal. 3:21). It was, as the Spirit declares, a ministration of death and condemnation (II Cor. 3:7, 9). With the coming of Messiah to Israel the testing was complete. Israel had failed in responsibility. Mankind in the first Adam was proven universally corrupt and ruined. At the rejection of Messiah, God judged and condemned the entire world (John 12:31). Every mouth was stopped and all the world became guilty before God (Rom. 3:19).

Galatians 3:10

"For as many as are of the works of the law are under the curse; for it is written, "Cursed is everyone who does not continue in all things which are written in the book of the law, to do them."

From the time at Mt. Sinai until the destruction of Jerusalem and the temple in 70 AD the entire nation of Israel were the 'many' that were 'of the works of the law.' Those 'of the law' are always under a curse. During that time Israel existed with cursing and condemnation individually and corporately, although God always kept a remnant. The law was external requirements demanding human righteousness of man in Adam, in the flesh, and sinners already. It could only be an administration of death and condemnation. In this period of time, whether Israel was a complete nation or partially represented, they were always a cursed people. Not one individual among them could 'continue in all things...to do them.'

Judaism is God's religion of the Earth

The law is simply a grand appeal in itself to the flesh of man, and to his senses. It had to be exactly this because of the original circumstances in which it was given – to man in Adam and in the flesh. The law was never a walk of faith, but rather always a walk by sight and senses. It is earthly in its character. But here is another perspective we must understand concerning God giving the law to Israel. Even though the law was a ministration of death and condemnation to man in the first Adam, it still remains the religion God gave to the earthly calling, the nation of Israel.

In all respects, Judaism is God's religion of the earth. Those of Judaism, by the religion itself, are connected to the earth and of this world. When the law was given to Israel it served to separate this nation in their worship of Jehovah from all the false religions in the world. Jehovah was the one true God among all the gods that mankind worshiped (Rom. 1:18-25). Judaism distinguished Israel from everybody else – they worshiped the one true God. The nations around them would soon come to know that there was a God in the midst of Israel.

Please note this important point – Judaism always kept Israel connected to the earth and of the world. Judaism never separated Israel from this world. The law only separated the Jews from the Gentiles. This was an obvious external separation in the flesh. Yet there never was a separation of Israel from the world. If we look for the biblical understanding of the composition of the world, what is it? The world is made up of unbelieving Jews and Gentiles. Israel remains an integral part of this world.

What do I mean by saying Judaism is God's religion of the earth? It is the one and only religion God ever gave to man in Adam. The first man was of the earth, made of dust (I Cor. 15:47). As long as there is man on the earth and in Adam, Judaism is God's intended religion for them. There will be man in Adam on this earth throughout the entire millennium. The saved remnant of Israel will have the law, as a new covenant, written on their hearts and minds by the finger of God (Heb. 8:7-13, Jer. 31:31-34). Yet this Jewish remnant is still man in Adam, in the flesh, and connected to this world. As the greatest nation on the face of the earth at that time they will perfectly practice the law by the sovereign grace and power of God. This will be the religion on the earth throughout the thousand years. Judaism is God's religion of the earth.

It is an amazing privilege for the believer to be invited by God to know His counsels and understand His ways. Israel was never given this privilege and they will never have this privilege. By their religion they are always servants and in bondage (Gal. 4:24-25). They are never made friends, brethren, or sons in God's house (John 15:15, Rom. 8:29, Heb. 2:10-11, Gal. 3:26, John 8:34-38).

I speak of this privilege in order to share a further insight into the ways of God. In every situation in man's history where God has given him responsibility, the outcome has always been failure. These failures were usually immediate. Yet during the millennium every previous failure of man in responsibility will be made good by the sovereign grace and power of God. Where there was failure and ruin by the first Adam, God makes good in the rule and reign over all the earth by the second Adam, the Son of Man. Where there was failure in the royal line by Solomon, the son of David, and the kingdom divided, God will make good by the true Son of David, the Messiah reigning over a united Israel. Where the Jews failed in their responsibility when given the law, God will write it on their hearts and by His sovereign power they will fulfill it perfectly. Every failure of man in responsibility, God takes responsibility to make good. The means and end of all the ways of God are for what purpose? The eternal glory of God alone.

Judaism – an Appeal to the Flesh and Senses of Man

Judaism is a religion of the senses. It is walking by sight, by the senses. The Law of Moses is not a walk by faith, but a religion designed for the flesh. It had its thundering and lightening and smoke on Mt. Sinai and tablets of stone. It had God as a cloud by day and a pillar of fire by night. It had its tabernacle and furniture, made after the pattern of heavenly things no less, but still only a pattern, a similitude, and very much still on the earth. In Jerusalem they built a temple that was very beautiful and ornate and pleasing to behold. Certainly Solomon's temple was glorious, while its replacement had an inferior glory compared to the first. Regardless, it caught the disciples' eyes one day. They had animal sacrifices and blood and gold and brass coverings, beautiful vestments, candlesticks and trumpets to sound.

They had the burning of incense and the ark of covenant and the artifacts hidden therein. Their washings were of the outer flesh. The sprinkling of blood and anointing with oil was of the same effect. The sign of God's covenant with Israel was circumcision in the outer flesh. They had pilgrimages back to Jerusalem to worship and sacrifice. They had businesses set up in the outer courts selling everything you might need to worship properly once you arrived. Judaism, simply put, is God's religion of the earth and of this world. It is a religion for the eyes and flesh of man, according to the weak and beggarly elements of this world (Gal. 4:9). It is the religion of the earthly calling.

Hagar, the Slave Woman – a Type of the Covenant of Law and the Nation of Israel

If we look in Galatians chapter four, we see what should be an unmistakable connection of Israel with the earth and the flesh (Gal. 4:21-5:3). Hagar, the slave woman, and her offspring Ishmael, the slave son of Abraham, is a type used by the Spirit of God prefiguring a whole list of things. It includes the workings of the flesh and the covenant from Sinai (the Law of Moses – Judaism). This is said to be a covenant that only gives birth to bondage. Further, the type is said to correspond to an earthly Jerusalem, a city that is in bondage with her children (the Jews). It would be hard to say anything different as to the meaning of this type, because the Spirit of God provides the exactness of the interpretation. As it was from the time Israel was at Mt. Sinai it remains the same today. Those who are of Judaism (the law) entangle themselves in bondage (Gal. 5:1). They are connected with the weak and beggarly elements of the earth and world (Gal. 4:9), and are involved in the workings of the flesh (Gal. 4:23).

This chapter shows the attachment of Israel in the promises of God to the earth. All the above establishes Israel as the earthly calling. In Deuteronomy we view the counsels of God concerning Israel as the center of the earth when God divided the nations.

Deuteronomy 32:8
"When the Most High divided their inheritance to the nations, When He separated the sons of Adam, and He set the boundaries of the peoples According to the number of the children of Israel."

In the End, God Makes Israel the Center of the Earth

In the end, during the millennial reign of Christ, Israel will be the center of Christ's earthly glory, and the center of God's earthly government. He will reign from Jerusalem over a restored and united earthly people. The Gentile nations will be gathered and blessed in them. We discussed briefly in a previous chapter how this name for God as 'Most High' points to millennial government and blessing. This is what God will bring to pass on the earth during the millennium, in the earthly kingdom and glory of the Son of Man (Luke 21:27, Matt. 25:31, Dan. 7:13-14). These are the counsels of God established by His promises in prophecy and to be fulfilled by God in His own faithfulness and sovereign power and grace.

Abraham's many seeds, in the flesh and on the earth, will eventually be as innumerable as the sands of the seashore (Gen. 22:17, Heb. 11:12). In the counsels of God, the earthly calling of Israel will be fulfilled by twelve tribes united and restored in the Promised Land in an earthly Messianic kingdom. These are the earthly things. In the fullness of the times all things on the earth will be gathered into Christ (Eph. 1:10). This is the earthly glory of Christ.

Chapter 13:

The Heavenly Calling

Hebrews 3:1

"Therefore, holy brethren, partakers of the heavenly calling, consider the Apostle and High Priest of our confession, Christ Jesus,"

If there is an earthly calling of Israel, then there is a heavenly calling of the believer and the Body of Christ. Through Christ we have been made partakers of this specific calling, presently by title and spiritual position in Him. At a certain point in the future it will be physically made so by the sovereign work and power of God. As the believer goes through the scriptural references in this chapter, we learn to turn our eyes and attention elsewhere, to the heavens. We are simply strangers on this earth. What we will see is who we are, what we are, and what we have in Jesus Christ. God does not have us as strangers to the earth now, just to make us dwellers on the earth later on. No, our eyes should be lifted up from the earth, because in every Biblical sense, our life is not to be found here.

Colossians 3:1-3

"If then you were raised with Christ, seek those things which are above, where Christ is, sitting at the right hand of God. Set your mind on things above, not on things on the earth. For you died, and your life is hidden with Christ in God."

The Believer's Life is Christ, and He is Hidden Now, at the Right Hand of God

The believer is supposed to be seeking those things above and setting his mind on such things. If we were to give a quiz to Christians as to exactly what these things above are, most would be hard pressed to list anything. How can we set our minds on them then? One of the things we can see from this passage is that the believer's entire life is there because the Son of Man is sitting at the right hand of God. Christ is hidden in God there. Our life is Christ. Paul said, it is not I who live, but Christ lives in me (Gal. 2:20, Col. 3:4). Our life presently is hidden in God, because Christ is presently hidden. Why hidden? It is the opposite of the next verse.

Colossians 3:4

"When the Christ is manifested who is our life, then will you also be manifested with him in glory."

It states when Christ appears (and this manifestation is to the world, because the hiding in God is in relation to the world and this earth) we are manifested with Him in the glory (Rom. 8:18-19 parallels these thoughts). Our life is hidden now as out of the world as Christ is apart from this world. We can understand then that we should act and live and walk on this earth accordingly, as apart from it. Our life is not connected to this world. Therefore, in every possible way, we should not involve ourselves in the things of the world or the cares of this life down here.

Ephesians 4:1-4

"I, therefore, the prisoner of the Lord, beseech you to walk worthy of the calling with which you were called, with all lowliness and gentleness, with longsuffering, bearing with one another in love, endeavoring to keep the unity of the Spirit in the bond of peace. There is one body and one Spirit, just as you were called in one hope of your calling."

Our calling is not connected with this world. Believers should always endeavor to have a walk worthy of our heavenly calling. If we had an earthly calling our attention would be to this world and earth, to the cares of this world, and the cares of life here. But our life is above and our calling heavenly.

The Believer's Position before God is the same as the Glorified Son of Man

Ephesians 1:3

"Blessed be the God and Father of our Lord Jesus Christ, who has blessed us with every spiritual blessing in the heavenlies in Christ."

Biblical truths concerning the individual believer is the attention of the Spirit in the first half of the first chapter of Ephesians. The believer is shown to be in the counsels of God in Christ from before the world began. Verse 3 is another 'in Christ' reality and truth concerning us. Our loving heavenly Father has blessed the Christian with everything He knows we may ever need in the heavens. We are blessed as Christ is blessed in the heavens.

Ephesians 1:6

"...to the praise of the glory of His grace, by which He made us accepted in the Beloved."

This verse shows us again the basis of all this incredible favor and blessing. It is the display of the glory of the Father's grace by which He has enabled us as completely acceptable to Him, as in Christ who is His Beloved. We are beloved of the Father as Christ is beloved. We are loved by the Father with the same love the Father has for Him (John 17:23). We are seen by the Father as He sees Christ. It doesn't get any better than this.

The Body of Christ in the Heavens

Ephesians 1:19-23

"...and what is the exceeding greatness of His power toward us who believe, according to the working of His mighty power which He worked in Christ when He raised Him from the dead and seated Him at His right hand in the heavenly places, far above all principality and power and might and

dominion, and every name that is named, not only in this age but also in that which is to come.

And He put all things under His feet, and gave Him to be head over all things to the church, which is His body, the fullness of Him who fills all in all."

These verses are truly marvelous. We have Christ raised out of death as the Son of Man. We have Christ then exalted far above all things as the glorified Man, even to the right hand in the heavens. Yet this portion of Scripture starts as God's grace towards us, believers, in resurrection power. The passage ends with Christ's body, the church, exalted in Him far above all principalities and powers. At the end the church is the fullness of Him, while He fills all in all. Again, this is at the Father's right hand in heavenly places.

Ephesians 2:6-7

"...and raised us up together, and made us sit together in the heavenly places in Christ Jesus, that in the ages to come He might show the exceeding riches of His grace in His kindness toward us in Christ Jesus."

Seated in Christ in the heavens is at the Father's right hand. It is the establishing in Christ, by the redemptive work of the second Adam and the Father's consequent glorifying of Him, the believer/Body of Christ in the heavenly calling. The believer is seated in the heavens, as far as the mind of God and His counsels toward us, in all spiritual truth and position. But it is verse 7 where we begin to catch sight of the depth of truth and glory that we share in Christ. The Father has in store for us exceeding riches of His grace. When? It is throughout the ages to come. How? It is by His loving kindness for us in Christ. Christ has been glorified by the Father, this is true. He in turn, shares His glory with us (John 17:22). The truth of the heavenly calling is further established in Philippians;

Philippians 3:14

"I press toward the goal for the prize of the upward call of God in Christ Jesus."

Philippians 3:18-19

"For many walk, of whom I have told you often, and now tell you even weeping, that they are the enemies of the cross of Christ: whose end is destruction, whose god is their belly, and whose glory is in their shame— who set their mind on earthly things."

Philippians 3:20

"For our citizenship is in heaven, from which we also eagerly wait for the Savior, the Lord Jesus Christ."

The teaching here by the Spirit should be unmistakable. The heavenly call of the believer is described as the upward call of God, again in Christ Jesus. And a definite understanding is given, that we have a citizenship in heaven, making the believer on the earth a stranger, a pilgrim, and an ambassador. The citizenship does not change for all eternity. It would be a mistake if the believer had the idea that their dwelling and abode is somewhere on the earth. We are not among the Gentile nations who will present themselves once a year to worship the Son of Man who sits on His throne of glory in Jerusalem. We are not placed under His dominion and rule on the earth. (Certainly this is in prophecy concerning the Son of Man's millennial kingdom over the earth, but the believer has been placed in Christ, in a position where he is no longer Jew or Gentile, and so, no longer of this world.)

The Believer's Relationship with the Father is as a Son

Allow me to explain some distinctions I see concerning the believer's heavenly calling and the character of our relationship with the Father and with Jesus Christ. As we have previously discussed, this relationship with the Father is as many sons in glory (Rom. 8:16-17, Gal. 4:5), and that as having been sealed with the Spirit of adoption of sonship (Rom. 8:15). It is by the presence of the Spirit in the believer and this established eternal relationship with the Father (Gal. 4:6), whereby we cry, "Abba, Father." It is the Father who gave this seal of the Spirit as asked by Jesus (John 14:16), and so, the sealing becomes our guarantee of glory, inheritance, and all heavenly blessing.

1 Pet. 1:3-4

"Blessed be the God and Father of our Lord Jesus Christ, who according to His abundant mercy has begotten us again to a living hope through the resurrection of Jesus Christ from the dead, to an inheritance incorruptible and undefiled and that does not fade away, reserved in heaven for you,"

We are heirs of God as sons of the Father (Rom. 8:17). It is the Father who gives the inheritance to His sons. Our inheritance is reserved in heaven. We are not heirs of Christ, but rather co-heirs with Him. The Son of Man Himself is an heir of the Father. And all this makes Christ our brother, the firstborn among many brethren (Rom. 8:29).

The Work of the Son of Man prepares a Place in the Heavens for the Believer

Also we know Christ went away to prepare a place for us in the Father's house (John 14:1-3). Where He went, we know. He went back to the Father, back into the heavens, to the right hand of the throne of God. The place He prepared for us is in the heavens. The preparations were all complete when the blood was brought into the holy place, and Jesus sat down as the glorified Man at the right hand of God. All the necessary work for bringing many others into the presence of God, to live there in the house of the Father as sons, is completely finished.

For a certainty, Jesus was speaking of going away into the heavens. He did not go away to somewhere in Jerusalem or anywhere else on this earth. The Father's house is in the heavens. We are sons in the Father's house (here we are speaking of individual believers, not corporately of the church), as Christ is a Son of the Father as well. This, I believe, is very clear from what the Lord says after His resurrection;

John 20:17

"Jesus said to her, "Do not cling to Me, for I have not yet ascended to My Father; but go to My brethren and say to them, 'I am ascending to My Father and your Father, and to My God and your God.'""

He places the believer in the same position and relationship that He is in with His Father and God. He says this consequent to His being raised from the dead by the Father. For believers it is the same. We were crucified with Christ and we died with Him (Gal. 2:20, Col. 3:3, Rom. 6:3, 5). Then the Father, with the same exceeding greatness of power towards us who believe (Eph. 1:19), raises us up with Him from the dead (Eph. 2:1, 5-6, Rom. 6:4-5). In Christ, the Father exalts us as Christ's body far above all principality and power (Eph. 1:20-23). He seats us in Christ, at His right hand (Eph. 2:6). What we may notice from the above verse is that only after His resurrection, for the first time, He calls the disciples His brethren. In the Son of Man title and by the redemptive work of the second Adam, we are associated with Christ as brothers.

Adam and Eve – Christ, the Son of Man, and His Bride

Let us look at another relationship we have in Scripture through the work of the Son of Man that we will find has a distinct character as well -- the Bride of Christ. As we have previously discussed, the first Adam and his wife, Eve, are types of Christ and the church (Eph. 5:32). This type prefiguring the greater reality of Christ and the church is valid only as seen before sin entered into the world. As a type (Rom. 5:14), Adam was to rule over God's creation. Eve was made from Adam and not part of the original creation. She was to rule with him as his help-meet. She was to be his companion in the government and inheritance of all things, all the works of God's hand. When we consider Christ as the second Adam, then His bride, the church, is the antitype of Eve (Eph. 5:25-32). The church will be the Son of Man's help-meet in His rule, dominion, and kingdom over the entire earth. We must also see we are co-heirs with Him in the inheritance of all things. This will be the character and role of the church as the Bride of Christ, and it also speaks to believers as being made kings and priests in Christ.

[When we study the book of Revelation and begin to understand the prophetic symbols used there, we see twenty-four elders on endowed thrones of authority in chapter four. This is the Body of Christ as made kings. In chapter five these same twenty-four elders are depicted as priests. This is the Body of Christ as made priests. It is the positioning of the church and the giving of the title of these things (Rev. 1:6). It is not the church functioning in the ministry of these roles yet, which is reserved for the millennial kingdom of the Son of Man. Yet these two chapters show certain realities concerning the heavenly calling. When chapter four begins, the church is seen in the heavens, and associated with the throne of God's government. The church is no longer on the earth.]

The First and Second Adams

In the chapter on types and shadows we discussed how these things are based on similarities. A shadow is shaped similar to the object that is casting it. A shadow has a measure of reality, but nothing at all like the substance of the object itself. This makes a distinction that is important to see and understand. Christ, as the second Adam, is distinct from the first.

1 Corinthians 15:45-47

"And so it is written, "The first man Adam became a living being." The last Adam became a life-giving spirit.

However, the spiritual is not first, but the natural, and afterward the spiritual. The first man was of the earth, made of dust; the second Man is from heaven."

When Paul says, "...the spiritual is not first, but the natural," one point being made is that all types and shadows precede and prefigure the greater reality and substance. In verse 45 we have the first distinction made. The first man is a living being, while the second man is a life-giving spirit. The first Adam, as a living being, soon fell into sin and ruin. By contrast, in the last Adam is eternal life. But the specific point I make, and that related to the heavenly calling, is the second distinction made in verse 47. The first Adam was of the earth. The second Man is from heaven. The reach and scope of the title and influence of the second Man far outweighs that of the first.

The Son of Man and the Inheritance of All Things

All things will be gathered into Christ, the second Adam. He will have the Headship of all things (Col. 1:17-18), both in heaven and on earth (Eph. 1:10). This includes everything – all of creation, things visible and invisible (Col. 1:16). This is His inheritance. The basis and means of Christ receiving and possessing the inheritance is revealed to us in Scripture as well:

1.) He has a right to inherit as the Creator (John 1:1-3, Col. 1:15-17)

2.) As the true Son of God, He is appointed heir of all things (Heb. 1:2)

3.) As the raised and glorified Son of Man (Ps. 8:4-6, Heb. 2:6-9, Eph. 1:22, I Cor. 15:25-27)

In the first point above, Christ as Creator speaks of His divinity. He created everything, visible or invisible. His divinity is unchanging, and in this we have no part or sharing. Peter does tell us that in Christ we have been made partakers of the divine nature (II Pet. 1:2-4). This however is the Spirit within and pertains to the new life we have. It is the life of God and godliness, and the new creation we are – it does not refer to His divine attributes. It is by a divine nature we can have a relationship with God, enjoy God, and be in His presence.

In the second point above Jesus is the Son of God. We share in this, but only in a certain understanding. We do not share in His divinity ever. But believers are made sons of God through faith in Christ (Gal. 3:26). We are enabled to share in the same relationship He has with the Father – as adopted sons of God, having the Spirit of adoption. Therefore He says, "…go to My brethren and say to them…" We can clearly see that this new position we have been given in Christ was by the Son of God as the Son of Man. We received the adoption of sonship through His death.

In this book we concentrate on the title, role, and character of Christ as the Son of Man, the second Adam. Christ, in this role, accomplishes the work of redemption, and then is Man raised and glorified in His present position. He is the Son of Man, at the very least, through the end of the millennium. *He is Jesus Christ, who, being in the form of God, did not consider it robbery to be equal with God...coming in the likeness of men* (Phil. 2:6). How God accomplished this is never explained in any detail in Scripture. But what we clearly see in the revelation of Scripture is the title, role, and character of Christ as the Son of Man, and the truths the Spirit of God associates with it.

It is as the glorified Man that He will take the inheritance (the third point above). As the Creator, it is His right to possess. As the Son, it is appointed to Him by the Father. It is only as having reconciled it all through His death as the Son of Man, that He will take the inheritance of all things (Col.1:20). It is only through the death of the Son of Man that many brethren will share as co-heirs with Him of the inheritance given (Col. 1:21-22). This is an important understanding – He redeems the inheritance of all things as a Man in order that the church, His body redeemed by His blood, will share as co-heir of all things with Him.

The understanding of the title of Son of Man in the counsels of God is of great importance. But to be clear so that there are no misunderstandings, in Christ the fullness of the Godhead dwells bodily, and He is the image of the invisible God (Col.1:15, 19). The divinity of Christ remains intact.

The two Headships of Christ, the Son of Man

When Scripture speaks of Christ receiving an inheritance, it is not the same as His Headships. Christ is Head over all creation as well as the church (Col. 1:15, 18). But just as Eve in type was not part of the original creation to be ruled over by Adam, so also the church is not part of Christ's inheritance to be ruled over. No, we will be co-heirs with Him (Rom. 8:17) of the inheritance given by the Father. His Bride is His companion in His kingdom and government over all creation during the millennial age to come.

Now do not be tempted to think that we will be residents of this earth when ruling with the Son of Man over it. Allow me to remind you of the lesson God taught to man when He first set up the Gentiles to rule the earth.

The Heavens rule the Earth

Daniel 4:26

"And whereas it was commanded to leave the stump of the roots of the tree; thy kingdom shall remain unto thee, after that thou shalt know that the heavens do rule."

The heavens rule the affairs of this earth. This is readily seen in the book of Daniel with God's use of angelic administrations in the heavens and their influence over the kingdoms of men. But God's judgment of Nebuchadnezzar – seven years he lives as a beast – teaches the lesson that the heavens rule the earth. This is obviously quite symbolic when you consider the beast symbols used in the prophetic language depicting the four Gentile world empires in Daniel (Dan. 7).

When the glory and presence of God was in the tabernacle and Solomon's temple, God ruled the earth from the midst of Israel. The heavens ruling the earth would not have been true at this time. It was only when God's presence left Israel, and the Jews were no longer acknowledged by God, that angelic administrations were established – principalities and powers in heavenly places.

The heavenly Man came down to give His life (I Cor. 15:47-49). Being raised up by God, the Son of Man returns to heaven. This serves to establish the beginnings of the kingdom of heaven, which is only spoken of in Matthew's gospel. Nevertheless, the King of this kingdom is away in heaven. The reality of the kingdom of heaven would involve the rule and authority of this kingdom from the heavens. All power and authority in heaven and on earth was given to the Son of Man when He was resurrected (Luke 24:7, Matt. 28:18). Without a detailed explanation, believers must know their association with the glorified Son of Man who sits at the right hand of the Power on High.

Presently, on the earth, the true church wrestles and struggles against principalities and powers in the heavens (Eph. 6:12). There may be multiple reasons for this. The body of Christ has already been exalted in Christ far above all principality and power and might and dominion (Eph. 1:19-23) – however, we do not exercise this authority as yet. Why? One particular reason being we are still on the earth and in these bodies of flesh. We are not yet conformed into the image of His Son (Rom. 8:29). When this event occurs, we will have glorified bodies, and the church will be taken from the earth into the heavens as the body of the glorified Son of Man. Shortly thereafter, as a consequence of the church positioned in the heavens, Satan and his forces will be cast out and down to the earth (Rev. 12).

Back in the time of Daniel, as it is now, there are principalities and powers. In the age to come (the millennium) the angels, good or bad, will have been replaced by the true church (Heb. 2:5-11). If you carefully look at this chapter in Hebrews 2 you will see that the world to come is in subjection to man. However it is not just any man, but the glorified Son of Man and the many sons together as His body and bride. The Son of Man will rule from His throne in Jerusalem and His body, the church, from its position in the heavens. It will still remain that the affairs of the earth will be ruled by the heavens.

This relationship of the church and the angels now in heavenly places is subtly hinted at in Ephesians. There are three separate times principalities and powers are mentioned in this epistle, and each time it is in relation to the church. The church is raised and exalted in Christ by the Father, far above all principality and power and might and dominion (Eph. 1:21-23). We know that at this present time and in this present age, while the church is still on the earth, we wrestle not against flesh and blood (Eph. 6:12). And finally, in the eternal counsels of God, He shows forth His abundant wisdom in and by the church to the principalities and powers in the heavens (Eph.3:10). How is this done? God's eternal purpose is His own glory, of which Christ is the centerpiece (Eph. 1:9-10, 3:11). The church is His Body and we are in Christ. We are seen by the Father as Christ (Heb. 2:11) and loved by the Father with the very same love (John 17:23). When the Spirit speaks of the Father exalting Christ -- the Body, the church, is found there at the right hand of God (Eph. 1:19-23). This is the positioning of the church by the Father, and His manifold wisdom now made known; these are things into which angels desire to look (I Pet. 1:12).

The Character of Prophecy

Prophecy involves God's dealings with Israel and God's governmental dealings with the earth. This is the major theme of all of prophecy. As long as God does not acknowledge Israel as His people, and until He takes them up again in the end, Israel remains set aside and desolate. With Israel set aside, then prophecy is set aside. If prophecy is set aside, then the earth is not being dealt with. The final thought that completes this sequence is that time stands still, as we can easily see in Daniel's 70 week prophecy (Dan. 9:24-27). Time is not counted in heaven, or with heavenly things like the church, but is associated with Israel and the earth in prophecy.

The Mystery of Christ -- Hidden from Prophecy

What God is currently doing is not found in prophecy. It is hidden from the prophets of old and all their writings. It is not related to His government of the earth, and has nothing to do with Israel as a people and nation. What God is doing now through grace and the redemptive work of the Son of Man is His mystery. It is that which He purposely kept hidden. Further He does not reveal His mystery until after the Son of Man was glorified, and the Holy Spirit was sent.

Ephesians 3:1-11

"For this reason I, Paul, the prisoner of Christ Jesus for you Gentiles— if indeed you have heard of the dispensation of the grace of God which was given to me for you, how that by revelation He made known to me the mystery (as I have briefly written already, by which, when you read, you may understand my knowledge in the mystery of Christ), which in other ages was not made known to the sons of men, as it has now been revealed by the Spirit to His holy apostles and prophets: that the Gentiles should be fellow heirs, of the same body, and partakers of His promise in Christ through the

gospel, of which I became a minister according to the gift of the grace of God given to me by the effective working of His power.

To me, who am less than the least of all the saints, this grace was given, that I should preach among the Gentiles the unsearchable riches of Christ, and to make all see what is the fellowship of the mystery, which from the beginning of the ages has been hidden in God who created all things through Jesus Christ, to the intent that now the manifold wisdom of God might be made known by the church to the principalities and powers in the heavenly places, according to the eternal purpose which He accomplished in Christ Jesus our Lord,"

There are numerous truths and important understandings found in these eleven verses; important in seeing clearly and comprehending by the Spirit. These I attempt to bring out in the list below and then add more scriptural support.

1.) The mystery was God's and He kept it hidden and unrevealed from (before) the foundations of the world – *which in other ages was not made known to the sons of men...which from the beginning of the ages has been hidden in God...* Note: The mystery was hidden in God, and the prophets of old would have no possibility of discovering it, or be able to speak concerning it.

2.) Although hidden in God, the mystery existed in God's counsels and plans before He created the world – *according to the eternal purpose...*

3.) The mystery was kept hidden by God until the work of redemption was finished. After the Son of Man was glorified and sat down, the Holy Spirit was sent to bring forth this revelation of the mystery – *as it has now been revealed by the Spirit...to the intent that now the manifold wisdom of God might be made known...*

4.) The mystery was specifically given to Paul to reveal by the Spirit, as a personal stewardship of the grace of God, a dispensation of the mystery of Christ – *For this reason, I, Paul,...if indeed you have heard of the dispensation of the grace of God which was given to me for you, how that by revelation He made known to me the mystery...my knowledge in the mystery of Christ...of which I became a minister...to me... this grace was given...and to make all people see what is the fellowship (dispensation) of the mystery...*

5.) This mystery of God's is now revealed by the Spirit with the purpose of being understood and comprehended by the believer, and not to remain hidden any longer – *by which, when you read, you may understand my knowledge in the mystery...to make all people see what is the fellowship of the mystery...*

The Mystery of Christ Given Specifically to Paul to Reveal

It is not just in Ephesians that Paul speaks of the mystery; it is found in passages elsewhere and confirms the above points made.

Rom. 16:25

"Now to Him who is able to establish you according to my gospel and the preaching of Jesus Christ, according to the revelation of the mystery kept secret since the world began..."

Ephesians 1:8-9,

"...which He made to abound toward us in all wisdom and prudence, having made known to us the mystery of His will, according to His good pleasure which He purposed in Himself,"

Colossians 1:25-27,

"...of which I became a minister according to the stewardship (dispensation) from God which was given to me for you, to fulfill the word of God, the mystery which has been hidden from ages and from generations, but now has been revealed to His saints. To them God willed to make known what are the riches of the glory of this mystery among the Gentiles: which is Christ in you, the hope of glory."

Colossians 2:2-3,

"...that their hearts may be encouraged, being knit together in love, and attaining to all riches of the full assurance of understanding, to the knowledge of the mystery of God, in whom are hidden all the treasures of wisdom and knowledge."

The Mystery of Christ – God forms the Body of the Glorified Man

What is this mystery God kept hidden but now reveals by the Spirit? It is the Body of Christ (Eph. 2:11-22). The passage from Ephesians 3 concerning the mystery follows the explanation of the Body of Christ in Ephesians 2, and starts with Paul saying, "For this reason..." (Eph. 3:1) Think about it. We now know through this revelation to Paul the reality of the idea that God would form, through redemption, a mystical body that would be gathered and joined to the Son of Man raised and exalted into glory. Many members are made one through faith by one Spirit into one body, with Christ as its Head. This is simply unthinkable for man and foreign to Jewish thought. Yet this is the bulk of the mystery that God held hidden for ages.

Christ dwelling in the individual believer is part of the mystery as well, 'Christ in you, the hope of glory.' He is in us, and we are in Him (John 14:20). Christ in us is our life. For the believer to live is Christ. We have no life on our own any longer. The life the believer had in Adam was put to death on the cross. The old man, that life in Adam, was crucified with Christ (Rom. 6:6). The only life the believer has is the resurrected Christ (Rom. 6:5, 8). All these redemptive truths are part of the mystery of Christ.

Also the steadfast certainty of the believer's hopes in Christ's glory, and our sharing in that glory, would be part of the mystery. Finally, what also seems hidden from prophecy is the Priesthood of Christ (not referring to the order of His Priesthood, but the ministry and function of it presently).

When the believer looks for the doctrine and teaching concerning the Body of Christ in Scripture, it can only be found in Paul's writings. This reinforces the idea that the revelation of the mystery of Christ was specifically given to Paul to reveal by the Spirit. The other New Testament writers never broach the subject. At best there are vague references to assemblies in various cities and localities. But it is never one Body, one Spirit, one hope of your calling; one Lord, one faith, one baptism. It is never gifts given by Christ to the Body for its growth and edification, to the measure of the stature of the fullness of Christ (Eph. 4:4-16).

What does the mystery have to do with the heavenly calling? The Body of Christ and the individual believer are those of the heavenly calling. But beyond this, during God's dealings with the mystery and the Spirit sent down from heaven, prophecy is suspended. Israel and the earth are set aside, and time is not counted. The mystery is all about heavenly things. So much so, that as far as prophecy goes and the times of the Gentiles, even the fourth beast has disappeared from the landscape of the prophetic earth.

The Biblical Differences between Judaism and Christianity

The differences between Christianity and Judaism are profound, especially seen in the discourse with the woman at the well (John 4). Christianity is worship in spirit and truth (John 4:23-24), and a walk of faith (II Cor. 5:7). Judaism is worship in the flesh (Heb. 9:9-10) and a walk by sight. It was given to a people in the flesh and of the world, and ministered to their flesh and their senses. As true believers, we worship what we do not see in the flesh (Rom. 8:24). We worship in the Spirit. Christianity is in the heavens while Judaism is all on this earth with a temple in Jerusalem or a mountain top in Samaria (John 4:20-21). Those of Judaism are still looking for a Christ to come in the flesh. Christians know Christ no longer after the flesh. We know Him as the Son of Man gone up into the glory, into the heavens.

God does not come to live on the earth until at least an external redemption is accomplished with Israel. Christians, through the blood of Christ and faith in His blood, are the fulfillment of the Red Sea event of Israel in type. Christianity, by the redemptive work of the Son of Man, then comes in as God's religion of the heavens.

These are believers who have the circumcision of the Spirit, who received the seal of the Spirit, who worship God in the Spirit, and this not in the flesh at all. Believers are being built-up as the house of God, with Christ as the cornerstone of this very house (Eph.2:19-21). We are members one of another, lively stones being built around Him, the body of Christ. So now God, by His Spirit, lives individually in the believer (I Cor. 6:19, II Cor. 6:16), as well as corporately in the body (I Cor. 3:16, Eph. 2:22) on the earth (while the body remains on the earth). Redemption through Christ Jesus is accomplished on our behalf, not externally in the flesh or in types and shadows.

The Believer's Citizenship is in Heaven

I say Christianity is the religion of the heavens for our citizenship is there. We are seated in heavenly places in Christ, and He said He would come again and take us there, having prepared a place for us (John 14:1-3). The Head of the Body is seated at the right hand of the Father. He will not take His inheritance until His Body is united to Him physically in the heavens. He will come for His Body because we are His fellow co-heirs and brethren.

1 Corinthians 15:48

"As was the man of dust, so also are those who are made of dust; and as is the heavenly Man, so also are those who are heavenly."

Colossians 1:5

"...because of the hope which is laid up for you in heaven, of which you heard before in the word of the truth of the gospel,"

Individual believers and the church are those who are heavenly and who will follow the heavenly Man there (John 17:24, 14:2-3). They are those whose hopes and inheritance are laid up in heaven (I Pet. 1:3-4). We are holy brethren of Christ and partakers of the heavenly calling. And in Abraham, his spiritual seed are children by faith (not by the flesh or physical decent), centered and contained in his one Seed, who is Christ. As our calling is above, we will be as innumerable as the stars of the heavens (Gen. 15:5).

Israel	The Believer/ body of Christ
The earthly calling according to prophecy. Connected to the earth and a promised land. Only saved as an earthly remnant.	The heavenly calling according to the mystery of Christ, hidden from the prophets. Citizenship in heaven (Phil. 3:20).
Judaism – the religion of the flesh and of the earth. A yoke of bondage that only produces slaves (Gal. 4:21-25, 5:1). A walk by sight.	Christianity – the religion of the heavens. Worship of God in spirit and truth. A walk of faith. Seated with Christ in heavenly places.
Circumcision in the flesh, made with hands (Eph. 2:11).	Circumcision in the Spirit, made without hands (Phil. 3:3, Col. 2:11)
Only ever bondservants and slaves in the House of God. No security of abiding forever (John 8:34-35).	Sons of God who abide in the House of God forever (John 8:35-36, Gal. 3:26). Heirs of God and co-heirs with Christ.
The sands of the seashore	The stars of the heavens

Once we understand the truths concerning the earthly and heavenly callings it becomes important to maintain the distinctions between them. We should never mix the two of them as one. If we do this our teachings and beliefs become confounded. Inevitably all our hopes will sink to the lesser value of the earthly. The character of those believers that understand their calling as heavenly in Christ is depicted in Colossians;

Colossians 3:1-2

"If then you were raised with Christ, seek those things which are above, where Christ is, sitting at the right hand of God. Set your mind on things above, not on things on the earth."

The Believer's Life is not Down Here on the Earth

Be on your guard for teachings that encourage you to pursue things here below, and to set your mind on things of the earth. This is not the character of the true Christian. We should know we are not of this world. We do not dwell on this earth, but instead are strangers here.

When you were justified by faith in Christ, becoming a member of His body, you gave up citizenship on this earth. Once you are established as a believer, there is no teaching or prophecy of Scripture that makes you a dweller of the earth. This is true throughout eternity. Our habitation is in heavenly places. We are the heavenly Jerusalem. Our Father's house has many mansions, and Christ has prepared all by going there ahead of us. We are truly strangers and pilgrims here on the earth.

Be on guard for teachings about living your life down here. The cares of living and the cares of life are the cares of this world. They are thorns that rise up, choking the word in those who merely profess Christianity (Matt. 13:22). For true believers, they only serve to turn your attention to this world, connecting you to this earth. Their end result is unfruitfulness. But the believer's life is located somewhere else:

Colossians 3:3-4

"...For you died, and your life is hidden with Christ in God. When Christ who is our life appears, then you also will appear with Him in glory."

As a believer, when you look for your life down here, the motivation and character of that is all wrong and displeasing to the Lord. When ministers and ministries teach you as if your life is down here, their motivation and emphasis is wrong as well. I understand how most people only choose to see what is in front of them, and that is their physical life lived out day by day on the earth. Ministries take advantage of this emphasis and profit by it. When you tangle yourself up with the cares of living in this world, it is simply not befitting of the saint. Our life is Christ, and Christ is where? Christ is hidden in God at this time, in the heavens. Our life therefore is hidden in God, in the heavens as well. It is not to be found down here, on this earth or of this world.

Is the Believer to Reign in Life Down Here?

Then how are you to reign in life down here if your life can't be found here? You can't. Are you going to reign without Christ? Will you reign before Christ reigns? Those verses in Romans five have nothing to do with our walk on this earth and are not speaking of our life down here. Yet whole ministries are built on such applications of scripture.

If you want to know about the believer in his walk, it is found later in Romans;

Romans 8:17-18

"…and if children, then heirs—heirs of God and joint heirs with Christ, if indeed we suffer with Him, that we may also be glorified together.

For I consider that the sufferings of this present time are not worthy to be compared with the glory which shall be revealed in us."

The inheritance the Spirit speaks of is ours with Christ when it is given by the Father, and not until then. The believer will not reign until we have been joined with Christ in glory. Then we will reign in life, as in eternal life in the glory, reigning with Christ as kings, when He is revealed and manifested as King of kings and Lord of lords. What is our portion at this present time? Sufferings, if indeed we suffer with Christ.

Christ did not reign as a king in His walk on this earth. They rejected Him as their king and crucified Him. He does not reign as a King at this present time. Now He is hidden in God (Col. 3:1-3). He is patiently waiting there, until His enemies be made His footstool (Heb. 10:13). In the meantime, the Holy Spirit has been sent down to gather the co-heirs that will be with Him in His glory. That is the glory that will be revealed in us. That is when we reign.

What is the Believer's Portion Presently on the Earth?

But now what is our portion to be? We are to suffer with Him. We are to love one another as He loved us, giving Himself for us (Eph. 5:2). We are to keep the word of His patience and wait as He waits (Rev. 1:9, 3:10). We are to have the constant expectation of His coming for us. This truth purifies us now as He is pure (I John 3:2-3). If a person can be known by the ends he is pursuing, than his life will bear the impress of what future outcomes he is expecting. This should be valid for the Christian. The believer's expectation is to be conformed into His image when He comes for us. This hope has a sanctifying influence on our walk here on earth.

Those whose ambition is position and power, those who are seeking earthly riches and investments, and those who are pursuing only the pleasures of this world, will live and act according to the desires in their heart. Their behavior will reflect their longings. This will be true for believers who understand and are faithful to their heavenly calling. We are destined to share with Christ in the heavenly glory – this future hope and expectation must have its effect on us now.

Embracing our heavenly calling, we walk as pilgrims and strangers in this world. We will not be confused by the earthly promises made to the Jews in the prophetic scriptures, but rather will distinguish these promises from the heavenly promises for the church. As not of the world, we will keep ourselves from many cares and distractions that are hurtful to the Christian life. Having heavenly hopes founded in our heavenly calling, we become faithful in fulfilling any duties that flow out of it. We are to walk on this earth as He walked on this earth. He was despised and rejected of men. We should be also.

John 15:18-19

"If the world hates you, you know that it hated Me before it hated you. If you were of the world, the world would love its own. Yet because you are not of the world, but I chose you out of the world, therefore the world hates you."

We do not reign in this present life on earth. We are pilgrims here, not kings. And besides, are we ever to take what Christ did not? Everything about the believer is as Christ and in Christ and with Christ. *It is never apart from Christ.* We will not reign until Christ reigns, for we are His body. Presently we suffer with Him, so that later we will reign with Him in glory. Is this not the mind and truth of God?

The Biblical Hope of the Believer is not presently seen

The Father will have the heavenly calling conformed to the image of His Son. He predestined it to be so (Rom. 8:29). If you carefully read Rom. 8:19-25 it is all pointing to this counsel. It says this specific hope (conformed to the image of His Son) is the earnest expectation of both the believer and creation. But hope that is seen is not hope at all. So then, presently, we eagerly wait for it with perseverance;

as does creation. At this time, in these bodies of the flesh, we groan within ourselves, eagerly waiting. We do not reign in life on earth.

The Believer is on a walk out of this World

As disciples, our life is not here on this earth, and we cannot seek our life in the world, or attach ourselves to this world. It is always considered a walk (Eph. 5:1-2, and 8), because we are not of this world, nor dwellers of the earth, but are walking on a road out of it, following Jesus (John 1:43). If you think a little about it, the roads are only in this present world and on this earth for us to walk. There were no roads in paradise with Adam, and there will be no roads in glory with the Father and Son. Both of these define the rest of God, the sabbath (Heb. 4:9-11). The original rest of God was ruined by man and sin. The future rest of God is entered into by all believers, through the sovereign power of God, when He takes us there, into the glory of God (Heb. 4:1-3, John 14:2-3). Presently, on this earth, there is no rest of God to be found. That is why there are roads here, and believers are on a walk out of this world.

John 12:25

"He who loves his life will lose it, and he who hates his life in this world will keep it for eternal life."

If you love life down here, you will lose everything, and end up with nothing. 'Life in this world,' and what you can make of it, cannot be your objective or your interest as a believer. You cannot even become a disciple this way. You must hate your life in this world, in order to receive or possess eternal life. It is so you can lay this life, in this world, down and die, following the Son of Man through death, so that you can be where He is;

John 12:26

"If anyone serves Me, let him follow Me; and where I am, there My servant will be also. If anyone serves Me, him My Father will honor."

The Believer's Life is Christ

The "Me" we are to follow is Jesus, the Son of Man, who first goes down into death, and then is glorified; this is clear from the previous verses (John 12:23-24). How are you to be where He is? I can tell you this from v. 26, that when you are where He is, then there will be honor from the Father. That is because you will be in glory with the glorified Son of Man, as in Christ, and with Christ. You will be where He is. But again, how can you get there? The only way to be where He is, is to follow the same path. If we hate our life in this world, we will die with Christ and end that life. Truly eternal life can only be found beyond our death. How is this? The Son of Man glorified is beyond death, for His death had to come first. Eternal life is in the resurrected Christ, beyond death. We have to follow Him down into death and beyond, to a new life, a resurrected life. And so, I am crucified with Christ (Gal. 2:20). My old life in this world is no longer alive – it is no longer I who live. My life is now a resurrected Christ living in me. This is eternal life, and it has no connection with life in this world.

This is what it really means to follow Him. It is not stressing, straining, and sweating in human performance to be pleasing to God. It is a redemptive truth found in the work of Jesus Christ, the Son of Man. We die with Him so we may possess eternal life by having Him as our life (John 5:39-40). He lives in us as this resurrected life. Now we are disciples. And precious truth -- He will come for us personally, so that we may be with Him where He is, in His glory (John 14:1-3, and 17:24). Take up your cross and follow Him? When you take up a cross, it can only mean certain death (Luke 14:27). But for us, it is what is beyond the death that is all important. It is eternal life received now in our soul and spirit. It then becomes discipleship that has a certain walk in this world. Finally it is with Him in glory as possessing this life, our bodies glorified, and where there are no roads leading out.

The Son of Man lifted up from the Earth

I want to be crystal clear in portraying what Jesus is saying in all this. Your walk on this earth as a disciple can only be after you become a disciple. You only become a disciple after you die with the Son of Man, and then you are raised with Him (Rom. 6:3-5, Col. 2:11-13). Then you possess eternal life in possessing Christ as your life (John 1:4, 6:47-51, 10:28, and 11:25). You are a disciple, and you can walk in this world as a disciple.

This walk has a certain character, to be sure. It is walking as Jesus walked (1 John 2:6), loving the brethren as Jesus loved us (John 15:12, 1 John 3:16, and Eph. 5:2), and walking as children of light, as our Father is light (Eph. 5:1, 8, and Phil. 2:15). It is a walk that is apart from the world, as a stranger and pilgrim on the earth, on a road following Jesus out of this world. This is a big part of the meaning of the Son of Man being lifted up in John 12:32. The lifting up is from the earth, apart from the world, because He was hated and rejected by the world. His lifting up is the severing of all His relationship with the world. It is the world judged and condemned by God when the Son of Man was lifted up apart from it (John 12:31-32). The Son of God is not of the world, as the Son of Man lifted up. [The same thing cannot be said of the title of Messiah; it is of this world and of this earth.] Our walk then, as disciples, is one rejected by the world and hated by the world, as they rejected and hated Him (John 15:18-19, Gal. 6:14). I cannot be genuine and teach you that in your walk as a disciple of Christ in this world you should reign as a king.

The true Christian's life is not down here, though while on the earth we are passing through the wilderness. We are on the journey, not in the rest. It is not yet the life in the rest and glory of Christ. Let us look at Israel in the types and shadows that present these greater truths and realities for the believer.

Israel Passes through the Wilderness in Type

Our walk as believers in the world and on the earth is symbolized by Israel passing through the wilderness. The Passover lamb they ate and the blood they placed on the doors, the day before their exit from Egypt, kept the hand of God's righteous judgment from them. Passing on dry land through the Red Sea is the salvation of the Lord in type, their justification by faith. Entrance into the Promised Land, from the book of Hebrews, is obviously entrance of the believer into the rest of God – entrance physically into the very presence and glory of God eternally.

These are broad strokes concerning the shadows God uses to teach truth – types God uses to show forth greater realities. For Israel, it is all shadows of a true redemption. For them it is an external redemption in the flesh, an external separation, and an external deliverance. The Law of Moses, their religion of Judaism, is geared by God for man externally, in the flesh (Heb. 9:9-10, 10:1-4). It is a religion of the world (Col. 2:8, Gal. 4:9). But the types and shadows continue.

Hebrews 3:16-19

"For who, having heard, rebelled? Indeed, was it not all who came out of Egypt, led by Moses? Now with whom was He angry forty years? Was it not with those who sinned, whose corpses fell in the wilderness? And to whom did He swear that they would not enter His rest, but to those who did not obey? So we see that they could not enter in because of unbelief."

The Promised Land is a Type of the Glory and Rest of God

What I want you to see is that all Israel in mass came out of Egypt. They came out as a nation, as a large corporate group. But those in unbelief were judged by God in the wilderness and did not enter into God's rest – the land as a type. We have the same reality today in the Christian world – the corporate group of all those who profess Christ. This is depicted by the spoiled crop of tares and wheat in the field of the world, in the parable in Matt. 13:24-30. Its interpretation is in Matt. 13:37-43. The wheat and tares are mixed together as a corporate entity until removal of the wheat from the world. To be sure, the tares are bundled together and left in the world to be judged (more on this parable in a later chapter). But reading further in Hebrews:

Heb. 4:1-11

"Therefore, since a promise remains of entering His rest, let us fear lest any of you seem to have come short of it. For indeed the gospel was preached to

us as well as to them; but the word which they heard did not profit them, not being mixed with faith in those who heard it. For we who have believed do enter that rest, as He has said:

"So I swore in My wrath,
'They shall not enter My rest,'"

although the works were finished from the foundation of the world. For He has spoken in a certain place of the seventh day in this way: "And God rested on the seventh day from all His works"; and again in this place: "They shall not enter My rest."

Since therefore it remains that some must enter it, and those to whom it was first preached did not enter because of disobedience, again He designates a certain day, saying in David, "Today," after such a long time, as it has been said:

"Today, if you will hear His voice,
Do not harden your hearts."

For if Joshua had given them rest, then He would not afterward have spoken of another day. There remains therefore a rest for the people of God. For he who has entered His rest has himself also ceased from his works as God did from His.

Let us therefore be diligent to enter that rest, lest anyone fall according to the same example of disobedience."

We can see in this portion some of the things taught earlier in the chapter. Truly man placed in paradise was the rest of God. But Adam, in sin, ruined the rest of God on earth. God, in a great sense, had to go back to work (John 5:17). The work He does is the revealing of, and the accomplishing of, all the counsels of God. His counsels are His work, or what He is working out, and center on the two titles we've been discussing in the book. Joshua did not give them rest, even though he led some into the land; it was all shadows still (Heb. 4:8). Joshua, in his name, and in bringing those of faith into the land, is a type of Jesus Christ, the Son of Man who is Lord of the sabbath (Matt. 12:8, the true rest of God).

Israel Crossing the Jordan in Type

What should be exciting for the believer is what comes next. It is the type which corresponds to the believer's blessed hope and earnest expectation. We are in the wilderness and passing through while on this earth. It is a walk of faith on a road out of this world, heading to God's rest. And how do we enter? Through the Jordan, and once again it is on dry land (Josh. 4:23-24). This passage on dry land is symbolic of the work of the Sovereign God, and that by His power and purpose, according to His counsels. Israel passing through the Jordan by God's sovereign power is type of the removal of the body of Christ from the earth, and entrance into the rest and glory of God.

As soon as Israel crosses Jordan and enters the land, Joshua is told by God to circumcise the men (Josh. 5:2-9). This also is symbolic. At the time the body of Christ is removed from the earth, the glorification of our bodies is by the removal of sin from the flesh. Mortal will put on immortality, corruptible will put on incorruption – all by the sovereign power of God (I Cor. 15:51-56). The circumcision of Israel is a type prefiguring sin being removed from the flesh of the believer – the glorification of our bodies in order to enter into the presence and glory of God.

The Old Man is crucified with Christ

Jesus tells us in John 12:25 that you should hate your life in this world – that is the life you have before your death with Him. It is life in the first Adam, life in the flesh (Rom. 8:7-8), and life connected to this world. When you take up a cross and follow Him, it is to be for the death of your life in Adam, that life that is of the world and of the earth. It is the old man in Adam that is being crucified on that cross. It is the old man in Adam that died with Christ (Rom. 6:6). This is how your relationship with Adam ends – by death (Rom. 6:2-3). You know, till death do you part (Rom. 7:1-3). You had to change positions. You had to get out of Adam and into Christ, as a new creation, as a new life, and as an entirely new position (Rom. 6:4-5, Gal. 6:15, 2 Cor. 17).

Now you have better understanding about Jesus as the Son of Man. When Jesus says the Son of Man is Lord of the sabbath (Matt. 12:8), it is mainly because through His death and faith in His shed blood, believers have entrance into the rest of God (Heb. 4:3). When Jesus says, "Foxes have holes, and birds of the air have nests, but the Son of Man has nowhere to lay His head," it is because the Son of Man does not live on this earth, but is walking on a road out of this world (Luke 9:58). When He says to take up your cross and follow Him, it is because He is carrying a cross as well, and you go to die with Him. Therefore He says, "Follow Me," and walk after Me.

Leaven is Spreading in the Christian World

Be careful concerning many of the teachings and messages you hear in the Christian world. Leaven is being spread in the kingdom of heaven, and by the end it saturates the three lumps (Matt. 13:33). Can believers prevent this from happening? No, this is what will be, and there is no stopping it. The parable is a warning of what will happen in the kingdom of heaven while the King is away. The parable shows the failure of the church world in responsibility, from beginning to end while on the earth. It is a warning for this present age, for those He gives the privilege of understanding (i.e. the believer sealed with the Spirit of truth, being led by the Spirit into all truth – Matt. 13:11).

What is the believer to do? You turn away from evil and have no part in it. You turn away from false teachings, from systems of doctrine that deny the heavenly calling, and distort the counsels of God. There are and will be many ministers who will not acknowledge that a heavenly calling even exists in Christ for the believer. They will have us connected with Israel and the earth. One evil that the scriptures speak of as existing in the church world in the end is ministers who run greedily for profit in the error of Balaam (Jude 11). If I turn the attention of your eyes to the heavens where Christ is at the right hand of God, it serves to establish in faith your sure and steadfast hope as a believer. The only profit in this is your sanctification and godliness for your walk down here. It does not appeal to the things of life here, your cares and wishes, how you may live more in comfort and ease. It is not the contemporary self-help and self-improvement gospel, or the many other devised teachings for the flesh. However, for some ministries there is profit in the teachings of the flesh, and plenty of itching ears wanting to be scratched (2 Tim. 4:3-4). The Spirit says these are spots in your feasts (Jude 12).

The Truth of God is not well received

I know I've mentioned this previously but it bears repeating. Truth from God, as a general principle, was fully displayed in the coming of Christ.

John 1:17

"For the law was given through Moses, but grace and truth came through Jesus Christ."

Often I find believers do not look at this verse closely enough. The Spirit is contrasting the first part of the sentence with the second part. The word 'but' establishes that a difference and contrast is being made. Law is contrasted with grace and truth. They are not the same in the counsels of God. No doubt God gave both -- the law through Moses and then, much later, sending Jesus Christ. But that does not make them the same, nor express God's purpose and intentions. The law is what man ought to be before God, simple human righteousness, and a testing of Israel in responsibility. Jesus' coming is the revelation of what God would be for man, the righteousness of God in grace and truth. In the sending of Jesus Christ, God's purpose was to bring out grace and truth, something the law could never do. Jesus also reveals God's love which is something the law could never do. This wasn't God's purpose for giving the law.

But the truth of God in Christ is not received by man. Israel as the test case, representing all mankind as a chosen and highly privileged people, rejected the truth of God when He came. They simply rejected God. Understanding Israel's position when they were tested by God (still a people in Adam and in the flesh) is important for our spiritual understanding of scripture. Let us look at this passage;

John 2:24-25

"But Jesus himself did not trust himself to them, because he knew all men, and that he had not need that any should testify of man, for himself knew what was in man."

This is to say that God knows exactly what man is. In man's state and position, there are none that seek after God, no, not one (Rom. 3:10-12). This is why Israel, as a nation, rejected their Messiah, rejecting the truth of God. In the privileged position God had placed them they still had no ability to receive the truth. Were the Gentiles in a better position? No, they were in a far worse position than this, having no privileges from God. So Israel, as the test case for mankind failed. It was proven by God that man in the flesh could not have a relationship with God. The embodiment of the truth was soundly rejected and nailed to the cross. The point is; when does the truth of God ever attract crowds or make men popular? The opposite is proven by the ministry of Jesus Christ. And I do not believe that the simple passage of time has altered this insight at all.

God knows exactly what man is. Man does not realize it and refuses to admit it. This is the religious leaven that is always corrupting the ways of man with God. It is perfectly shown in Israel and their law. What God gave them for death and condemnation, they made into a working of righteousness and a means of obtaining life. How was this done? "...they did not seek it by faith, but as it were, by the works of the law." (Rom. 9:31-32). Man thinks he has the ability to prove himself and exalt himself in his own strength and by his own works. And this, to one extent or the other, is what he is trying to do.

The leaven moves on from here, progressively becoming more subtle and harder to detect. God knows what man is, but man refuses to admit it. In the early church you have a Judaizing influence attempting to destroy the Christian faith. What is its character? It is the adding of the works of man in Judaism to the absolute sufficiency of Christ. And if this is permitted then Christ will profit you nothing (Gal. 5:1-2).

When we move on in the history of the church we see Romanism dominating the landscape. What is its character? It is the same leaven – the exalting of man by his works, the things that he does, in superstition and earthly religiousness, with idolatry thrown in. After the blessed Reformation, we have Protestantism. What end does this come to? It will be professing Christianity saying, "I am rich, have become wealthy, and have need of nothing." It is man exalting himself, in what he has, what he does, and who he thinks he is (Rev. 3:15-17). The same leaven, although in this more subtle form, will saturate the entire lump (Gal. 5:9). God fully knows what is in man.

The Worldly Measures of Success are used in the Church

There are many ministers and ministries in the Christian world. Many are talented speakers able to turn a phrase and get you excited. There are those who build large followings and large buildings, declaring the blessing of God on themselves. They are very successful, at least in the eyes of those attracted to them. Popularity and numbers and size become the measure of godly and scriptural success for many believers. Unfortunately, the world uses the exact same criteria for judging success. The world's standards become our standards for determining God's truth. Our spiritual judgment becomes blindness to the truth of God.

The only way the believer can turn from evil is to have the spiritual understanding to recognize it. This is a responsibility that you cannot put off on others, or make naïve assumptions about. When the believer sinks down to the earth and focuses on the cares of this life, the world comes in and we become very comfortable. Believers may be in this present world, but we are not of the world. However, the line of separation between these two phrases becomes increasingly blurred for many Christians. We begin to allow our ears to be tickled and consequently, our spiritual perception suffers. We start judging what we hear and are taught, as to right or wrong, good or bad, by how comfortable we are with it. If we are comfortable and like what we hear, we reason this must be the truth from God. Our understanding and spiritual perception becomes dull.

Comfort, ease, popularity, and numbers are never the standard of spiritual judgment. If I teach the believer that you presently should reign as a king in your life, it is for comfort and ease. It is very popular to the flesh of man (or I should more properly say, very popular to man in the flesh – Rom. 8:8-9). The numbers attracted will soon bear this out. But if I teach that the believer is to suffer with Christ, there is no comfort and ease in this, nor popularity. And the numbers will soon bear this out as well.

Sin is in the Flesh of Man

In the cross of Christ, no doubt, sin in the flesh was condemned by God (Rom. 8:3). He judged it, and Jesus died as a consequence (Rom. 6:23). Now the believer has died with Christ and has been freed from sin (Rom. 6:1-7), certainly in the sense of no longer a slave of sin (John 8:34). We have this in title, but not the fullness of it yet, for sin still dwells in the flesh.

At the time Jesus comes to take us to the Father's house (John 14:1-3), we will be conformed into the image of Christ (Rom. 8:29). Sin in the flesh will be removed from the believer (I Cor. 15:54-57), and this by resurrection or change (I Cor. 15:51-53). Jesus tells us this event should be scriptural comfort for the believer, as we wait for it. However, until then, we walk on this earth, and do so by faith. One of the exercises of our faith is to 'reckon yourselves to be dead indeed to sin' (Rom. 6:11). Sin in the flesh that God condemned in Christ on the cross (Rom. 8:3) is the old man crucified with Christ (Rom. 6:6). By faith, we reckon the old man as dead, putting aside sin in the flesh, even though it is still there. A similar exercise of faith for the believer is to reckon ourselves to be dead to the world (Col. 2:20). As much as we possibly can, we walk in the example of Christ.

The Believer's Heavenly Calling – a Citizenship, Inheritance, and Habitation

In Christ, we are holy brethren, partakers of the heavenly calling. Instead of a kingdom with an earthly Messiah and an earthly calling, believers have the eternal glory of the Son of Man in heaven. In

God's counsels we are to be conformed to His Son's very image, to be like Him and with Him. This is the heavenly calling. We should always hold to this scriptural understanding and have faith and hopes accordingly. And our walk on this earth should reflect our calling in Christ. While we walk down here our eyes should be fixed on Christ in the heavens. Our life is there, our citizenship, inheritance, and habitation.

Hebrews 11:13-16

"These all died in faith, not having received the promises, but having seen them afar off were assured of them, embraced them and confessed that they were strangers and pilgrims on the earth. For those who say such things declare plainly that they seek a homeland. And truly if they had called to mind that country from which they had come out, they would have had opportunity to return. But now they desire a better, that is, a heavenly country. Therefore God is not ashamed to be called their God, for He has prepared a city for them."

Chapter 14:

Israel in the Counsels of God

Ephesians 1:9-10

"…having made known to us the mystery of His will, according to His good pleasure which He purposed in Himself, that in the dispensation of the fullness of the times He might gather together in one all things in Christ, both which are in heaven and which are on earth—in Him."

The above passage describes what I refer to as the counsels of God. This contains all the work of God birthed in His determined will for the purpose of His own glory. The divine glory of God is the end and culmination of all His counsels. Jesus Christ holds the central place in these counsels and by Him God will be glorified and exalted. In the dispensation of the fullness of times God will gather together all things in Christ (Eph. 1:10). This gathering into one has a two-fold fulfillment – all things in heaven, and distinct from this, all things on earth.

The Foundation of All of God's Counsels

The gathering is in Christ. However, it soon becomes clear that a foundation had to be laid as a basis for all the work that God would do – all the gathering that He would accomplish. This foundational work would be the means by which God could remain true to His own holy and righteous nature, and still bring about the reconciliation of a creation defiled by sin. This foundation is the death of Jesus Christ, the Son of Man. When this work was finished, it provided the basis for the unfolding of all God's counsels, not only towards man, but towards all of creation.

The understanding of this foundational work as related to the counsels of God is brought out in a remarkable way in the first chapter of the book of Colossians.

Colossians 1:14-22

14 "...in whom we have redemption through His blood, the forgiveness of sins.

15 He is the image of the invisible God, the firstborn over all creation. 16 For by Him all things were created that are in heaven and that are on earth, visible and invisible, whether thrones or dominions or principalities or powers. All things were created through Him and for Him. 17 And He is before all things, and in Him all things consist. 18 And He is the head of the body, the church, who is the beginning, the firstborn from the dead, that in all things He may have the preeminence.

19 For it pleased the Father that in Him all the fullness should dwell, 20 and by Him to reconcile all things to Himself, by Him, whether things on earth or things in heaven, having made peace through the blood of His cross.

21 And you, who once were alienated and enemies in your mind by wicked works, yet now He has reconciled 22 in the body of His flesh through death, to present you holy, and blameless, and above reproach in His sight."

The believer has redemption as a result of His death – through His blood (v. 14). Christ is the firstborn from the dead (v. 18), the beginning of all those that will be resurrected into glory. Therefore He is the Head of the Body for the church. Because He is also before all things, and in Him all things consist, then it stands to reason that in all things He has the preeminence. 'All things' is a reference to all of creation. This goes well beyond just a body of believers redeemed, although this is a most blessed truth. To be clear, it is all things in heaven and on earth, all things visible and invisible, thrones, dominions, principalities, and powers – all things He had created (v. 20). All this is reconciled by His death.

The Preeminence of Christ is as the Son of Man

Christ's preeminence over all creation can be viewed through a two-fold understanding. All things were created through Him and for Him (v. 16); therefore He is before all things as the Creator (v. 17). He made everything and has a right to it. However, as we have pointed out previously, He only takes possession of creation after reconciling it through His death (v. 20). He created it as God, but reconciles it back to God as a Man. This is the important understanding to gain here. All things of creation, as well as the body of Christ, have been reconciled to God by the death of the Son of Man.

When the counsels of God gather all things in heaven and on earth into Christ, it is after the Son of Man has been raised from the dead and glorified by God (John 13:31-32). This is easy to see if we go farther in this chapter in Ephesians to a passage that begins with the Son of Man in the grave.

Ephesians 1:19-23

"…and what is the exceeding greatness of His power toward us who believe, according to the working of His mighty power which He worked in Christ when He raised Him from the dead and seated Him at His right hand in the heavenly places, far above all principality and power and might and dominion, and every name that is named, not only in this age but also in that which is to come.

And He put all things under His feet, and gave Him to be head over all things to the church, which is His body, the fullness of Him who fills all in all."

Earlier in this book I showed how the title of the Son of Man is inseparably linked to the death of Jesus Christ. If it is the Son of Man in the grave, then it is the Son of Man who is raised up out of the grave (Luke 24:7). And if so, then it is the Son of Man seated at the right hand of God (Mark 14:62). He is the one who reconciled to God all things created. It is the Son of Man's body that is presently being gathered as the church. The counsels of God unfold in, and are centered upon, Jesus Christ, the Son of Man – all things gathered in heaven and on the earth.

Matthew 28:18

"And Jesus came and spoke to them, saying, "All authority has been given to Me in heaven and on earth."

After the resurrection, Jesus appeared to the eleven disciples in Galilee and said this to them. It connects the counsels of God -- the gathering of all things in heaven and on earth – to the foundational work of the resurrected Son of Man. All authority in heaven and earth is given to the Son of Man. This is the basis for God's gathering of all things into Christ. But it is and always will be Christ as the Son of Man.

The Heavenly Glory of Christ

In this book we have concentrated on the heavenly glory of Christ. It is our proper place and position in this glorified Man that the believer must be taught by the Spirit of God. We are in Christ. We are His body. We will be associated with Him in all He inherits and possesses. All the glory He now enters into beyond the cross, He shares with us, as His brethren. We are the heavenly calling in Jesus Christ.

I speak of these things as our proper place and position, but these must be statements totally devoid of human boasting. There simply cannot be any Arminian thought or philosophy behind this accomplishment. It is the Father who places the believer into this "proper position' in Christ. We must see that it is the work of the sovereign God. It was His choice, purpose and counsels alone, accomplished by His own sovereign will and good pleasure (Eph. 1:3-12). It was not by my will or my decision. It was not by the will of the flesh or the will of man to we are born of God (John 1:13).

When you think of the counsels of God, you realize He has only one plan and that He must be sovereign in that plan if the details of it are to be accomplished. It cannot be any other way. God cannot become dependent on the will of the creature. His counsels could not and would not be accomplished that way. He must maintain control down to the minutest detail or the whole plan would unravel.

As a believer, I will share Christ's glory. Also I am a co-heir with Him in all He inherits. I will be made like Him, conformed into His image by God (Rom. 8:29). I have been made a member of His body and of His Bride. Throughout the ages to come the Father will show an exceeding richness of grace to me because He placed me in Christ (Eph. 2:7). I am God's workmanship, created in Christ Jesus.

I did not make this stuff up. If I did it would be all pride and arrogance. But it is all found in God's word, where He reveals His counsels to the believer. It is what God has declared and His word will not return to Him void, because He is sovereign. It will accomplish everything He has sent it to do. It is a false humility for the believer to deny these truths. I embrace them as what my loving Father has provided for me, and I declare that God's sovereignty is shown by them. I fully realize it is all God's work – all of it. And this is how we should define the sovereignty of God, and how He has blessed the believer in Christ.

The Earthly Glory of Christ

Now I would like to share, with the Holy Spirit's help, the understanding of the earthly things in the counsels of God (John 3:12). All of biblical prophecy is about the earth. In the fullness of times, all things on earth will be gathered into Christ (Eph. 1:10). Again, this is for the glory of God. The simple understanding is that all prophecy can only be understood as it relates to Jesus Christ and the earthly things. All the objects and events found in prophecy can only be understood and properly interpreted in their relationship with and to Christ. The spirit of prophecy is the testimony of Jesus Christ (Rev. 19:10).

The Last Dispensation: The Millennium on Earth

The dispensation of the fullness of times in the above verse is the millennium (Rev. 20:6-7). During that time period, all things on earth will come under the dominion and reign of the Son of Man (Dan. 7:13-14). We can go on and make some general statements of interest concerning this dispensation. It is a time when Satan is bound and out of the way, until the end of the period when He will be set loose for a season to tempt and deceive (Rev. 20:7-9). The character of the millennium while Satan is bound is a reign of righteousness and peace. This is the character of the exercise of the Melchizedek order of priesthood in Christ – a royal and kingly priesthood.

Hebrews 7:1-3

"For this Melchizedek, king of Salem, priest of the Most High God, who met Abraham returning from the slaughter of the kings and blessed him, to whom also Abraham gave a tenth part of all, first being translated "king of righteousness," and then also king of Salem, meaning "king of peace," without father, without mother, without genealogy, having neither beginning of days nor end of life, but made like the Son of God, remains a priest continually."

The whole story of Melchizedek meeting Abraham is a type prefiguring the millennial glory of Christ. As King of kings and Lord of lords, the Son of Man will reign at this time as the King of righteousness and peace (Matt. 25:31). Melchizedek blessed Abraham after the defeat of all his enemies. Again this prefigures the future Jewish remnant blessed and prospering in the land after the defeat of their enemies. God's name as Most High always points to the millennial glory, as it does here. In Deut. 32:8-9 the Most High makes Israel the center of the earth for the dividing of all nations. God's direct government of the earth will once again go forth out of Jerusalem. In Daniel 7, the Most High is related to the earthly kingdom and dominion of the Son of Man. During the millennium the city of God's government of the earth is called, 'The Lord Our Righteousness.' (Jer. 33:16).

The character of the millennium is a King reigning over Israel (Messiah) and over the whole of creation (Son of Man). He is reigning by the exercise of judgments and power. It is a reign of peace and righteousness.

Jeremiah 33:14-17

"'Behold, the days are coming,' says the Lord, 'that I will perform that good thing which I have promised to the house of Israel and to the house of Judah:

'In those days and at that time
I will cause to grow up to David
A Branch of righteousness;
He shall execute judgment and righteousness in the earth.
In those days Judah will be saved,
And Jerusalem will dwell safely.
And this is the name by which she will be called:

THE LORD OUR RIGHTEOUSNESS.'

"For thus says the Lord: 'David shall never lack a man to sit on the throne of the house of Israel.'"

This prophecy is Messianic and shows that during the millennial reign of Messiah the two kingdoms of Israel and Judah will be reunited as one people. Worth noting is that the King uses His power to execute judgments in righteousness to bring peace. The inhabitants of the world will learn righteousness only when God's judgments are in the earth (Is. 26:9-10, 5:15-16).

The fullness of times of the millennium is the last counting of time before the eternal state of the new heavens and new earth. The end of the millennium, being the filling-up of time, is also the last fulfilling of prophecy. It is the end of this present earth. The millennium as a dispensation is the last one. The thought of a dispensation is not only the marking of a general period of time, but is related to the present earth. A dispensation is certainly more than this, but I am only establishing a connection – time being counted, the present earth, prophecy, and dispensations are all linked together. What lies beyond in the new heavens and new earth is a whole new world.

The Millennium: Natural bodies, Nationalities, and Genders

Where the millennium is a reign of righteousness by judgments and power, the eternal state will be where righteousness dwells (II Pet. 3:13). The big difference between the millennium and the eternal state is that the sin of Adam still remains in the flesh of all the inhabitants of the earth during the millennium. The saved Jewish remnant, and the remaining Gentile nations not judged as goats (Matt. 25:31-32), enter the millennium with natural bodies, male and female, in order to be fruitful and multiply.

Galatians 3:26-28

"For you are all sons of God through faith in Christ Jesus. For as many of you as were baptized into Christ have put on Christ. There is neither Jew nor Greek, there is neither slave nor free, there is neither male nor female; for you are all one in Christ Jesus."

The believers position in Christ in not only where there are no nationalities, but also where there is no male or female. Being in glory with Christ, the body of Christ will not be growing and increasing in numbers. In the heavens there is only one marriage. It is the body of Christ with the Lamb (Rev. 19:7-9). Nationalities are for the earth, as are genders. In Christ all believers are sons with the Father, sons of God; not male and female, but as it declares, 'you are all sons.' This is part of the believer's new position, out of the first Adam and into the second Adam. This new creation is the putting on Christ through faith.

Hebrews 2:10-11

"For it was fitting for Him, for whom are all things and by whom are all things, in bringing many sons to glory, to make the captain of their salvation perfect through sufferings. For both He who sanctifies and those who are being sanctified are all of one, for which reason He is not ashamed to call them brethren,"

He who sanctifies is Jesus Christ. Those that are sanctified are one, and as one, with Him who sanctifies (I Cor. 6:17). As the heavenly calling, when the body of Christ is taken from this earth, it will be in this character. However the earthly calling is never like this – they are always Israel in nationality and male and female. Those on the earth that survive the tribulation, and are not judged and condemned, enter the millennium as the dwellers on the earth. They will live and inhabit the earth, as belonging to it and being of it. Israel at that time acknowledged of God in the Jewish remnant, will receive the Promised Land as their inheritance (Ez. 28:24-26, Ez. 47:13-14).

Christ, not of this World

This is quite a distinction between Israel and the body of Christ. Believers are asked to follow Christ (John 1:43). Believers, on the earth and in this world, are described as having a walk (Col. 1:10). Our walk is a sojourn (Heb. 11:8-10, 13-16). When Jesus was raised from the dead in His glorified body, He could not stay here in this world.

John 17:11-16

"Now I am no longer in the world, but these are in the world, and I come to You. Holy Father, keep through Your name those whom You have given Me, that they may be one as We are. While I was with them in the world, I kept them in Your name. Those whom You gave Me I have kept; and none of them is lost except the son of perdition, that the Scripture might be fulfilled. But now I come to You, and these things I speak in the world, that they may have My joy fulfilled in themselves. I have given them Your word; and the world has hated them because they are not of the world, just as I am not of the world. I do not pray that You should take them out of the world, but that You should keep them from the evil one. They are not of the world, just as I am not of the world."

We get the sense that this world would no longer be fit for the resurrected Man to stay in, yet the disciples and believers would be left here. He is no longer in the world, but goes to the Father. These disciples are in the world and He does not ask the Father to take them out of the world. "They are not of the world, just as I am not of the world," – in this the believer is the same with Him. The difference is that Jesus would be in a raised and glorified body, and we would not, at least not yet. As the glorified Man, this sinful world would be nothing but defilement for Him if He were to stay.

The Glorified Body – not of this present World

We do not yet have the end of our salvation – the glorification of our bodies. The counsels of God have always been such that the many sons of the Father would be conformed into the image of His Son (Rom. 8:11, 17, and 29). When this occurs, we will no longer be fit for this world either, and will be taken out of it. If you think about it, all the bodies of every Christian there ever was are still on this earth. This thought alone is reason enough for the future event I speak of – the blessed hope of the church (Rom. 8:23-25). You are not a complete man, as created by God in His image, without your body. When a believer dies, spirit and soul go to be with the Lord (II Cor. 5:8, Phil. 1:23). But without the body we are naked. Our proper hope is not to be unclothed, but further clothed, that our mortal bodies would be swallowed up by life (II Cor. 5: 1-6).

Our bodies of flesh remain in the first man – the sin he gave us, resides in the flesh. Everything else about the believer is of the new creation in Christ – in the second Man. Our mortal bodies are our only remaining connection to Adam and this world. When sin is removed, our bodies will be glorified, and we will follow Christ out of this present evil world. Until then we remain here, and He asks the Father to keep us from the evil in it (John 17:15). We also have a High Priest. As we are on our walk in this evil world, our feet become dirty – we become defiled by the evil around us. Jesus is constantly washing the believer's feet and removing any defilement accumulated from our walk (John 13:7). When we are in glory, conformed into His very image, He will no longer have need to wash our feet. When we see Him we will be like Him (I John 3:2).

Believers chosen out of this World

Christ is not of this world, and the believer in Christ is not of this world (John 8:23, 15:19, 17:14, 16). We are in the world and on the earth presently, but viewed as being in Christ, we have no connections to it. All of this however is not the position of Israel, or any unbeliever. They are part of this world and have no connection to Christ. They are dwellers of the earth. The whole world is in unbelief. The entire world is condemned by God (John 12:31). Presently, while the mystery of Christ is at the forefront of the counsels of God, and prophecy is set aside, this is all that is taking place:

John 15:19

"If you were of the world, the world would love its own. Yet because you are not of the world, but I chose you out of the world, therefore the world hates you."

The Holy Spirit gathers Christ's body as those chosen by Him – chosen out of this world. But here He was speaking of disciples, of believers. When He spoke about His leaving this world to the nation of Israel, it wasn't at all the same message. Where He went they were not permitted to come. He was going away and they would continue to look for a Messiah, but He tells them they would not be able to find one and they would die in their sin (John 8:21, 7:33-34). The world was judged and condemned by God, but now He would choose some out of it.

Israel's New Covenant in the Millennium: The Sovereign Work of God

According to the prophecies concerning the end, Israel will be saved as a remnant (Rev. 7: 1-8, 11:26-28). They are the earthly calling and the earthly glory of Christ (Is. 60:1, 3), as well as the center of the government of God over the world (Is. 9:6-7, Ps. 2:8-9). What is remarkable is how this is accomplished – all by sovereign choice and power from God. They are chosen, they are marked, and they are preserved by the power of God in the midst of their enemies. When Jesus comes to them as their Messiah, they will look on Him whom they have pierced (Zech. 12:10). Their faith is a very earthly type of faith – a Thomas type of faith – they do not believe until they actually see (John 20:25). It is a walk by sight, and is characteristic of Judaism. But this is understandable, especially if we look at the new covenant that God makes with them in that day (the beginning of the millennium);

Jeremiah 31:31-34

"Behold, the days are coming, says the Lord, when I will make a new covenant with the house of Israel and with the house of Judah— not according to the covenant that I made with their fathers in the day that I took them by the hand to lead them out of the land of Egypt, My covenant which they broke, though I was a husband to them, says the Lord. But this is the covenant that I will make with the house of Israel after those days, says the Lord: I will put My law in their minds, and write it on their hearts; and I will be their God, and they shall be My people. No more shall every man teach his neighbor, and every man his brother, saying, 'Know the Lord,' for they all shall know Me, from the least of them to the greatest of them, says the Lord. For I will forgive their iniquity, and their sin I will remember no more."

This new covenant is also by the sovereign working of God. He writes His law on their hearts and puts it in their minds. This is not a learning process for He declares that no more shall they be taught. It is simply by sovereign power that they walk perfectly in His law. All of Israel will know the Lord and perfectly obey Him. God does this; it is not the work of man. They are still a people in the flesh and in Adam, and it is still the Law of Moses – God's religion of the earth and of the world. But it is accomplished by the sovereign choice and power of God. The finger of God writes His law on their hearts, the very law that was set aside by God when Jerusalem was destroyed. Now it is a new covenant with Israel, and it will be obeyed and fulfilled.

Matthew 5:18
"For assuredly, I say to you, till heaven and earth pass away, one jot or one tittle will by no means pass from the law till all is fulfilled."

The law will not pass away until all is fulfilled. It is a law given by God to Israel, and at best, represents the standard of human righteousness before God. By the sovereign power of God, Israel will perfectly obey the law of God, and fulfill these very words of Christ. They will do it during the millennium, before God brings about the new heavens and the new earth. The law will be fulfilled by Israel, every jot and tittle.

This new covenant for Israel is not the new covenant the believer has in Christ. We are in Him, and He in us (John 14:20, 17:26). We are His body, and His bride. We ate His flesh and drank His blood (John 6:53). In Christ we are made sons of God, and seated with Him and in Him in the heavens. We are never tied to the earth. Israel however, is always of the earth and servants in the house of God (John 8:35-36). This covenant is as to servants in the household, not to sons.

Israel's Two Covenants – One Covenant Given Twice

These two covenants are the only two covenants Israel will ever have. It is the law both times. Truly by the sovereign power of God, before He brings about the new heavens and the new earth, the law is perfectly fulfilled by those that He gave it to originally. The law was given to Israel to be done by Israel. At its first giving, it was a testing of man in responsibility. It was to see if man in Adam -- man in the flesh, and man in his own power -- could produce righteousness as a fruit before God. But this was not possible. Israel, as the test case for all mankind failed in responsibility.

What the law was and why it was given the first time at Mt. Sinai is important to understand. What it was -- it was a testing of man in responsibility. Why it was given – it was given for death and condemnation. As a new covenant made with Israel -- written on their hearts at the beginning of the millennium, and performed by the sovereign power of God in them (Ez. 36:24-28) – the what, and why is all for the glory of God. It is the earthly glory of Christ. God will be glorified in the earth by the exalting of Israel above all the nations.

Israel perfectly obeys the Law – Israel is Exalted, and Jehovah's Name Hallowed

Deuteronomy 28:1

"Now it shall come to pass, if you diligently obey the voice of the Lord your God, to observe carefully all His commandments which I command you

today, that the Lord your God will set you high above all nations of the earth."

When God originally gave the law to Israel, this was His promise to them. If the nation would perfectly obey the law of God, then He would make them the greatest nation on the face of the earth. In the end, when they are gathered back to the land, these very words will be fulfilled. Of course, God's word never returns back to Him void.

Isaiah 2:2

"Now it shall come to pass in the latter days
That the mountain of the Lord's house
Shall be established on the top of the mountains,
And shall be exalted above the hills;
And all nations shall flow to it."

Israel is the mountain of the Lord's house on the earth. The other mountains and hills are the remaining Gentile nations. In the millennium, as the earthly glory of Christ, Israel will be exalted above all, and the Gentile nations will be gathered to them for blessing. But we must remember this is all by God's sovereign plan and power, not by Israel doing anything to deserve it. Jehovah's name will be hallowed in Israel as well, by what He works in them and through them. God will glorify His name by all this, and His glory will fill the earth.

Leviticus 22:31-33

"Therefore you shall keep My commandments, and perform them: I am the Lord. You shall not profane My holy name, but I will be hallowed among the children of Israel. I am the Lord who sanctifies you, who brought you out of the land of Egypt, to be your God: I am the Lord."

The law given to Israel in Leviticus would not be done. It was not possible for man, already a sinner, to keep His commandments and obey them. The keeping and performing of the law by Israel would have meant their separation (sanctification) in the world and on the earth. If the law was perfectly done by Israel, God's holy name would have been hallowed in the earth. This is an example of how God is glorified by man. However, allow me to caution you to think correctly about this very point – it was impossible for Israel to do. As long as the basis of the performance of the law remained in the responsibility of man in Adam, there would be nothing but failure. Now contrast the above passage with a prophecy concerning Israel's history leading to their restoration in the land.

Ezekiel 36:16-38

16 "Moreover the word of the Lord came to me, saying: 17 "Son of man, when the house of Israel dwelt in their own land, they defiled it by their own ways and deeds; to Me their way was like the uncleanness of a woman in her customary impurity. 18 Therefore I poured out My fury on them for the blood they had shed on the land, and for their idols with which they had defiled it. 19 So I scattered them among the nations, and they were dispersed throughout the countries; I judged them according to their ways and their deeds. 20 When they came to the nations, wherever they went, they profaned My holy name—when they said of them, 'These are the people of the Lord, and yet they have gone out of His land.' 21 But I had concern for My holy name, which the house of Israel had profaned among the nations wherever they went."

22 "Therefore say to the house of Israel, 'Thus says the Lord God: "I do not do this for your sake, O house of Israel, but for My holy name's sake, which you have profaned among the nations wherever you went. 23 And I will sanctify My great name, which has been profaned among the nations, which you have profaned in their midst; and the nations shall know that I am the Lord," says the Lord God, "when I am hallowed in you before their eyes. 24 For I will take you from among the nations, gather you out of all countries, and bring you into your own land. 25 Then I will sprinkle clean water on you, and you shall be clean; I will cleanse you from all your filthiness and from all your idols. 26 I will give you a new heart and put a new spirit within you; I will take the heart of stone out of your flesh and give you a heart of flesh. 27 I will put My Spirit within you and cause you to walk in My statutes, and you will keep My judgments and do them. 28 Then you shall dwell in the land that I gave to your fathers; you shall be My people, and I will be your God. 29 I will deliver you from all your uncleanness. I will call for the grain and multiply it, and bring no famine upon you. 30 And I will multiply the fruit of your trees and the increase of your fields, so that you need never again bear the reproach of famine among the nations.

31 Then you will remember your evil ways and your deeds that were not good; and you will loathe yourselves in your own sight, for your iniquities and your abominations. 32 Not for your sake do I do this," says the Lord God, "let it be known to you. Be ashamed and confounded for your own ways, O house of Israel!"

33 "'Thus says the Lord God: "On the day that I cleanse you from all your iniquities, I will also enable you to dwell in the cities, and the ruins shall be rebuilt. 34 The desolate land shall be tilled instead of lying desolate in the sight of all who pass by. 35 So they will say, 'This land that was desolate has become like the garden of Eden; and the wasted, desolate, and ruined cities are now fortified and inhabited.' 36 Then the nations which are left all around you shall know that I, the Lord, have rebuilt the ruined places and planted what was desolate. I, the Lord, have spoken it, and I will do it."

37 "'Thus says the Lord God: "I will also let the house of Israel inquire of Me to do this for them: I will increase their men like a flock. 38 Like a flock offered as holy sacrifices, like the flock at Jerusalem on its feast days, so shall the ruined cities be filled with flocks of men. Then they shall know that I am the Lord."'

This passage shows Israel's failure in their history when they were tested in responsibility. The result was defilement of the land by their ways and deeds (v. 17). God scatters them (v.19), and His name is profaned in the earth among the Gentiles, because of this (v. 20-21). Israel is among the nations because God judged their failures in responsibility. They are among the Gentiles as not His people and not as a nation set apart for His glory.

In time, God will glorify His name on the earth. We see how God will do this. He will not be dependent on man, but He will sovereignly do a work. Jehovah's name is hallowed in all the earth because of what He works on His own. He does not do it for their sake, but for His own glory (v. 22-23). He alone is responsible for hallowing His own name. When the Gentiles see what God works in Israel -- a gathered and separated nation in their own land, and perfectly obeying His law (v.26-27) – then Jehovah is glorified in all the earth because Israel is exalted above all the nations. This is easily seen in the remainder of the passage.

Human Righteousness vs. the Righteousness of God

There is one more point I want to make concerning Israel's covenant -- the Law of Moses. If you keep in mind all that has been said previously in this book concerning the law and Judaism, this should be easier to see. The Law of God, given to Israel, only represents human righteousness. The performance of the law – whether you are doing it, or someone is doing it for you in your place – only results in a human type of righteousness. It is not the righteousness of God.

This can be seen on two different fronts. First, the law was made and given by God, while the righteousness of God is an attribute depicting the nature of God. God is holy and righteous. This is who God is, what He is, in his nature. God never makes a law, principle, or ordinance, that He is subject to or dependent on. This is impossible. Whenever He works and acts, He does so as being true to His own nature, true to Himself. God is never acting or working in obedience to some exterior law, even a law of His own making. How could this be, and God remain God? How could anything be above God, if He is transcendent in His nature? How could God make anything that He then becomes subject to?

Therefore the righteousness of God can never be viewed as obeying an exterior law. When we think about the righteousness of God, I would think we would be considering the nature of God Himself. If I could perfectly obey the Law of Moses, I would have produced a righteousness of the law, a righteousness of my own, and not that of God (Phil. 3:9-10). It would be a human righteousness associated with the earth and Judaism. When Israel perfectly obeys the law in the millennium, this is what it will be – the measure of what a man in Adam should be before a holy and righteous God.

Now let me clearly state what I've implied from the last three paragraphs. Jesus did not come to this earth to do the law for you and me under some thought of substitution. God never had this thought, and Jesus never had this intention. Jesus didn't fulfill the law, neither did He try to. When He is speaking of the law being fulfilled down to every jot and tittle, He is not speaking of Himself doing it. When you read the gospels of the walk of Christ on this earth, do you honestly get the impression that He was going out of His way to fulfill the Law of Moses? Quite frankly, it appears that many times He was going out of His way to make waves with the leaders of Israel concerning their law (John 15:24-25, 5:18).

As we explained above, the doing of the law does not represent the righteousness of God, even if it were Jesus as the one doing it. There could only be a human righteousness found in the law.

Galatians 3:21

"Is the law then against the promises of God? Certainly not! For if there had been a law given which could have given life, truly righteousness would have been by the law."

There was never a law given which could give life. Was there ever a possibility that the righteousness of God could come by the law – even someone doing it for us by substitution? Then the scriptures would say that Jesus did the law for us, and so, truly the righteousness of God came to us by the law being done. But there is a big 'if' in the above passage – if there had been a law given which could – but there never was a law given which could.

2 Corinthians 5:21

"For He made Him who knew no sin to be sin for us, that we might become the righteousness of God in Him."

This is the only way that the righteousness of God comes to the believer. It is by God making Christ to be sin for us. The believer becoming the righteousness of God is solely dependent on this truth – Christ made to be sin, and God judged and condemned Him on our behalf.

The Spotless Sacrifice – The Second Adam

Certainly, He knew no sin of His own, but this is so He could be the spotless sacrifice offered up. When the Passover was instituted the sacrifice was a lamb without blemish of the first year (Ex. 12:5). The choice of the lambs as fit for the sacrifice was based upon their birth

– without blemish. It was not based upon how the lambs lived their first year of life. Jesus Christ was born of a virgin, conceived by the Holy Spirit, the power of the Highest overshadowing Mary. What was born to her was the Holy One, the Son of God. This was not man being born in the first Adam. This is what made Jesus a fit sacrifice.

Jesus never walked on this earth as a man born in Adam. This understanding makes all the difference in the doctrines of redemption the church was to teach through the centuries. He came to Israel as the Son of God in human flesh, and His assignment as the Son was to obediently reveal the Father. This is how He walked in the flesh. When He walked on the water in the midst of the storm to the disciples in the boat half way across the sea, it was as the Son of God. And the same was true in raising Lazarus from the dead (John 11:4). All the works He did and all the words He spoke were as the Son obedient to the Father, who was always with Him and in Him (John 15:21-24, 14:6-11). Only God could reveal God, and the Son revealed the Father as He walked on this earth.

Could the Son of God commit sin and be guilty of sin? Not any more than the Father or the Holy Spirit could commit sin. It was impossible. Did the Son have His own will apart from the Father? Absolutely He did. However, the Son sets aside His own will, to be obedient to do the will of the Father alone, and therefore reveal the Father only. This is a similar understanding of what we are to have concerning the Holy Spirit as the Spirit of truth.

John 16:12-15

"I still have many things to say to you, but you cannot bear them now. However, when He, the Spirit of truth, has come, He will guide you into all truth; for He will not speak on His own authority, but whatever He hears He will speak; and He will tell you things to come. He will glorify Me, for He will take of what is Mine and declare it to you. All things that the Father has are Mine. Therefore I said that He will take of Mine and declare it to you."

The Holy Spirit is God. The believer's body is the temple of God because the Spirit of God dwells in us. But the Holy Spirit does not speak on His own authority – He does not do His own will. He takes of what is Christ's, and declares it to us. The point is we tend to misunderstand the Son being sent, taking on humanity, and walking in the midst of Israel. We also misunderstand the title of Christ as the Son of Man, and what that distinctly points to – it is not simply His humanity, but His death. His walk was always with the Father (John 16:32) as the Son of God. His death was as forsaken by the Father, or rather forsaken by God (Matt. 27:46). There is a big difference in how you should view the obedience He shows in each.

The Law of Moses is always associated with man in Adam

The Law of Moses was given to Israel. They represented mankind in the first Adam. The law always remains the testing of responsibility of man in the first Adam. It stays there. Christ was not born in the first Adam. He was the second Adam, the last Adam. He did not come to do the law for us. Even if in your thinking He did, His performance would only represent human righteousness. What would be the reason for Jesus to come and accomplish human righteousness? Man needed God's righteousness in order to enter the presence of God. The doing of the law does not touch the righteousness of God.

This is another example of man's thoughts opposed to God's thoughts. Israel thought the law made them righteous and gave them life, but it was the opposite. So also, man thinks Jesus came to do the law for us and to give us the righteousness of God. But God's righteousness is that He made Christ to be sin and Christ carried sins, and God judged and condemned Him on the cross – quite an opposite thought from Christ perfectly performing the law.

The Law of Moses was only ever given to Israel. As a covenant it is specifically identified with Israel only. They are to do it. In the millennium they will fulfill the law completely as a nation and a people still in the first Adam. Again, this will be done by the sovereign power of God and before the heavens and the earth pass away. But the conclusion is this – the Law of Moses is for man in Adam.

As a believer and a son of God, are you in Adam? No, you are in Christ, the second Adam, the Son of Man. The believer is the new creation of God (II Cor. 5:17). The believer is the work of the sovereign God – created in Christ Jesus (Eph. 2:10). This is a new position. This is beyond the death of the man in.Adam, concerning the believer. Our old man was crucified with Christ (Rom. 6:6). For the believer, the spiritual truth and understanding is that you, in Adam, died on the cross. This was substitution, for He suffered death for us – but it has to be our death. This is how the believer comes out of the first Adam and is placed in a new position in Christ. It is a new creation, because there was a death first, and we stopped existing in Adam. It is no longer I who live, but Christ lives in me (Gal. 2:20). It is a Christ in resurrected life. It is the Son of Man raised from the dead that we find ourselves in as a new creation.

The Contemporary Teaching on Faith

An example that may give us a similar understanding is what is sometimes taught as doctrine by some of the so called 'faith teachers.' At times faith is depicted as a law or force or power that even God must obey. However, as previously stated, there will never be a law that God is subject to. Also, faith is not a power or force that God uses to do anything. God has all power and does as He pleases with His power, because He is sovereign. If God wants to bring something to pass, He speaks, and it is so immediately. If His timing is involved in His plans, He speaks, and it comes to pass when He wants it to, according to His infinite wisdom and knowledge. It is never a matter of God exercising faith. He does not work in obedience to a principle of faith.

Often these same teachers point to the unbelieving world as exercising the creative power of faith, with the results of being blessed and prospering. It is explained as either a separate power of faith operating in the universe or as God having to obey His own laws of faith on their behalf, even when He may be hesitant to bless evil. This is simply contemporary human philosophy entering the Christian world. It is another example of how we mistakenly look at the circumstances of life around us and create doctrines to explain what we see. If we are looking for different circumstances, they are coming in the millennium, when God's direct government of the earth is established. Then evil is judged and directly punished during a reign of righteousness. The world will be changed by God at that time. However, these are not the principles of this present age.

Faith is a human thing. Truly in humans, faith requires an object that should be far beyond and above us – this object is God. That is why Jesus taught us to have faith in God (Mark 11: 22, John 12:44), and in Him, as the Son of God (John 6:40, 3:15-16, 11:26, and 14:1). It is the same lesson we learn from Abraham (Rom. 4:17, 21), and when we are encouraged in faith by the examples in Hebrews 11, it is the same – faith in God.

Hebrews 11:6

"But without faith it is impossible to please Him, for he who comes to God must believe that He is, and that He is a rewarder of those who diligently seek Him."

Faith is a human thing, and for the believer, it must always have its proper object – God. It is that He exists, and that He will reward. Now if it is true that Biblical faith must have an object beyond the one having faith, then how is God to exercise faith? Who is God to have faith in? What is beyond God? That would also be impossible.

Faith is also of the earth, for it is associated with the believer's walk down here – a walk of faith (II Cor. 5:7). Why the earth? It is while still here that we do not see any of the things hoped for (II Cor. 4:16 – 5:9). It is here on the earth for the believer that faith is the evidence of things not seen (Heb. 11:1). And let us stop twisting the meaning of these passages – as long as the believer remains on the earth we do not have the things hoped for, nor do we have the things not seen. All the things hoped for by the believer are in glory with Christ. The things not seen are all there as well. If the believer is hoping for anything different your faith is misguided and misplaced.

When a 'grace' ministry teaches the believer that God wants you, through the abundance of grace, to reign in life down here on this earth (Rom. 5:17), it is one of two possibilities. Either they do not understand the meaning of these scriptures, or they purposely build a business for their own profit. Both the 'faith teachers' and 'grace teachers' that fit into this mold have ministries that concentrate on the believer's life down here. Modern Christianity has discovered a profitable consumer industry from the world, and has brought it into the church with open arms. It is the industry of 'self.' How can I help you improve your life, get you the things you desire and want, and make life more comfortable and pleasurable for you?

How the Law of Moses Falls Short

The idea of 'self' brings us back to a certain understanding of the Law of Moses. When Jesus summed up the entire law, He said this;

Matthew 22:37-40

"Jesus said to him, "'You shall love the Lord your God with all your heart, with all your soul, and with all your mind.' This is the first and great commandment. And the second is like it: 'You shall love your neighbor as yourself.' On these two commandments hang all the Law and the Prophets."

As said previously, the measure of the law is human righteousness. It requires what you should be in the two relationships man has in life – with God, and with his fellow man. But noticeably missing from the law is any revelation of what God is for man. What is not shown at all is God's love. The revelation of the love of God is the cross, not the law (John 1:17, Rom. 5:5-8). This is why the adulteress brought before Jesus did not receive her just judgment according to the law (John 8:3-11). Instead, God was there, and His love and forgiveness goes well beyond the confines of the law. Besides, the very law they were using against her, and testing Jesus with, condemned each one of them of sin, from the oldest to the youngest.

The measure in the Law of Moses for human love is 'self' -- love your neighbor as yourself. This falls short of Christian love. This is not the believer's commandment (John 13:34, 15:12-13, Eph. 5:2). You will always be hard pressed to find any self-sacrifice in the law. But this is how we are to love fellow believers, just as Jesus loved us and gave

Himself for us. But my original thought was this – how can we look at the Law of Moses, and anyone perfectly fulfilling it, as the measure of what the righteousness of God is?

Prophecy -- the Earth, Israel, and Messiah

The prophecies are about the earth and the earthly calling that is this nation, Israel. They will be restored in the land. They will have God's religion of the earth and of the flesh restored to them. They will still be a people in the flesh with natural bodies. Israel and Judah will be united as one nation, and will be exalted over all the other nations. They will grow in numbers and be the most prosperous nation on the face of the earth (Ez. 36:10, 36:37-38). There will be one King over them, their Messiah of the house and lineage of David. The following passage from Ezekiel sums up these thoughts well.

Ezekiel 37:21-28

21 "Then say to them, 'Thus says the Lord God: "Surely I will take the children of Israel from among the nations, wherever they have gone, and will gather them from every side and bring them into their own land; 22 and I will make them one nation in the land, on the mountains of Israel; and one king shall be king over them all; they shall no longer be two nations, nor shall they ever be divided into two kingdoms again. 23 They shall not defile themselves anymore with their idols, nor with their detestable things, nor with any of their transgressions; but I will deliver them from all their dwelling places in which they have sinned, and will cleanse them. Then they shall be My people, and I will be their God."

24 "David My servant shall be king over them, and they shall all have one shepherd; they shall also walk in My judgments and observe My statutes, and do them. 25 Then they shall dwell in the land that I have given to Jacob My servant, where your fathers dwelt; and they shall dwell there, they, their children, and their children's children, forever; and My servant David shall be their prince forever. 26 Moreover I will make a covenant of peace with them, and it shall be an everlasting covenant with them; I will establish them and multiply them, and I will set My sanctuary in their midst forevermore. 27 My tabernacle also shall be with them; indeed I will be their

God, and they shall be My people. 28 The nations also will know that I, the Lord, sanctify Israel, when My sanctuary is in their midst forevermore.'"

Why Israel is Special

Support of Israel is a biblical principle. America, as a nation, should always remain allied and in support of Israel simply because God commands it in His Word. It remains a matter of obedience to God for all Gentile nations on the earth. In the end, after Christ returns, the beast, the Antichrist, and the nations that are with them will be judged and condemned to eternal punishment. This is because they make war against Jesus Christ and the earthly Jerusalem (Rev. 17:13-14). Jesus returns at his second advent and destroys them in direct judgment and use of His power (Rev. 19:15-21, Matt 24:28). The nations that remain on the earth will be judged by Christ at that time, based on how they have treated the Israeli remnant (Matt. 25:31-46).

Israel, the Center of the Earth

We see that Jesus Christ is the center of fulfillment of all prophecy, which serves to bring out the divine glory of God in the exaltation of Christ. However Israel and the Promised Land itself, in relation to God's dealings in prophecy with the world, becomes a center point of the earth. The major objects and agents in prophetic scripture, in the end, are focused there, in the Promised Land and around Jerusalem. Judgment for their actions will be based on this principle – the character of their relationship with Israel. Therefore Israel is special, in a sense, as being the center of the earth.

Israel, separated in the world

Another way in which Israel is special is the simple understanding that they are called and separated by God from the rest of the nations of the world. God raised up a wall of separation around them in the earth. God gave Israel the law, the ordinances, the customs, the eating of foods, and circumcision in the flesh. He gave them worship in the tabernacle and the temple – all these are part of this wall of separation from the Gentiles. So the thought of Israel being special becomes this – as a people, they were chosen by God on the earth and in the world, and simply separated from the Gentiles.

Jesus is not of the world, and His body is not of it as well (John 15:19). The Jews are of the world and connected to the earth. This present world is made up of two entities: the Jews and the Gentile nations – this is a Biblical truth. The church alone is not of this world (John 17:14, 16). When Jesus told the Jews that they were of their father the devil, it is because they were of the world and of the earth, and Satan is the god of the world (John 8:23, 44).

Two Principles of God's Workings in Israel – God's Government and God's Calling

A separate scene concerning Israel's failure in responsibility is found at the time of Ezekiel. But to fully understand this failure we must first understand the two principles of God's plans and workings in the earth that were involved with Israel as a nation. These two principles are the government of God and the calling of God.

The principle of government started when Noah stepped out of the ark and God placed the authority of the sword in man's hands to limit and restrict evil (Gen. 9:5-6). The principle of the calling of God started with Abraham. God separated him out of his country, kindred, and father's house (Gen. 12:1). These principles were united together in Israel, from the time of Mt. Sinai through Solomon's temple. God had called Israel as a people unto Himself, and His government of the earth would be by His presence and glory abiding in the midst of this nation. This arrangement existed as long as Israel remained somewhat responsible. God would use His prophets to be His voice and judge the nations from His throne in the tabernacle or temple. They were used of God to call His people back to the law He had given them.

The presence of God in His glory behind the veil, and dwelling on His throne between the cherubim, was for His direct government of the earth (Num. 7:89, Ps. 99:1). Israel eventually sank into apostasy and idolatry. Their failure in responsibility resulted in the separation of the two principles. Jehovah removes His glory out of Israel and off the earth (Ez. 10, 11), and brings judgment on Jerusalem by the hand of Nebuchadnezzar. The city and the temple are destroyed, and the Ark of the Covenant -- the throne of God -- is lost forever. The label 'Lo-Ammi' is attached to Israel at that time – "...you are not My people, and I will not be your God," (Hosea 1:9). When Israel is spoken of by God this way, the Gentile world dominates them until the very end. The existence of the civil world power of the four Gentile beasts (Dan. 7) comes about directly consequent to Israel's failure in responsibility. Israel is not recognized by God concerning two specific things: God's glory and presence is removed from among them, and God's throne of government is no longer on the earth. The obvious results – there was no presence and glory of God beyond this event, in the rebuilt temple of Nehemiah, and even during the coming of Messiah to Israel. The times of the Gentiles began. Gentile dominion in the earth marches on today, and will continue until the future millennium.

The separation of the principle of God's government from the principle of God's calling is easily seen when Judah went into captivity in Babylon. Daniel acknowledges civil governmental authority in Nebuchadnezzar, and he even works for his kingdom. Yet he never recognizes any religious authority in him. Nebuchadnezzar attempts to unite religion with government in Daniel 4, but is taught a lesson by God in judgment – he crawls and eats like a beast for seven years.

The two principles were together in Israel from Mt. Sinai through the entire time of Solomon's temple. The principles united depended on Israel's responsibility. Failure was the outcome and the two principles were separated. These principles will again be united together in a restored Israel during the millennium under the reign of Messiah. However, at this future time they will not be dependent on responsibility in man, but instead on the sovereign power of God. In between these two scenes when the two principles are together is a period of time called the 'times of the Gentiles.' The entire time the Gentiles are given civil power the two principles are to be separated. [This is another example of the need for the Bible student to understand general Biblical principles depicting the ways of God in His dealings with man. It is in understanding the general principles first that allows a clearer grasp of the detail of Scripture.]

It is important to recognize what God is working and why He works it. The presence and glory of Jehovah in Israel is for His government of the world. It was then, and it will be again in the millennium. In between these two are 'the times of the Gentiles,' where God sets up the Gentiles in civil government and world rule. This is part of prophecy, involves the earth, and the succession of Gentile dynasties that rule over the Jews. If you want to understand this period of time, you must put together the vision of the four beasts in Daniel 7 with the dream of the statue in Daniel 2. The prophetic books of Daniel, Zechariah, and Revelations speak of these 'times of the Gentiles' with their results and effects.

Some further points can be made about 'the times of the Gentiles.' The two presentations of Messiah to Israel happen during this period. When Messiah came the first time, three of the four beasts had already come and gone on the face of the earth. In the time of Christ, the fourth beast of Daniel, the Roman Empire, had been ruling the prophetic world for some time. Between the two presentations of Messiah to Israel there is a parenthesis of time, prophecy, and God's dealings with the earth, as the Jews are morally set aside by God. This parenthetical period is called the mystery of Christ – not of prophecy or the earth, but rather hidden from the prophets and pointing to the heavens. It is not Judaism of the earthly calling, but Christianity of the heavenly calling. The parenthesis must be completed entirely, before time starts ticking again, and prophecy can be fulfilled.

The Calling of God -- Israel set aside Morally

As for the principle of the calling of God in Israel, at this present time, it has been set aside. The Jews are not acknowledged by God as His people. Morally they were set aside when Messiah was rejected by what was left of the nation. Previous to this, Israel had the law of God for hundreds of years, yet could not please God. Besides, God never desired, nor had pleasure in any of the sacrifices offered by the law that He had given them (Heb. 10:1-7). God's sending Messiah to Israel was the last testing of responsibility of man in the flesh. God brought an end to the practice of Judaism when Jerusalem and the temple were destroyed in 70 AD (Dan. 9:26). At that time what remained of the nation was scattered into the world of the Gentiles – God having His hand in this dispersion (Ez. 36:19). Scattered, unrecognized by God, and without their earthly temple, they live as the Gentiles.

Earlier in this book we taught how the title and promises of Messiah have been set aside by God. This also was consequent to Israel's rejection of Messiah, they did this as a people and a nation (John 19:15, Matt. 27:22-25). When this understanding of God's determinate counsels is accepted (Acts 2:23, 4:27-28), it is easier for the believer to see how prophecy, Israel, Judaism, the earth, and time being counted, has all been set aside by God as well (Dan. 9:25-26). The earthly calling by God of Israel is set aside for this present age. It is not that God has totally cast away His earthly people (Rom. 11:1). The gifts and callings of God are without repentance (Rom. 11:29). But during this present age, the calling of Israel has been set aside by God (Rom. 11:25), with all the above discussed spiritual truths and consequences.

The Present Question of Messiah

This raises important questions if Messiah and all the prophetic promises associated with Him are presently set aside in God's counsels. God is working something entirely different in revealing His mystery by the Spirit. Is it possible for Jesus Christ today to be found as Messiah? This is an easy answer for all Gentiles. It was never a possibility for them. Messiah was always a prophetic promise to Israel alone. But can Jesus Christ be found as Messiah today by a Jew? How would this be possible if Messiah is set aside by God and He does not recognize them as a people? It isn't possible. These two thoughts in the counsels of God presently cannot be circumvented. Messiah cannot be found today by Israel or even the individual Jew.

These are two truths of great importance for understanding Scripture. This is God's plan and counsel as found in His Word, but it was graphically displayed by His judgment of Israel in 70 AD. God uses the Romans as a rod of judgment against Israel, destroying Jerusalem and the temple. This was Israel's house being made desolate by the hidden hand of God (Matt. 23:37-24:2). As I've said previously, what God effectively does is set aside the Law of Moses and brings a halt to the practice of the earthly religion, Judaism. Messiah and all associated with Him are set aside, including the house of Israel.

The promise of Messiah, as we see in Scripture, is limited to Israel. What we also need to understand is that this promise will only be fulfilled to Israel on the earth and in the flesh. His second coming to Israel will be a physical presence in Zion for a very physical deliverance from their enemies (Rom. 11:26-27). It will not be all of Israel delivered, but a remnant saved (Rom. 9:27-29, Matt. 24:21-22). They will be sealed with a physical earthly seal (Rev. 7:3), and preserved in the counsels of God through the 3 ½ years of Jacob's trouble (Jer. 30:7, Rev. 12:6, 14). This is how the earthly calling of Israel is fulfilled by God. It will not be until the end. Only then will He recognize them again as His people and He as their God. Until the end, there is no Messiah, there are no Messianic promises, there are no Messianic Jews, and there is no earthly calling of Israel. All has been set aside in the counsels of God. And this will be for the entire time of this present age, the entire time of God's mystery, and the entire time that the Body of Christ remains on the earth.

However, as we previously remarked, all the gifts and callings of God are without repentance (Rom. 11:29). This will certainly be true concerning Israel. God will be faithful to fulfill all He has promised. In the end God again acknowledges the elect remnant of Israel (the remnant in the end are the only real Messianic Jews). In the prophetic scriptures that speak of the millennium we see this acknowledgement by God. When Israel is delivered and restored in the land, God refers again to Israel as His people and He as their God (Ez. 36:23-28, 28:25-26, Jer. 30:18-22, Joel 2:26-27). We must understand it will be according to His counsels, and not in variance to how He has chosen. As I've said from the beginning of the book, we've been invited by God, as His sons, to know His counsels, even those that concern the earthly calling. He gave us the Spirit of truth so we may understand these things.

Christians are a New Creation, and Members of the Body

What then can we say about the individual Jew who is drawn by God to faith in Jesus Christ? There are many things that are said in the church world, some that are scriptural and some that are not. The Scriptures seem to indicate that God always keeps a remnant of sorts. As there was a remnant from Israel into the Body of Christ at the beginning of the church in Paul's time (Rom. 11:5-7), so too, I believe there is always a remnant. What is also clear in this same passage is that Israel, as a whole, has been hardened (Rom. 11:7-10). Israel, as a nation, had rejected the Son of Man, nailed Him to the cross, and also then rejected the testimony of the Holy Spirit sent from heaven (Acts 7:51, John 15:26-27, Heb.2:3-4). However, this stumbling and fall of the nation does mean riches for the Gentiles (Rom. 11:11-14). The Body of Christ has always been a Gentile mass with an Israeli remnant, however small that remnant may be.

But this is not Jesus Christ as Messiah. This is not the promise of Messiah to Israel. To reiterate, as far as the counsels of God presently, Messiah, the promises, and Israel as a people are not acknowledged by God. The individual drawn to faith in Christ becomes a believer, a saint, and a Christian. When one gains entrance into the Body of Christ and the kingdom of God through justification by faith, it is by a new creation (II Cor. 5:17). What God does is entirely new. It is not a make-over or a sprucing-up. This new creation is of God (II Cor. 5:18). It is not connected to the old creation at all, the first Adam, or the world. It is a new creation in Christ, and not of this world, and certainly no longer belonging to the nation of Israel.

This new creation has no earthly attachments. The believer is also a member of a heavenly body, the Body of Christ, members one of another, but members of one body. The new creation and the Body of Christ have no nationalities. If it was connected to the earth and this world it would have these things. But it isn't in any way.

Colossians 3:10-11

"...and have put on the new man who is renewed in knowledge according to the image of Him who created him, where there is neither Greek nor Jew, circumcised nor uncircumcised, barbarian, Scythian, slave nor free, but Christ is all and in all."

Galatians 3:26-28

"For you are all sons of God through faith in Christ Jesus. For as many of you as were baptized into Christ have put on Christ. There is neither Jew nor Greek, there is neither slave nor free, there is neither male nor female; for you are all one in Christ Jesus."

The new man is the new creation after the image of God, who alone could and does create it. There are no nationalities, none of these earthly labels exist in Christ. As for the Body of Christ the same applies (Eph. 2:14-16). According to the teaching of Scripture then, there are no Jews or Gentiles.

Christians Conformed into the Image of the Son

When the Body of Christ is removed from the earth to the heavens, it will be as follows. The dead in Christ in the graves, being corrupted, will put on incorruption, while those alive in Christ at the time, being mortal, will put on immortality. Every believer will either be raised or changed (I Cor. 15:48-54). What this event accomplishes is the removal of the Body of Christ from the earth. What this event accomplishes is the glorification of every believer's physical body. What this event accomplishes is every believer conformed by the Father into the image of His Son.

Romans 8:29-30

"For whom He foreknew, He also predestined to be conformed to the image of His Son, that He might be the firstborn among many brethren. Moreover

whom He predestined, these He also called; whom He called, these He also justified; and whom He justified, these He also glorified."

What I clearly recognize from these scriptures and all we have been saying is that this certainly is the determined counsels and plan of God. The Father foreknew and the Father predestined this specified conforming of believers to the very image of His Son. This was His plan before time began (II Tim. 1:9-10). Moreover the Father called the believer, justified the believer, and glorified the believer. All this is in the past tense as already accomplished in His counsels. Now I've come in this direction to show the reader one of the purposes why the believer's body must be glorified. When the body of Christ is taken, Jesus brings us to the Father's house, as sons of the Father (John 14:1-3). We enter into the glory of the Father, into His presence (not falling short of the glory of God any longer, Rom. 3:23). I think it is easy to see that we can only enter into God's presence, in a glorified body, sin removed from our flesh by resurrection.

Further, it becomes clear with a little study of the scriptures that Israel restored in the Promised Land will prosper, increase, and bring blessing to the Gentile nations. Yet they are there with earthly natural bodies still, only prolonged in days by the Lord. They are in these natural bodies, as male and female, as are all the remaining Gentile nations. The curse on the earth and creation will be lifted, as will the female pain and sorrow in childbearing (Gen. 3:16-19).

Christians and Christianity – not Messianic Jews, Israel, and Judaism

Again we ask what can be said about the individual Jew who is drawn to faith in Christ? All the above was the scriptural part of the answer. They are in Christ as Christians. They are new creations of God, not part of the old creation, nor of the first Adam, and not of Israel any longer. They are a part of the heavenly calling in Christ. They are part and equal members of the one body, the body of the glorified Man, Jesus Christ. Paul speaks of some of the truths involved in the forming of the Body of Christ in Ephesians.

Eph. 2:14-16

"For He Himself is our peace, who has made both one, and has broken down the middle wall of separation, having abolished in His flesh the enmity, that is, the law of commandments contained in ordinances, so as to create in Himself one new man from the two, thus making peace, and that He might reconcile them both to God in one body through the cross, thereby putting to death the enmity."

The middle wall of separation is the law of commandments of Moses, the religion of the Jews. It effectively separated Jews from Gentiles in this world and on this earth. In the Body of Christ the religion of the Jew has been abolished. It was abolished in His flesh, that is, by His death. In Col. 2:14, the Law of Moses was nailed to the cross, completely removed out of the way. The individual Jew drawn to faith in Christ is reconciled to God in the one body, right along with the Gentiles in faith. The individual Jew in Christ is no longer a Jew, but now a Christian.

Now, consider the unscriptural part of what is said, and in doing so, we take up the term, 'Messianic Jew.' I'm very hesitant to comment on this designation because of the apparent human emotions. Yet I feel I must be true to God's word. If Messiah and all the promises concerning Him are put aside in the counsels of God for this present age, how can an individual be Messianic? If the individual is in Christ by faith as a new creation, how can they claim a nationality? Both of these, 'Messianic' and 'Jew', as this relates to the believer's position in Christ, are an impossibility in this age. It is a man-made thought and term that has no scriptural basis and is not acknowledged by God. Further, as we have understood, in Christ there is no distinction between Jew and Gentile (Rom. 10:12). This makes the counsels of God simple and clear.

Judaism, the Confidence of the Flesh

We see in Paul's testimony found in Phil. 3:3-10, that he leaves his former religion of Judaism behind. He counts it as rubbish, and absolutely not something to be held on to, but loss, in his pursuit for the excellency of the knowledge of Christ Jesus our Lord. He calls his accomplishments in Judaism his confidences in the flesh (Phil. 3:4). But he is careful to preface this boasting with the spiritual truth and reality of the believer.

Philippians 3:3

"For we are the circumcision, who worship in the Spirit of God, rejoice in Christ Jesus, and have no confidence in the flesh,"

For all believers everywhere, there are no confidences whatsoever in the flesh. Our confidence and boasting is solely in Christ. This is true concerning the believer's justification as well as his subsequent walk on this earth. If we boast in the condition of the flesh, it is not in anything we have done, but rather in our infirmities, persecutions, distresses, etc. In this we learn that His grace is always sufficient to meet the need (II Cor. 12:9-10). And Christ is magnified; not ourselves, and not our flesh.

The Threat of Judaizing the Christian Faith

But seeing these spiritual truths raises another question. Did Paul feel that a believer could mix Judaism with Christianity? Not in any conceivable way. In Gal. 5:1-6, he refers directly to Judaism as a yoke of bondage not to be entangled with. He says that, as believers, if you become entangled in it, Christ will profit you nothing. The term, 'Messianic Jew' and all that is associated with it, has a Judaizing influence. It mixes Judaism with the Christian faith. It brings the believer back down to the earth and to this world, establishing connections here. It is only confidences in the flesh because Judaism is God's religion of the flesh and this world. It is the taking up of that which Christ, our Savior, has abolished in His body. *It is an adding to Jesus Christ as if He is not enough.* Adding anything to Christ is denying the perfection of the work of Christ in redemption, and denying the sufficiency of His death. God has shown that He accepts nothing else but the death of Christ in that He raised Christ up from among the dead. The spiritually minded believer must come to see that Jesus Christ is more than enough, certainly for justification, but also for our walk here on this earth. Nothing else is needed.

Allow me to give you some food for thought. I believe that all the provisions and consequences of the one-time redemptive work of the Son of Man also include the new heavens and a new earth. Certainly then, there is more than enough provision in that work for me to walk at this present time on this earth as a believer, until He returns to take me to His Father's and my Father's house. There is absolutely no reason for the believer to ever add anything to the provision that is Christ.

Much of the heartache for Paul in his ministry to the Gentiles was combating the influence of the Judaizers in his time. They had a great corrupting influence on Gentile Christians. In Galatia, believers were being taught to be circumcised in the flesh (Gal. 5:2-4) and to observe days (Gal. 4:9-11) according to the Law of Moses, the religion of the weak and beggarly elements of the world. It is of the flesh and of the earth.

Galatians 3:3

"Are you so foolish? Having begun in the Spirit, are you now being made perfect by the flesh?"

The believer taking up Judaism in any measure is trying to sanctify his walk on earth by fleshly means. Believers are not in the flesh as the Jews (Rom. 8:8-9). Your justification was not in the flesh. Your walk on this earth as a believer is not a perfection of the flesh as well. We know Christ no longer according to the flesh (II Cor. 5:16). However, if you entangle yourself in these earthly things, Christ will profit you nothing (Gal. 5:1-2).

How God Views Israel Set Aside in Unbelief

So now let us look at some other scriptures concerning Israel, and God's view of them. We should keep in mind John 6:29, where Jesus says, *"This is the work of God, that you believe in Him whom He sent."* In John 15:20-25, *"...they will also persecute you...because they do not know Him who sent Me...but now they have no excuse for their sin. He who hates Me hates My Father also...but now they have seen and also hated both Me and My Father."* The 'they' Jesus is talking about is Israel. Again in John 16:2-3,...*yes, the time is coming that whoever kills you will think that he offers God service...they have not known the Father nor Me.*" Luke 10:10-16...*he who rejects you rejects Me, and he who rejects Me rejects Him who sent Me.*" This is not very complimentary. What is Jesus saying concerning Israel's relationship with God? He recognizes that they rejected both the Father and the Son. They crucified the Son of Man and He does not count them as among His brethren (John 20:17). There is no relationship. Israel really had not known God.

John 8:54-55

"Jesus answered, "If I honor Myself, My honor is nothing. It is My Father who honors Me, of whom you say that He is your God. Yet you have not known Him, but I know Him. And if I say, 'I do not know Him,' I shall be a liar like you; but I do know Him and keep His word."

They say that He is their God and He is who they worship, but they have not known Him. In Matt.21:18-19 the cursing of the fig tree was a picture of how God viewed the state of Israel as a test case for all mankind in the first Adam. The parable of the landowner and vineyard in verses 33-41 is a description of Israel's testing in responsibility by God (the landowner). This particular parable (Matt. 21:33-41) is so descriptive of God's view of the history of Israel, as a nation, that it is hard to see it any other possible way. In verses 42-46 Jesus spells out God's viewpoint of Israel clearly, and what God would do about it, saying, *"the kingdom of God will be taken from you..."* When Jesus speaks of the guilt associated with all the righteous blood shed on the earth in Matt. 23:34-35, here again, Israel as a whole, stands guilty. In Matt. 23:37-39, Israel's house is left by God desolate...that is abandoned by God, and set aside by God as a nation. In Matt. 27:6 the leaders of Israel discuss what to do with the money returned by Judas, as the price of blood...this was the blood of their Messiah. In Matt. 27:25 the people cried out, *"His blood be on us and on our children."* It is still to this day in the eyes of God.

Acts 7:51-54

"You stiff-necked and uncircumcised in heart and ears! You always resist the Holy Spirit; as your fathers did, so do you. Which of the prophets did your fathers not persecute? And they killed those who foretold the coming of the Just One, of whom you now have become the betrayers and murderers, who have received the law by the direction of angels and have not kept it."

"When they heard these things they were cut to the heart, and they gnashed at him with their teeth."

These are Stephen's last words spoken to the Jews in Acts 7:51-53. This man, full of the Holy Ghost, brings a searing indictment against the Jews. And also, by the Spirit of God, Paul finishes his ministry in Rome by speaking to the Jews there (Acts 28:23-28), saying, *"Therefore let it be known to you that the salvation of God has been sent to the Gentiles, and they will hear it!"* In Rom. 10:21, God says concerning Israel, *"All day long I have held out my hands to a disobedient and contrary people."*

Israel's History – a Failure in Responsibility

Let us view some of Israel's history from God's perspective. From the time of Israel before God at Mt. Sinai, through King David and Solomon, the presence and glory of God remained in Israel, either in the tabernacle or the temple in Jerusalem. Even when Israel rebelled and sinned in many ways, God's presence remained on the earth, the glory behind the veil. This was not a presence that brought spiritual relationship and communion with Jehovah and the people of Israel. It was a presence by which God governed the earth from Israel. By and by, Israel's rebellion and apostasy was too much for God to still honor by His presence. In Ez.10:18, the glory of the Lord, departs the temple, departs Jerusalem and the earth. God then, in His providence, brings Nebuchadnezzar to destroy Jerusalem and the temple. The ark of God is gone forever from Jerusalem, and God turns over civil government to the Gentiles. When the presence of God is removed from the earth 'the Times of the Gentiles' began.

We understand what is said in Hosea 1:9," *...Lo-Ammi...you are not My people, and I will not be your God."* We see this in the book of Daniel, where God says always to Daniel," *your people."* From that time forward, from Nebuchadnezzar and the captivity of Judah, and the destruction of the temple and Jerusalem, the presence of God was no longer in Judah. The Jews were no longer considered God's people by God. It remains so to this day. Nothing has changed God's view of Israel since that time, especially the rejection of Messiah. From the time of Israel's captivity in Babylon, God had set aside Israel concerning His glory and government of the earth. With the rejection of Messiah, God set aside Israel morally, and turned to the Gentiles.

The Counsels of God for Israel – the Jewish Remnant

There is a future time, when God will take up Israel again, calling them 'His people.' The gifts and callings of God are without repentance (Rom. 11:28-29), even concerning this disobedient and contrary people (Rom. 10:21). What we need to fully realize is that God's purposes in Israel center on a future remnant. The term 'Messianic Jew' is a label that has only one Biblical application. It is an apt description of the 144,000 Israeli remnant in the last 3 ½ years before Christ's return to this earth. They will be looking for the true Messiah and will not be fooled by a false one (Matt. 24:24). However, the rest of Israel will receive a false Messiah in the Antichrist (John 5:43). When Jesus returns He is Messiah for this remnant. They alone, of all Israel, are truly Messianic. And they alone, in Israel, will be acknowledged by God (they have the earthly seal of Jehovah). They alone are the real Jews. [Compare Rom. 9:6-8 with Rom. 2:28-29 and Luke 3:8.]

A remnant in the end is the counsels of God for Israel. *It is to the remnant alone God will fulfill all the true Messianic promises and prophecies.* In Rev. 12 God's counsels concerning Israel are depicted for the believer to know through the vision given to John. The following is a small portion of a bible study on prophecy that addressed a part of this chapter. I include it here to show the future Jewish remnant in God's counsels.

A woman (Israel, a vessel without strength) seen in the heavens (that is, agreeable to the thoughts and counsels of God), clothed in the glory of the sun (having the spiritual authority of God). She rides with the moon under her feet (all legal ordinances under her, subordinate authority of Mosaic Law) and crowned with twelve stars (complete subordinate administrative authority of man on the earth/ or the twelve patriarchs). The woman should be viewed as the divine purpose of God in His people Israel, not simply Israel as a nation (because the woman is seen in the heavens, in the divine thoughts of God, and in the perfection of His purposes). The woman is with child, a male Child (Christ, and the church, His body in Him, in Christ), who is the object of all the counsels of God and the vessel of His power on earth (Rev. 12:5, Rev. 2:26-27). The Man-Child does not act in His might yet, but is caught up to the throne of God, hidden (Col 3:1-3, hidden in God, and the church hidden there as well). Satan is seen as a great red dragon in the form of the imperial Roman Empire, the seven heads being the perfection of evil, opposed to the coming forth of the Male-Child. The Empire is not seen historically here, but rather as the power of Satan. The woman flees into the world, her house in desolation, but finds a place of protection and sustenance from God (here she is the sealed and sovereignly protected remnant of Israel during the last 3½ years of Jacob's trouble).

It is beautiful to see how the character of prophecy is maintained in the vision, and this is done in a number of ways. For starters, the mystery of God, the body of Christ, is kept as hidden from the prophecy itself, as it is in all prophetic scriptures. Then Rev. 12:6 identifies the location as the earth, again prophecy concerning God's dealings with the earth. The woman is specifically seen in God's counsels and purposes as the remnant of Israel preserved on the earth and protected by God in the world for a certain period of time. Here the character of prophecy is the counting of time on the earth concerning the remnant (Rev. 12:6, 14).

This is the earthly glory of Jesus Christ, the remnant of Israel restored in the Promised Land. The remnant is the woman of Rev. 12, seen in the divine counsels of God concerning Israel. She is truly the only one, who can properly say,

"For unto us a Child is born,
Unto us a Son is given;
And the government will be upon His shoulder.
And His name will be called
Wonderful, Counselor, Mighty God,
Everlasting Father, Prince of Peace.

Of the increase of His government and peace
There will be no end,
Upon the throne of David and over His kingdom,
To order it and establish it with judgment and justice
From that time forward, even forever.
The zeal of the Lord of hosts will perform this." (Isaiah 9:6-7)

She alone will in the end cry out, "Blessed is He who comes in the name of the Lord!"

Chapter 15:

Rightly Dividing the
Word of Truth

This book is an involved study of Scripture. The serious minded believer may prayerfully gain spiritual truths and insights by its reading. I say this in all humility of spirit – the Holy Spirit is the revealer of truth, and He has taught me many things from God's word. In the end, the reader will judge what I have written. What God requires of you is that your judgment be by the Word and through the Word.

There are many scriptures in the text of the chapters that support the thoughts being presented. There are many other scripture references listed in parenthesis that benefit your study. They help to direct you in searching the Scriptures to find out whether these things are true (Acts 17:10-11). If there are multiple scriptures given in presenting a thought and making a point of instruction, then it is far less likely that twisting and turning of Scripture is being done to accommodate human imaginations or systems of doctrine. It is only God's thoughts out of God's Word as taught by the Spirit that should be of interest to us.

Believers Must Depend on the Holy Spirit to Teach

It will take some time on your part to go through all the references. As believers we should all desire to gain an in-depth understanding of God's Word. That usually takes study and effort. If it seems to us like work, that's because it is (II Tim.2:15). But the rewards are great and eternal, if we use prayerful diligence. And we should, as believers, have an ever increasing dependence on the Comforter's divine ability to teach.

John 16:13

"However, when He, the Spirit of truth, has come, He will guide you into all truth; for He will not speak on His own authority, but whatever He hears He will speak; and He will tell you things to come."

These are precious words from the Lord before His departure. The disciples were troubled in heart because of His frequent discourses about His leaving. The Holy Spirit was the promised Helper and Comforter, very much what they needed in His absence (John 14:16-17). The Spirit would come as sent from the Father to the many brethren of Christ, consequent to the glorification of the Son of Man (John 7:38-39). This is the same Holy Spirit that is the seal of God in all believers. And the Spirit of God knows the things of God...Now we have received...the Spirit who is from God. (I Cor. 2:11-12) Believers need to pray and ask God to open up the Scriptures, that the eyes of our understanding will be enlightened.

Also the ministry gifts were given by the Son of Man when He was raised and exalted above the heavens (Eph. 4:8). These gifts were given to His Body for the equipping of the saints and the edifying of the Body. By them the Body is to come into the unity of the faith and the knowledge of the Son of God, to a mature man, to the measure of the stature of the fullness of Christ (Eph.4:11-13). There are also subtle warnings in this passage. Believers should always be watching out, not to be carried about in all directions by winds of doctrines, presented to the Body by men of trickery, in cunning craftiness of their deceptions (Eph.4:14). False teachers try to creep in unnoticed or rise up among us innocently, and believers need to be equipped to earnestly contend for the faith (Jude 3-20).

The Need to Rightly Divide the Word of Truth

Another error that is mixed in with false teachers, which all believers need to be watchful for, is the title of our chapter and what is mentioned in Timothy;

II Tim. 2:15

"Be diligent to present yourself approved to God, a worker who does not need to be ashamed, rightly dividing the word of truth."

It is one thing to say, "All Scripture is given by inspiration of God...", that most of us agree on. And then, "All Scripture...is profitable for doctrine...", again most would agree on this (II Tim. 3:16). But if that is as far as our qualification and judgment of teaching and doctrine reaches, then we remain very naïve and easily deceived. Of importance is how the Scriptures are used, and how they are divided. The Word of God is easily and often wrongly divided, even unknowingly by good men, as teachings and doctrines are presented. We assume that good men teach only the truth of God's word, yet this thought is only a human assumption, and a dangerous one at times. It is held in the minds of a large percentage of believers; attempting to mask spiritual laziness. We hold these unspoken thoughts that it is the minister's job. We reason he is paid to do it. If the scriptures need to be rightly divided, it stands to reason that the scriptures can easily be wrongly divided, leading to false teachings and confusion.

The Finishing Point of All God's Counsels – God will be All in All

In the counsels of God He has an overall grand design and plan. The end point is the glory of God, Himself. In the far off eternal state of the new heavens and the new earth, it will be that God may be all in all (I Cor. 15:28). When Paul finished the doctrinal part of the epistle to the Romans and before turning to practical teaching, he makes this statement;

Rom. 11:36

"For of Him and through Him and to Him are all things, to whom be glory forever. Amen."

This is God's grand design to which all His purposes and counsels are pointing. The center object of the plan, and this understood as before the foundations of the world, is the exaltation of Jesus Christ. Everything in God's counsels revolves around this centerpiece as the means of fully bringing out the eternal glory of God. And there is a heavenly portion to this glory as well as an earthly portion;

Ephesians 1:9-10

"...having made known to us the mystery of His will, according to His good pleasure which He purposed in Himself, that in the dispensation of the fullness of the times He might gather together in one all things in Christ, both which are in heaven and which are on earth—in Him."

The passage speaks of God's will, God's good pleasure, and His purpose in Himself. This is referring to the counsels of God. All things are to be gathered into Christ as the Head, whether they are things in the heavens or things on the earth. We have already discussed in previous chapters that the Body of Christ, as the heavenly Bride and heavenly Jerusalem, will share in all the heavenly glory of Christ. *Israel, as a remnant preserved and restored in the Promised Land on the earth under their returned Messiah, and the Gentile nations gathered to them and blessed in them, are the object of the earthly glory of Christ.* These are some of the distinctions found in God's counsels made clear by the Spirit, for our spiritual enlightenment.

The Distinctions between Different Groups of People in Scripture

Let's begin by looking at some things that help our understanding of Scripture. First we may start by discussing the different groups of people separated in Scripture, and in the purpose and plan of God. We have already seen that in the counsels of God there is an earthly calling of Israel and a heavenly calling of the Body of Christ. They are similar to each other in that both groups are specifically called by God and that God authenticates this calling by a distinctive seal on each group. That is where the similarities end and the differences begin. In the callings, one is heavenly and the other is earthly. In the seal of authenticity, one is by the Spirit of God (Eph. 1:13-14), and the other by a physical mark on their foreheads (Rev. 7:3).

These two groups are totally separate from each other, but find their association with Christ through His two distinct titles, that of Messiah and that of the Son of Man. The one group will have possession of a land mass on earth as an inheritance with Jehovah dwelling in their midst. The other group has citizenship in heaven and habitation prepared there, in their Father's house, as sons of God, and brethren of the glorified Son of Man.

Many believers have the thought that everyone ends up in one big happy family of God, but where do we actually find that in Scripture? They see Israel as the people of God and Christians as the people of God, and so reason all are the same and all are together. And further still, if all are the same, then the reasoning is that all of God's teaching in all of God's word is equally applied to all, Jews and Christians alike. This certainly speaks to simplicity, because all are made to be the same and the teachings are the same. No need to rightly divide truth, if we equally apply everything to all.

God Distinctly Separated Israel, and this by His Own Sovereign Choice

This is a popular thought no doubt, birthed in human reasoning, but it has no basis or support in God's word. There were many existing Gentile nations and peoples when God chose Israel and delivered them by His sovereign power out of Egypt. At the very least in our understanding, we have to see that this was a separation accomplished by God, and a separation apart from the rest of the human race. God gives them the Law of Moses, and this builds up a wall of separation around this nation in the world (Eph. 2:14). Again, this was done by God, to the exclusion of all other nations. But let us look at God's own words to confirm what I'm saying;

Deuteronomy 7:6-7

"For you are a holy people to the Lord your God; the Lord your God has chosen you to be a people for Himself, a special treasure above all the peoples on the face of the earth. The Lord did not set His love on you nor choose you because you were more in number than any other people, for you were the least of all peoples;"

A holy people to the Lord means they are a people set apart, and this by the choice of God. The only thought of explanation for the choice is found in God's love. He set His love on them. Further, this choosing by God of Israel made them special, a special treasure to God. This is not the only place in Scripture where we find words like this spoken by Jehovah concerning Israel (Deut. 10:15, 14:2, Ez. 20:5-6).

There are important truths to understand and acknowledge here – these come by asking some big questions about a big subject, the sovereignty of God. I believe that the proper understanding of this Biblical topic by the believer is the only path to seeing the grand preeminence of God and His full undefiled majesty and glory – as truly seeing and holding God as all in all. All other paths seem to involve in measure, to a greater or less degree, the boasting of man (Rom. 3:27, 4:2, I Cor. 3:21, 4:6-7, 9:16, II Cor. 11:17-18, 12:1-11, Gal. 6:13-14, Eph. 2:9). And we should all be wary of man's affinity to boast.

Asking the tough but important Questions -- How was Israel Special to God?

Allow me to work backwards from the final thought above by asking the reader a few thoughtful questions. If Israel, as a nation, is special to God, how are they special? What does God mean by this word special? And in comparison to what are they special? An object can only possibly be special in comparison to other objects. The other objects in the above passage are all the other nations and peoples. Israel is special to God in comparison to the rest of mankind. How then did they come to be special to God? Was it their might and strength and numbers? Was it some previous great accomplishment, or some future work that God saw they would perform? Was it that Israel had secretly chosen God and that God was reciprocating? It wasn't any of these, which are the usual thoughts of human reasoning. They were special simply because they were chosen by God, nothing more, and nothing less.

And what was the reason for God choosing them? It was His love, and this basically unexplained. We know that the scriptures in other places speak about God's love, God is love (1 John 4:8, 16). Love is God's essential nature. God is light (1 John 1:5). The essential nature of God is love and light. He is these things in and of Himself. This is different than all His attributes. God showing love is never dependent on an object to give Him motive -- the motivation is always within His own nature, within Himself. Our exercise of love, even at the highest level, must have an object that provides a motivation. For example -- at the highest level, the object of our love would be the Father or Jesus Christ, and beholding the object the source of all motivation. But God isn't like this, He is an infinite Being. We, and all that is created, are finite.

If God made Israel Special, then God is showing Special Love

If God is making choices in His love, these choices are solely within His essential nature, within Himself. The choices have objects, this is true; but the objects of His choices are never the source of His motivation. His motivation, when and wherever He shows His love, has to be Himself alone. Now if Israel was special to God, chosen and set apart in His love, what does it show about the love of God in this situation? God is showing special love. Special love? Love to a specific object of His choosing, to the exclusion of other objects around it. To deny these things, these truths, is tantamount to denying the existence of Israel.

If the motivation for God's love is hidden from us in His essential nature, then it follows that the explanations and reasons for His choices are there as well. If we cannot see His motivation, how can we comprehend His reasoning? This is why we will never be able to explain the choice of God in His love and sovereign grace. We cannot know God in this way. We will never know God in this way. It would be the finite reaching to the infinite, the relative comprehending the absolute. It is simply impossible. Only God fully knows Himself.

Ephesians 1:9

"...having made known to us the mystery of His will, according to His good pleasure which He purposed in Himself,"

We, as believers, are the objects of God's love and grace shown in Christ, but never the recipients because something about us or in us drew this out of Him. He always accomplishes His own good pleasure. This is always His own purposes, only found in Himself, in His essential nature. The truth of Scripture is that God acted towards us while we were yet sinners (Rom. 5:8), when we were enemies (Rom. 5:10), and by nature, children of wrath (Eph. 2:3). He purposed in His counsels concerning us, placing us in Christ, before the foundation of the world (II Tim. 1:9).

God's Choices serve to Glorify Him

We can see the choice of God in love and grace, because we can see the objects of His choices. Israel coming through the Red Sea on dry land was the object of God's choice and special love. Pharaoh and the Egyptian army were not. We can see the choice of God in love, but we will never be able to explain His reasons. The things we can know as believers are those which God has revealed to us in His Word. I can see the choice of God in His love and grace all over the pages of Scripture. I can no longer deny it, nor feebly explain it away. I only now glorify God in it.

I am the product of the choice of God in Christ. If you are sealed with His Spirit then you are the product of His choice in grace. How can this not bring glory alone to God? All God's counsels, from before the world began, have only one objective – God's very own glory. All these counsels center on Jesus Christ. If we are the choice of God's love and sovereign grace in Christ, how do we not see the connection here? The glory of God then becomes the only reason and explanation revealed to us for the choices of God.

Ephesians 1:3-6

"Blessed be the God and Father of our Lord Jesus Christ, who has blessed us with every spiritual blessing in the heavenly places in Christ, just as He chose us in Him before the foundation of the world, that we should be holy and without blame before Him in love, having predestined us to adoption as sons by Jesus Christ to Himself, according to the good pleasure of His will, to the praise of the glory of His grace, by which He made us accepted in the Beloved."

Ephesians 1:10-12

"...that in the dispensation of the fullness of the times He might gather together in one all things in Christ, both which are in heaven and which are on earth—in Him. In Him also we have obtained an inheritance, being predestined according to the purpose of Him who works all things according to the counsel of His will; that we who first trusted in Christ should be to the praise of His glory."

These two passages of Scripture show the majority of points we've been discussing. You have all the counsels of God centered in on exalting Christ, as all things in the heavens and on earth are gathered into Him. You also have the choice of God of the believer in His love and grace in Christ. It reads the Father chose the believer in Christ before the foundation of the world. And the reasoning is? It is simply stated – it was in love and to the praise of the Father's glory.

There is another portion of Scripture on this subject that is extremely difficult for most believers to read, let alone accept the principle it teaches. It is a sad reality that entire portions of God's Word may be purposely avoided by His children because we find the teaching objectionable to our understanding. I print it here, not to teach it in depth, but to bring out from it one distinct and clear truth related to the counsels of God;

Romans 9:14-24

14 "What shall we say then? Is there unrighteousness with God? Certainly not! 15 For He says to Moses, "I will have mercy on whomever I will have mercy, and I will have compassion on whomever I will have compassion." 16 So then it is not of him who wills, nor of him who runs, but of God who shows mercy. 17 For the Scripture says to the Pharaoh, "For this very purpose I have raised you up, that I may show My power in you, and that My name may be declared in all the earth." 18 Therefore He has mercy on whom He wills, and whom He wills He hardens.

19 You will say to me then, "Why does He still find fault? For who has resisted His will?" 20 But indeed, O man, who are you to reply against God? Will the thing formed say to him who formed it, "Why have you made me like this?" 21 Does not the potter have power over the clay, from the same lump to make one vessel for honor and another for dishonor?

22 What if God, wanting to show His wrath and to make His power known, endured with much longsuffering the vessels of wrath prepared for destruction, 23 and that He might make known the riches of His glory on the vessels of mercy, which He had prepared beforehand for glory, 24 even us whom He called, not of the Jews only, but also of the Gentiles?"

God's Judgments Serve to Glorify Him

The one point I make, that I believe is clearly said in this passage, is that whenever God has made a choice, regardless of what that choice is, it always serves the purpose of glorifying Him. In verse 17 above, God says to Pharaoh, "For this very purpose I raised you up..." This is reason for the choice, and shows God's intention. And what was the reason revealed? It is to show God's power and to declare His name in all the known earth. The reason for His choice, and the means and actions He uses to carry out His choice is for the display of His own glory. As we said previously, this is the overall objective of the plan and counsel of God -- His very own glory.

Closely related to this line of thinking is what we see in verse 22 above -- God showing His wrath and making His power known in judgment. This is a poorly understood principle of God's ways. God's judgments, as displayed in the earth, result in the glory of God filling the earth. I'll say it again for emphasis; *it is the judgments of God in righteousness that accomplishes the filling the earth with His glory as well as the knowledge of Him.* And verse 23 follows this by saying, "...and that He might make known...His glory..." There it is; there is a biblical truth. You have just learned one of the Biblical principles in the counsels of God. [The judgment of God is discussed in greater detail farther on in the chapter.]

Is There Unrighteousness with God?

Before leaving the above passage, I point out what seems to me to be a sticky point of sorts. In verse 14 the question, or more so, the accusation is voiced, "Is there unrighteousness with God?" This accusation was voiced against God in the days of Paul's teaching and continues to be so today. In this difficult passage the Spirit through Paul abruptly brings out this question. Have you ever asked yourself why? The question gets to the heart of the matter if you hold one of two viewpoints.

- First: Your feathers are ruffled and you are angry at his doctrine – that of a God making decisions and choices you can't explain, or don't feel He has a right to make – so this accusation automatically pops up in our minds.

- Second: the leaven of doctrine we hold dismisses the teaching outright that leads to the question. We easily answer in the negative – there is no unrighteousness in God! By the leaven we hold dear, we are convinced that God sits back and waits, and only reacts to the choices and decisions that man makes.

The Spirit of God does answer the question. We don't see and understand the answer, or we can't accept the answer as it is given. What happens then, and innocently I'm sure, is the setting up and maintaining contradictions in one's thoughts and faith. The problem with this is that there are no contradictions in God. If you have this thought as a believer, that there seems to you to be unrighteousness in God's dealings, then you have a contradiction. The truth of Scripture is that there is absolutely no unrighteousness with God. Do not be content with having in your thoughts contradictions of Scripture. They are detrimental to the health of your faith and spiritual walk.

As I said, this is a great subject. And our thoughts and questions go on from here, even without all the answers. I also realize how emotionally charged this can be, and I apologize if I have offended anyone in what I have said. But the verses above remain. They are all God's own words. There is no mistaking what He is saying. These are His thoughts. It reveals to us the true God. He has His own personal will out of which His choices flowed, and reveals to us more clearly His ways. But this has been a side-bar to the point I was making, that God's Word separates certain groups of people in His counsels.

The Two Titles and the Two Separate Groups

In the Scriptures we have seen that the Son of Man and Messiah titles are clearly distinct in Christ, although the two thrones and reigns are simultaneous in the end during the millennium. Although simultaneous, the distinctions are recognizable and maintained. The titles, being distinct themselves, set up differences in all that is associated with each, *and clearly help guide the separation and rightly dividing of the Word of truth today.* With this in mind, let us set up a table showing these distinctions.

Messiah	Son of Man
Prophetic Promises, the Anointed One, the definite subject of prophecy for Israel. When He comes, He remains forever	Redemptive realities, reconciles creation and the believer. The Mystery of God. Last Adam. The Son of Man goes away to receive a kingdom
Israel – the center of the earthly glory of Christ as Messiah	The Body of Christ and individual believer – the center of the heavenly glory of Christ
Earthly calling, in the flesh, of the world and on the earth, fulfilled in a Promised Land, and the earthly Jerusalem restored	Heavenly calling, in the Spirit, not of this world, and seated in heavenly places, the New Jerusalem, the city of His God. The Father's house
The law of Moses, Judaism – the religion of the earth and for man in the flesh	Christianity – the religion of the heavens with a definite heavenly citizenship (Phil. 3:20)
The earthly seal in the flesh (Rev. 7:3)	The seal of the Spirit inwardly (Eph. 1:13)

Rightly Dividing Scripture

Understanding Scripture and rightly dividing the Word of truth requires that you give attention to any distinctions made and brought out. The truths concerning Messiah and the promises associated with Him are quite distinct in nature and character from those surrounding the Son of Man. These promises in Messiah are solely found in Old Testament Scripture, given there in prophecy, and directed to Israel. The Law of Moses, the religion of the earthly calling, is found there as well, along with the earthly tabernacle, the earthly service and ministry, and fleshly ordinances and rituals (Heb. 9:8-10). The exhortations of their prophets, efforts by these servants to turn the nation back to their law (Jer. 25:2-7), and God's teachings to the earthly calling are all found in the Old Testament. And finally, we find there the prophecies for the end declaring the counsels of God concerning Israel and the earth, Jehovah being ever faithful to fulfill all He has promised to this earthly people.

Where we find the Doctrine of the Body of Christ is where we find its Teachings

In contrast to all this and separate from it in God's Word is the gospel of the glory of Christ. We find it only in the New Testament. There we find the epistles – *the teachings specifically from the Father and the Son through the Comforter to the Body of Christ.* They are the specific work of the Comforter, only possible after the Son of Man was glorified. The epistles are the specific communications of the Father to the many sons (Rom. 8:14-17, Gal. 4:5-7), consequent upon the resurrection of Christ from the dead (John 20:17). *The teachings for the Body of Christ will be specifically found where we find the doctrine concerning the existence of the Body of Christ.* This makes sound spiritual sense.

The mystery of God is directly related to the glorified Son of Man as well, and it further establishes the above point about the epistles. This mystery was not revealed by the Father through the Comforter until after Christ sat down at God's right hand. This mystery is the revelation and teaching of this glorified Man and a mystical Body joined to Him, the Body of Christ, exalted and sharing in His glory and inheritance. Part of the mystery now revealed is Christ in the believer, the sure and steadfast hope of the glory. [The mystery of God was previously discussed in detail in the heavenly calling chapter.]

The recognition of this mystery and the timing of its revelation have great importance for rightly dividing the Word of truth. The mystery is hidden in God and not revealed to the prophets of old. It is not contained or found in the Old Testament. Hidden does not mean it can be found with a little hard work. Hidden means absolutely impossible to be found, for it was hidden in God's counsels by God Himself. *Further, if the mystery was hidden, then teaching and instruction for the mystery does not exist in the Old Testament as well.* As far as help for the believer in understanding scripture, this truth in the counsel of God is of paramount importance to grasp. The church, the Body of Christ, the mystery revealed, is further isolated by the Spirit to Paul's writings. He was given responsibility by God to reveal God's mystery (a dispensation given to him – Eph. 3:2-3).

The Gospels form a Period of Transition between the Two Titles

The gospels, although filled with wonderful instruction for the believer, must be rightly divided. They are to be seen as a transition. They include the Messiah presented to Israel (Luke 4:16-21), the kingdom of God present with Emanuel (Luke 8:1, 9:2, 11, 10:9-11, 11:20, 16:16), Messiah being rejected, the kingdom of heaven at hand (Matt. 10:7, 11:11-12, 13:11, 24), the Son of Man glorifying the Father (John 17:4), and then the Father glorifying the Son of Man (John 12:23).

In the gospels, Jesus speaks to Israel as a people under the law (Matt. 22:35-46, Mark 12:19-34) or blinded by unbelief (John 12:37-40, 10:26, Matt. 13:10-17). They cannot hear with their ears nor see with their eyes, as the prophet Isaiah judged of them eight hundred years previously. When He instructs His disciples or comforts them, it is always in the context of those He has personally chosen (John 10:27-

29, 13:18, 15:16, 19, 17:6-16). When Jesus speaks prophetically, the character and themes of Old Testament prophecy are maintained. His topics include Israel and the Gentile nations in the end. He speaks of God's judgments establishing His government of the earth in the power and kingdom of the Son of Man (Matt. 24:30, 16:28). In His prophecies He refers to the Jewish remnant in the end times preserved by the faithfulness of God to fulfill His promises (Matt. 24:22, 24, 31, 18:7, Is. 45:4, 65:9, 22). The mystery is maintained as hidden in the gospels, except in one short comment when He declares that He would build His church (Matt. 16:18, note; future tense).

The Transition from Responsibility in Man to God's Sovereign Grace

The gospels should also be seen as the transition between man's final testing in responsibility and God bringing in sovereign grace (John 1:17). The presentation of Messiah is the final test of mankind. After Israel's failure in rejecting Messiah, God condemns the world (John 12:31). Everything after that is God working in sovereign grace through the redemptive work of the Son of Man. God chooses men from out of the world and brings them to faith in Christ (John 15:9, 17:6, 17:2, 6:44, 6:37-39). This He does by the Holy Spirit sent down to gather Christ's Body.

This transition between God testing mankind and God bringing in sovereign grace is uniquely depicted in back to back parables found in Matthew. The first speaks of mankind being tested through Israel (Matt. 21:33-40). What is proven is man's total failure in responsibility (Matt. 21:41-44). The second parable is God's offer in grace (Matt. 22:2-14). A unique feature about this parable is that it depicts certain aspects of the kingdom of heaven, while the other parable about responsibility does not. The reason is that all the testing of man in Adam was completed before the kingdom of heaven is set up. Also we see certain events in this parable, such as Israel's rejection of the invitation of grace, God's judgment and destruction of Jerusalem, and God's removal of tares in professing Christianity from any part in the marriage feast.

An Example of the Misapplication of Scripture, and Its Consequences

The following is an example of the need and value of rightly dividing the word of truth in the Christian world.

Matthew 16:18
"And I also say to you that you are Peter, and on this rock I will build My church, and the gates of Hades shall not prevail against it."

Now for centuries this one verse, out of all of Scripture amazingly, has been used by the Church world to justify its man-made doctrines of apostolic authority and succession, and further, the infallibility of popes. But believers should resoundingly reject such teachings as the vain creations of the carnal mind. Yet these teachings have held their influence for hundreds of years, and still hold sway over many today.

The rock is the confession of Christ as the Son of God. Peter is the little stone of insignificance in view of Christ saying, 'I will build my church.' He builds by His sovereign power and grace, not by man or human authority. Nothing can stop the sovereign working of God or Christ, and that is the thought here concerning the gates of Hades. Yet it remains the largest of the ecclesiastical systems of man has been built-up and maintained in the Christian world on the basis of wrongly dividing a single verse of Scripture. This may be a slight oversimplification of the beliefs of Roman Catholicism, and if it is, please forgive me. It remains that the misunderstanding of this verse by man is central to catholic teaching and doctrine, as well as all they build up on the earth.

The Two Titles and the Two Groups (continued)

The message (gospels) associated with both titles, Messiah and the Son of Man, are different from each other. The mission and work associated with both are unique. The groups of people related to both the titles of Christ are quite distinct also.

- One is the earthly calling of Israel. They are a remnant only in the end, with their Messiah come out of Zion to destroy their enemies. He will reign on the throne of David from earthly Jerusalem over twelve tribes of a united Israel in their land.

- The other is the heavenly calling of the believer/body of Christ in the title and work of the Son of Man. He is the one Seed of Abraham (not the many seeds of Gal. 3:16), of whom Isaac served as a shadow. The spiritual seed of Abraham (Gal. 3:7-9, 26, 29) are the sons of God through faith in Christ Jesus (Gal. 3:26, 4:5-7). The Son of Man is the seed of the woman, the second Adam, who is now glorified into the heavens. This group is seated with Him in heavenly places, as the Body united to Christ and as believers found in Christ, the glorified Son of Man. He is the Head of His own mystical Body in the heavens (Eph. 1:17-23, 2:5-7).

The Composition of the Unbelieving World – Jews and Gentiles

The world as apart from God is constantly spoken of in scripture. The composition of its groups is Jews (John 8:23) and Gentiles. God set apart Israel in the world. A wall of separation was built up around the Jews by God in giving them their law (Judaism, Eph. 2:14-15). It is all in the flesh, of the world, and on the earth. Their setting apart was an external redemption in type, God bringing them through the Red Sea and into the wilderness to meet Jehovah at Mt. Sinai. Egypt serves as a type of the world from which they were delivered. Pharaoh is a type of Satan, the ruler of this world. Israel is a people in the flesh, of the world, and in the first Adam, as are all unbelievers. The entire world is guilty before God and under judgment (Rom. 3:19) -- all have sinned and come short of the glory of God (Rom. 3:23).

A distinction important in dividing truth is that believers are apart from the world (John 17:14, 16). We are not part of the unbelieving Jews and Gentiles. Believers are saved individually, but then become members of a Body, a corporate entity called the Body of Christ. This Body is truly what Christ builds in sovereign grace and power, and is not of this world. What is of the world is what man builds on the earth that he calls the church. This is a structure erected through the use of wood, hay, and straw. On the earth man builds a great house for God that is filled with many things, good and bad, vessels of honor and dishonor (II Tim. 2:20). Yet what Christ builds is the Body and is not connected to the earth. This Body is seated in heavenly places in Christ (Eph. 2:6) and has a heavenly citizenship (Phil. 3:20). The believer has been blessed with every spiritual blessing in heavenly places (Eph. 1:3).

The Distinct Groups of Professing Christianity – the Parable of the Wheat and Tares

Matthew 13:24-30

"Another parable He put forth to them, saying: "The kingdom of heaven is like a man who sowed good seed in his field; but while men slept, his enemy came and sowed tares among the wheat and went his way. But when the grain had sprouted and produced a crop, then the tares also appeared. So the servants of the owner came and said to him, 'Sir, did you not sow good seed in your field? How then does it have tares?' He said to them, 'An enemy has done this.' The servants said to him, 'Do you want us then to go and gather them up?' But he said, 'No, lest while you gather up the tares you also uproot the wheat with them. Let both grow together until the harvest, and at the time of harvest I will say to the reapers, "First gather together the tares and bind them in bundles to burn them, but gather the wheat into my barn."

This parable depicts the kingdom of heaven. It is prophetic in its character, as are the other parables that follow it in this chapter. This parable shows another distinct group that is separated in Scripture. The field is the world – unbelieving Jews and Gentiles. But there is a distinct crop in the field, separate from the field itself. The crop's composition is wheat and tares mixed together. The wheat is sown by the Son of Man, the tares by the evil one. These are distinct from each other in their nature, but in the present age they are mixed together without separation. They are only distinct from each other to the eye of the Son of Man, who knows those that are His (II Tim. 2:19), and to the eye of Satan, who knows his as well, as those planted by him.

The wheat is the Body of Christ on the earth presently. They are in the world (field), but not a part of the world (not part of the field). The wheat represents individual members making up this corporate entity, the Body of Christ. *The tares form a special group*, no longer part of the field in a certain sense, but part of the crop, and spoiling the crop. *The crop is the Christian world, Christendom. The tares are professing Christians, as are the wheat.* The wheat has true faith. They are the righteousness of God by faith, and *have been sealed by the Spirit of God*. The wheat is the work and planting of the Son of Man, and in every sense He takes responsibility for them. Men cannot see the Body of Christ in the crop, not clearly, and so judgment and separation is not given to the hands of man (in the history of Christendom, from time to time, we have seen man take judgment into his own hands, only to end in unrighteous and evil results). Jesus says, 'Allow both to grow together until the harvest...'

The Parable is a Picture of the Present State of the Kingdom of Heaven

This parable affords the believer certain important understandings of the counsels of God. The crop is spoiled and remains so for the entire age, worsening and ripening in evil. Does the Lord tell us that the wheat will rid itself of the evil around it? Are there any symbols used by the Lord in the parable by which the wheat, on their own, exercises the power of the gospel to change the tares or the unbelieving field into wheat? Will the crop in the field get better and more pure towards the end through the hard work of the wheat? Will the wheat in any sense, rise up and prepare the field as presenting a kingdom to the Son of Man when He returns, as we are taught in some circles?

The answers to these questions are simple for any believer who actually reads the parable. The wheat has no power or authority to rid itself of the evil around. All the wheat can do is turn away from the evil individually, and not be part of it (II Tim. 2:19-21, 3:5). The actual separation of the wheat from the tares is towards the end during a time of harvest, when the wheat is removed from the world (field). The tares are bundled together in the world (field) and left there for judgment.

As for the gospel, it will not change the field or the tares. The Son of Man planted the wheat, and did so by sovereign work. To believe and preach otherwise is the presumptuous teaching of ministers and men. The saving and changing of the world is not the promised result of the preaching of the gospel. This isn't true in the counsels of God, the Word of God, or in this parable. The Biblical principle associated with the results of the preaching of the gospel in this age of grace is individual. That principle is equally true when considering the Body of Christ or the kingdom of heaven. The principle of the results of the gospel preached is not national or global. The world does not change by the preaching of the gospel. America does not change by the preaching of the gospel. Truthfully, I have never heard of any nation ever being saved, in the history of Christendom, by the preaching of the gospel.

The crop in the field, a spoiling mixture of wheat and tares, is a picture of the progression of the kingdom of heaven today. We have to be willing to accept this truth, or immediately we step into blindness and presumption. It is man exalting himself, in what he does and what he builds, that keeps him from seeing God's truth – this is the leaven that saturates to the end (Matt. 13:33). Christendom is built up by man as a great corrupt power in the world (Matt. 13:31-32). It is not coincidence that these two parables immediately follow the wheat and tares parable. The gospel and its effects (results) during the time of the crop in the field are stated by the Lord in John and Mark.

John 3:18

"He who believes in Him is not condemned; but he who does not believe is condemned already, because he has not believed in the name of the only begotten Son of God."

Mark 16:15-16

"And He said to them, "Go into all the world and preach the gospel to every creature. He who believes and is baptized will be saved; but he who does not believe will be condemned."

These are the results of the preaching of the gospel, some will believe, and some will not (II Cor. 4:1-4). This is what the Scriptures promise, nothing more, nothing less. Man is given responsibility to go into all the world and preach the gospel. Man is not responsible for the results – God is responsible. When God works it will last for eternity. Christ will build His church. The Holy Spirit is sent down to gather the Body. By one Spirit we are baptized into one Body, the Body of Christ. This is the sovereign work of God, that which is made without hands (Col. 2:11, Mark 14:58). When we reason that God has placed in our hands the eternal destiny of another human being, and we made responsible for it, then we are thinking of ourselves more highly than we ought to think (Rom. 12:3).

In their past histories, England, Germany, and Italy have declared acceptable state religions politically mandated to their governed populaces. Here the floodgates were opened for entrance into the crop with barely any sincerity of profession required. And further back in the history of Christendom, the earthly wisdom of responsible men was the assimilating of heathen festivals into the church. They decided it better that the heathen have their drunkenness and revelry in the church rather than outside. Well, it certainly made for church growth, but I'll end my sarcasm there. Revelation 2, 3 is the telling of the progressive prophetic history of the crop (Christendom) in the field of the world. The spiritual fornication of the churches is the crop's unholy relationship and union with the world, where Satan has his throne, and is the god thereof.

The Failure of Man in Responsibility in Christendom

While men are sleeping, tares are sown among the wheat, and a spoiled crop is the result. The wheat is the body of Christ. What is true about all the wheat, and this individually, is the seal of the Spirit of adoption of sonship. The seal is the guarantee of authenticity. This is the seal of God, as given only by God, and not by man (Eph. 1:13-14, Gal. 4:5-7, Rom. 8:15-17). All true believers have this seal of authenticity, by which, from their hearts they can sincerely cry, "Abba, Father!"

In contrast, the entire crop in the field, wheat and tares together, has a different seal of approval upon entrance into it. This seal is the work of men and under the responsibility of men. It is water baptism. We see it in the above verse, as well as immediately on the day of Pentecost (Acts 2:38) and at the conversion of Paul (Acts 9:18). It is man's seal of approval of all that enters the crop in the field. It is a human work in the hands of men and therefore the responsibility of men before God. Failure in responsibility can easily be seen by the several contrasting doctrines of baptism conceived by men. It is not that water baptism isn't of God and doesn't have a proper godly place. It is just that it was only meant for the wheat, an outward show of our death with Christ and separation from the world. But through the centuries it was used for the opposite result, to mix the world with the church, for tares to enter in, and to further grow a spoiled crop.

What actually will change the World?

Will the preaching of the gospel change America, or change the world? That just isn't God's counsel. Will its preaching change some? That happens to be God's counsel and part of His plan. The preaching of the good news is the main means the Father uses to draw those He quickens to faith in Christ (John 6:37, 44). But allow me to remind you that there was no one preaching the gospel of Christ out on the road to Damascus when Saul came by. God does as He pleases, according to His eternal purpose and will (John 5:21).

If the gospel doesn't change America or the world, what will? *The answer to this eventually becomes clear. Change only comes by the direct judgments of God. This is a truth in principle in the counsels of God, the Word of God, and in the above parable in Matthew.* The tares are bundled together, left in the field, to be burned later. In the book of Revelation we have seals opened, trumpets blown, and vials poured out. All are judgments from the throne of God upon the world. Then we have the Son of Man returning on the white horse with a two-edged sword of judgment out of His mouth (II Thess. 2:8, Rev. 19:21). This will be the destroying of the two beasts and all those with them (Rev. 19:11-21), and the binding of Satan for a thousand years (Rev. 20:1-3).

This is what changes the world. When Satan is removed from the heavens, doesn't this limit his influence and power? (Rev. 12) If Satan is bound for a thousand years, wouldn't this have an effect on the world? (Rev. 20) If the two beasts and all their armies are cast into the lake of fire, doesn't this change things? (Rev. 19) Will it not result in the glory of the Son of Man spreading throughout all the earth, and His name being exalted among the Gentiles? When the remaining Gentile nations are addressed at that point, it is the separating of the sheep from the goats by the judgment of the Son of Man (Matt. 25:31-33). As for God's thoughts on this particular matter, it is clearly shown in the following passage:

Isaiah 26:9-10

"With my soul I have desired You in the night,
Yes, by my spirit within me I will seek You early;
For when Your judgments are in the earth,
The inhabitants of the world will learn righteousness.
Let grace be shown to the wicked,
Yet he will not learn righteousness;
In the land of uprightness he will deal unjustly,
And will not behold the majesty of the Lord."

Here then is the Biblical understanding on this topic. By the gospel of grace, the heathen will never learn righteousness. The world will not be changed by grace, and America will not be won by the gospel. This is how people are so deceiving themselves— Christians as well. We believe we will change and improve the world. All the while we know that Christ was in the world and did not improve it. Christians will do what Christ could not! This is the foolishness of even true believers. Christ was rejected by the world. He then condemned it (John 12:31). Yet we reason that the church has a mission to set the world right! But this is the time of the gathering of the church -- those who are to be Christ's companions. Certainly light coming in does improve the world in a certain sense. Men do not do in the light what they would in the dark. But this is the benefit, and it is superficial at best.

In all the centuries that the gospel has been present, the world has remained the same, not better. Christ didn't change it. We flatter ourselves thinking we will.

America is the World

America is a good example of what the Scriptures refer to as the world. We have in this country wealth, prosperity, luxury, materialism, and greed. We also have lying, cheating, adultery, harlotry, and fornication. We have a lot of pride, arrogance, and self. Finally, apostasy from God is a part of life in America, so much so, that it seems to be legislated upon us by the civil powers. I will say this, I wouldn't want to live anywhere else, and in a certain sense, I am proud to be an American. Yet I do have my eyes open. America started well in its beginnings, just like the church had a good start at Pentecost. But America isn't the same now, and neither is Christendom. *The evil only grows and ripens and gets worse; it never improves, regardless of the object it is in.* This is a principle one can easily see in Scripture.

Matthew 13:33

"He spoke another parable to them: The kingdom of the heavens is like leaven, which a woman took and hid in three measures of meal until it had been all leavened."

Leaven is always symbolic of evil and false doctrine (I Cor. 5:6, Gal. 5:9, Matt. 16:12). And it grows and spreads and worsens. Paul said that evil was at work in the church already in his day (II Thess. 2:7), and that in the last days perilous times will come (II Tim. 3:1-6, 13). Paul also said this by the Spirit to the Ephesian elders;

Acts 20:29-30

"For I know this, that after my departure savage wolves will come in among you, not sparing the flock. Also from among yourselves men will rise up, speaking perverse things, to draw away the disciples after themselves."

The Mystery of Sin Started in the Church in Apostolic Days

There was evil lurking in the church then, and it has only taken root and grown since. Ephesus, as representing Christendom, had departed its first position and had fallen (Rev. 2:4-5). They would not return. The steady decay and decline had started. According to the counsel of Christ, as the Son of Man judging the candlesticks, the evil would progress and ripen unto the end. The results would be Thyatira and its prophetess judged, and Laodicea spewed out of His mouth. The problem is that men refuse to recognize and admit the evil's presence and man's failure in responsibility in keeping it out. To deny these things and to teach the opposite is at best credulity, and at worse, a form of dangerous presumption. It seems to me to also be a willful disregard for the obvious teaching of Scripture, which along with the Holy Spirit are the only things we have, as believers, that reveals the mind of God on these matters.

Is it Possible for Christendom to Return to Apostolic Power?

Let's consider some other related questions in view of the parable of the wheat and tares. Will the church world be restored to apostolic power? Is this even possible? Is this thought in the counsels of God, supported by the Word of God, and found in the parable? I would answer these questions by considerations on a number of fronts.

- First, no thought of this is found in the parable at all. No apostolic authority bringing purity to the crop and no apostolic power at the end to further establish the wheat (Acts 5:12, II Cor. 12:12).

- Second, and this simply put, you need apostles present to have apostolic power and authority. This we do not have. And this cannot be imitated; the position, nor the power and authority. Apostles are eye-witnesses of Christ in their testimony.

- Third, Ephesus never repented and never returned to her first position; she never remembered from where she had fallen (Rev. 2:4-5).

The first position of the church (Ephesus) was Pentecost and the sovereign working of the Holy Spirit sent down from heaven. Apostolic power and authority were present. Ephesus, representing the first century church world with the last apostle banished to Patmos, embarks on a path of steady decay and decline. Its candlestick, threatened by the Son of Man with removal if they do not repent (Rev. 2:5), would be removed in the end with the spewing out of Laodicea (Rev. 3:16). This is how the prophetic progression of Christianity on the earth is brought to an end.

So then, the wheat and tares is a parable that actually contains four separate and distinct groups existing during this present age of grace and of the kingdom of heaven on earth. Wheat and tares mixed together profess Christ while unbelieving Jews and Gentiles together do not. Jews and Gentiles are mixed in the world because the Jews are not recognized as a people by God. When God destroyed Jerusalem and the temple in 70 AD, this effectively ended the practice of Judaism. God scattered the remaining Jews into the Gentile nations, to live there as the Gentiles in unbelief. Again, it is an important understanding for rightly dividing the Word of truth and knowing the ways of God in this present age.

In the end there are other groups separate and distinct. An Israeli remnant of 144,000 is separated from Israel itself (Rev. 7:1-8). Also we see tribulation saints separated out of the unbelieving Gentile nations (Rev. 7:9-17), tribulation martyrs under the altar (Rev. 6:9-11), Old Testament saints, and those born during the millennium, etc.

The Judaizing of the Christian Faith is a mixing of Israel with the Body of Christ

These distinctions are clearly made throughout the Word of God, and we must see and understand them by the Spirit in order to keep them separate and maintained in our faith and teachings. As an apostle Paul fought a spiritual fight protecting Christian truth and doctrine. This fight that he waged by the Spirit of God and the Word of God was not against an outright heathen influence. The evil was a Judaizing dominance that was constantly deceiving and corrupting the foundational truths of the Christian faith.

As an example of distinctions made by the Spirit and Paul's spiritual fight to maintain these truths, we have the entire book of Galatians. In the first two chapters the Holy Spirit fully distinguishes the apostleship of Paul from the other twelve in Jerusalem, particularly from the apostleship of Peter. In the very first verse he says his apostleship is not from men, nor through man, but through Jesus Christ and God the Father. This brings out two important points:

- First, there is never the thought by God of approving apostolic authority by succession in and among men (that is, apostles being called and made by men, and authority being handed down in the church through men, as we discussed earlier in the chapter).

- Second, the apostleship of Paul was distinct from the twelve, as well as separate from their authority and influence. This separation is clearly delineated in scope of ministry in Gal. 2:5-9; Paul to the uncircumcised, Peter and the twelve to the circumcised.

This last distinction certainly proved important in the history of the early church. The results proved this separation and distinction was made by the wisdom of God. In the historical record of the Book of Acts, it is Paul empowered by the Spirit and grace of God taking the gospel to the known world. God's dealings with Paul, starting in Acts 9, are the pivotal point of the historical account, marking a definite division for the whole book. God at that time, by sovereign power and grace, uses Paul for the bringing out the revelation of His mystery, and the bringing in of the Gentiles.

In the Fullness of Time God sent His Son

Another important perspective, that is insightful and leads to greater understanding, is found in two New Testament passages;

Galatians 4:4-5

"But when the fullness of the time had come, God sent forth His Son, born of a woman, born under the law, to redeem those who were under the law, that we might receive the adoption as sons."

Hebrews 9:26

"He then would have had to suffer often since the foundation of the world; but now, once at the end of the ages, He has appeared to put away sin by the sacrifice of Himself."

What is this 'fullness of the time' that the Spirit speaks of in Galatians? What is this 'once at the end of the ages' in Hebrews? The verses are obviously referring to when Christ came, redeeming us (in Galatians) and appearing to put away sin by the sacrifice of Himself (in Hebrews). This work was done by the Son of God, as the Son of Man, doing the will of the Father and going to the cross. This was after Messiah was rejected and set aside. There is the subtle hint that God is turning from one thing to another. Something comes to an end that precipitates the sending forth of the Son. Obviously, what He turns to is the redemptive work. But still, how was this the fullness of time, or the end of the ages, if it was two thousand years ago? What exactly had been filled up as far as time? What had caused the ending of the ages?

The Testing by God of Man in Responsibility

This is what we must see, and bear with me in this explanation. If we go back to paradise, we see man tested by God with one commandment to obey. '...of the tree of the knowledge of good and evil you shall not eat.' This was a testing of responsibility in man. Man distrusts God and believes the serpent, throwing the human race under sin and death. All men are sinners, and sin is in the flesh of man, as all men are in Adam, as their head.

God does many things after this with Abel, Enoch, Noah, and Abraham. But Israel, delivered out of Egypt, is a corporate people (a nation) externally redeemed, separated by God in the world from the Gentiles. The giving of the law to Israel was God fully testing man in the first Adam, man in the flesh, to see if man might produce fruit to God (especially righteousness, for the law given raises the question of righteousness in man).

Israel, in a great sense, represented the whole human race in this testing. How was this? The law was never given to the Gentiles, but to Israel. When you realistically compare Israel to all other nations at that time, they simply had every advantage possible that God could give man in order to produce fruit unto God (fruit being the measure of responsibility). Jehovah had drawn as close as a holy God possibly could to fallen man. *Therefore Israel was the test case.* If they failed there was no hope for man in Adam.

There is no doubt that God knew what the outcome would be of this testing. He knew the results before the foundation of the world. This is similar to His presenting Messiah to Israel, whose rejection God foreknew as well. Still, both had to be done, in the sense of fulfilling all righteousness and promise. *But man in the flesh cannot please God, nor can the mind of the flesh be subject to the law of God (Rom. 8:7-8).* Israel failed, being in the flesh. God never found any fruit on the tree. God's conclusion was that all, Jew and Gentile alike, were by nature children of wrath (Eph. 2:3, Rom. 3:19-20, 23). The testing of man was finished. The test case had resoundingly failed.

Israel's double culpability was when the scriptures say of God, "Then last of all he sent his son to them, saying, 'they will respect my son.' "But when the vinedressers saw the son, they said among themselves, 'This is the heir. Come, let us kill him...' *This was the fullness of time and the end of the ages (Matt. 21:33-43).* God was completely finished and had fully tested man, giving Israel every advantage. It was conclusively proven impossible for man in Adam to produce fruit unto God. The rejection of Messiah by Israel was the last straw. From this point forward, Israel is set aside as the earthly calling, prophecy grinds to a halt (even the Roman beast, the last great Gentile power on the earth, disappears when prophecy is set aside by God) and the earth will have to wait.

The Consequences of Israel's Failure in Responsibility

Israel fully and morally set aside by God came about in His providence (God's hidden hand), in a very physical and dramatic way. The Romans destroyed everything under Titus in 70 AD. As Jesus predicted, not one stone left upon another (Matt. 24:2). And what became of the Jewish people? They were scattered into all the existing nations of the world. All this was the result of the test case failing and Messiah being rejected by Israel. But there is more we can see here in the ways of God in accomplishing His counsels.

Galatians 3:19

"What purpose then does the law serve? It was added because of transgressions, till the Seed should come to whom the promise was made; and it was appointed through angels by the hand of a mediator."

With the destruction of Jerusalem, the temple, and the scattering of the people, we have the effective and practical setting aside of the Law of Moses, the religion of the Jews. There would be no sacrifices, no priesthood, and no temple. By judgment, God sets aside the practice of Judaism. Was this not His counsel? The law was added until the Seed should come. And it had to be so for what God would do next.

As Biblical Principles, The Law and Grace are Opposite

God now acts towards man by an entirely different principle (Rom. 11:6, 6:14). It is an opposite principle to that of law. God works in sovereign grace by the redemptive work of Jesus Christ, the Son of Man. This is where the righteousness of God would be manifested, in the gospel of Jesus Christ. "...He has appeared to put away sin by the sacrifice of Himself." God calls, yet not another earthly people, but a heavenly people by a heavenly calling. God's counsels concerning this new calling were before the foundation of the world, yet they remained hidden and contained in His very own well-kept mystery. The mystery of God is now revealed by the Holy Spirit sent down, after the glorifying of the Son of Man.

Responsibility in man as a biblical principle is of great importance. In the history of man as told by Scripture, when this principle is looked at or tested, it always comes to a constant and sure result -- failure. Man failed in the garden, eating the forbidden fruit. Man failed at the base of Sinai, making the golden idol. Also the kings beginning with Saul had immediate failure. Through Samuel, God warns Israel of the consequences of their fleshly desire, but to no avail (I Sam. 8:6-9:2). Israel wanted to be like the other Gentile nations, while God wanted Israel set apart and distinct. The prophets fail beginning with the rejection of Samuel as prophet and judge (I Sam. 8:7-8). The priesthood failed, first in the sons of Aaron, and finally in the sons of Eli. The prophets fail in Baal and Ashtoreth, and the Gentiles in Nebuchadnezzar, the first civil world government head. The pattern remained the same -- responsibility always ending in failure, at least with man in the flesh and in Adam.

If we look at responsibility of man before God as a category, there are a number of similar ideas that would fall under such a heading. There is disobedience in the garden, lawlessness without the law, transgressors of the law when man has the law, and unrighteous abuse of power by Hebrew kings or Gentile heads and rulers. Also we must include all man's works as in Adam and the flesh. This is all his righteousness as filthy rags before God (Is. 64:6). All men will be judged according to their works (Rev. 20:12-13, Rom.3:5-6). *Man's works are his sins.* The judging of man by his works carries the absolute certainty of condemnation, because they are his sins and must be judged accordingly by a holy God.

One more separate listing in this category of responsibility is that man's original failure resulted in a far-reaching defilement of creation and this earth (all of which the first Adam was responsible to govern and rule over, only ending up defiling it). We see in the religion of the Jews, the many washings and cleansings, external attempts in types and shadows to deal with this defilement.

When the subject of responsibility is taken up in Scripture the analogy is of God planting a vineyard and expecting good fruit (Isaiah 5:1-7, Matt. 21:33-34). As I have said previously, when God tested man in responsibility, He came to Israel looking for fruit on the fig tree. When He found no fruit He cursed it, putting an end to the testing. In some of the parables about the kingdom of heaven and this present age, failure in responsibility is spoken of as men sleeping (Matt. 13:25), virgins sleeping (Matt. 25:5), or wicked and lazy servants (Matt. 25:26). This later are those who beat their fellow servants and eat and drink with the drunkards (Matt. 24:49).

The Principle of Responsibility, the Spoiled Crop in the Field, and Candlesticks

In the parable of the wheat and tares we saw that while men slept, Satan came in and sowed tares. As we said, this is failure and God holds men responsible for evil coming in while they sleep. But there is another aspect of responsibility that we can garner from the symbols here and the passing of the age. It involves the spoiled crop in the field. This crop represents all of professing Christendom. As professing the name of Jesus Christ and regardless of whether being a wheat or tare, all of it together corporately, as one crop, is responsible before God. And the responsibility associated with professing the name of Christ is to be a light shining to this world of darkness (Matt. 5:14-15, Phil. 2:15). We see this accountability of the crop symbolized by the seven golden candlesticks in Revelation 1, in the midst of which the Son of Man walks. When we read Rev. 1:13-16 the Son of Man has the distinct character of judgment. He is there to judge the responsibility of the crop, to judge the light from the candlesticks.

This He does in Revelation 2, 3. These two chapters show a prophetic picture of the spoiled crop progressing through all the times of the Body of Christ on the earth. Please remember, the crop, as a corporate entity, is wheat and tares together, and represents all of professing Christendom. The body of Christ however, is just the wheat. The first three chapters of Revelation, I would think, should be a fascinating study for all believers. It is a prophetic history taking place now. Unfortunately, the details are complicated and symbolic; regardless, the subject matter should be quite intriguing for the Christian.

While Christ was in the world, He was the light of the world (John 9:5). But He told His disciples it was imperative for Him to go out of the world (John 16:5, 7). The short version is that He represents us at the right hand of God, and so, while we are on the earth, professing Christianity represents Christ to this world. Therefore, we are to be the light of God to this world. *In the parable of the virgins, all ten had candlesticks, regardless of whether they were wise or foolish (Matt. 25:1-4).* The entire crop of wheat and tares is responsible for the light of the golden candlestick. Now, if tares give no light for they have no oil, then the amount of light from the mixed crop is diminished. And as time goes on and the evil grows and worsens, as it always does, the light from the candlestick simply grows less and less. This is what we see in the prophetic progression of pictures of the crop in the field that the Son of Man judges in Revelations two and three -- this is what is happening in Christendom today.

God judges our Responsibility on the Cross – the Son of Man bears Sins and is made Sin

The testing of man in Adam and the presenting of Messiah to Israel clearly show the absolute failure of fallen man. The outcome of this failure in the counsels of God is that man in Adam is judged as lost. When God condemned the world, the Son of Man was lifted up on the cross (John 12:31-32). Represented in the cross are the height of man's hatred and enmity against God, and the full extent of man's failures in Adam. Man's animosity toward God is shown here;

John 15:23-25

"He who hates Me hates My Father also. If I had not done among them the works which no one else did, they would have no sin; but now they have seen and also hated both Me and My Father. But this happened that the word might be fulfilled which is written in their law, 'They hated Me without a cause.'"

There certainly was hatred towards Jesus. They gnashed their teeth at Him and plotted His death. They said, '...let us kill him and seize his inheritance,' as well as, 'We have no king but Caesar!' The hatred of man towards Christ is simply equated to the Father. And the Lord said of them in John 8, "You do the deeds of your father...You are of your father the devil, and the desires of your father you want to do." Israel legitimately represents all men in their hatred of Christ, and therefore of God. This enmity against God is brought to the cross, man providing the sins and the nails, hanging the Son of Man to the tree.

Man's failure in responsibility was brought to the cross as well. *This failure not only was proven by God, but then had to be judged by God.* The wages of sin is death, and the proof of this certainly was the cross on which the Son of Man died. Our responsibility, our righteousness as filthy rags in His sight, our works to be judged, our sins to be borne, and sin in the flesh, was all brought to the cross as the contributions of man in Adam.

The Cross is the Full Revelation of God's Love toward Us

If man brought these things, then the cross is also the revelation of what God brought as well. God so loved the world that He gave His Son. This was the pouring out of God's love for us, as we see here in Romans:

Rom. 5:5-8

"Now hope does not disappoint, because the love of God has been poured out in our hearts by the Holy Spirit who was given to us.

For when we were still without strength, in due time Christ died for the ungodly. For scarcely for a righteous man will one die; yet perhaps for a good man someone would even dare to die. But God demonstrates His own love toward us, in that while we were still sinners, Christ died for us."

The fullness of God's own love for us was shown when we were without strength (in the flesh), and when we were still sinners (in Adam). The depths of God's love fully met the hatred of man for Him on the cross. This was never revealed in the Law, not the love of God as demonstrated in Christ. The adulterous women brought before Jesus was spared, when the law would have rightly and justly condemned her to stoning. The love of God in Christ goes far beyond any revelation in the law. To the point, the law isn't at all the revelation of God's love for man. It is always the measure of what man should be before God. The law revealed what man's love for God must be, what man's love for his neighbor should be, and then demanded obedience (Matt. 22:36-40). And all there was for 'those of the works of the law' was a curse (judgment, condemnation, Gal. 3:10). This is not the revelation of God's love. All there is for man with the law (Jews), and man without the law (Gentiles), is a falling short of the glory of God (Rom. 3:19, 23). How is this the love of God, if, with the law man is still found to be without strength and a sinner? It is the cross, and only the cross, that is the epitome of the expression of God's love for us, and that as meeting the heights of man's hatred and rebellion against Him.

More Redemptive Truths Displayed in the Cross

There are more revelations and redemptive truths to be found in the cross of Christ, the Son of Man. The work of redemption was perfect and complete and fully satisfying to God, His Father. This is what is revealed in Romans;

Rom. 3:25-26

"...whom God set forth as a propitiation by His blood, through faith, to demonstrate His righteousness, because in His forbearance God had passed over the sins that were previously committed, to demonstrate at the present time His righteousness, that He might be just and the justifier of the one who has faith in Jesus."

Propitiation carries the idea of fully satisfying a debt by payment. What is propitiated is God. *His holy and righteous character is vindicated and fully satisfied by the shedding of Christ's blood.* By the cross, God has fully dealt with our sin and sins, and done so in such a way that He remains just – that is, He always remains true to Himself, in all His character and attributes. The Son of Man glorified God by means of the cross and His shed blood. This is the righteousness of God – God is fully and completely satisfied. His holiness and righteousness as to sin in man, and judgment of it, is maintained by how He rightly deals with it and puts it away, by the death of the Son of Man.

It is truly a wonderful meditation to think of the convergence of all these redemptive truths in the cross of Christ. In the title of the Son of Man, Jesus had certain objectives to accomplish.

1. There was the propitiating of sins (Heb. 2:17) in which He satisfied and glorified God. He was wounded for our transgressions, He was bruised for our iniquities, the chastisement of our peace was upon Him (Is. 53:3).

2. There was the overcoming of the power of Satan (Heb. 2:14) by His willingness to go down under the power of death without any sins of His own.

3. There is the entering into all our infirmities, temptations, and weaknesses (Heb. 2:18, 4:15-16).

This should fill the saint with joy and confidence in Christ, and lead to rejoicing in the full knowledge of our steadfast hope of glory with Him (Heb. 2:10). These understandings are the result of the Son of God, as the Son of Man, coming into the world. God had prepared a body for Him; in the volume of the book it is written of Him, He came to do Your will, O God (Heb. 10:5-10). The more we look at the cross, the more we realize that God could not be glorified any other way.

The Gospel of the Son of Man – the One True Gospel that Paul Preached

Switching gears somewhat, let us consider other distinctions and differences found in God's Word that help to divide the truth. The one true gospel is made a major point of emphasis by the Spirit in Galatians. After the introduction of the letter (Gal. 1:1-5) we see right away Paul marveling and questioning the corruption of the true gospel among them (Gal. 1:6-10). But look how the Spirit of God impresses upon the reader the distinctions of this gospel.

1. In verse 6 it is a turning to a different gospel.

2. In verse 7 it actually isn't a different gospel, but a perversion of the one true gospel.

3. In verse 8 the true gospel is the one Paul preached to the Galatians originally. If he comes again to them with any changes or additions or something different, or even an angelic being from the presence of God Himself preaching something different, they are pronounced accursed.

4. In verse 9, the charge of being accursed for preaching a different gospel is repeated, a means of communicating emphasis (similar to Jesus saying, "Verily, verily...").

5. In verses 11, 12 the gospel Paul preached absolutely did not come from men, not from the twelve in any way, but was a direct revelation given to him by Jesus Christ (Acts 9:3-9, II Cor. 12:1-7). He did not immediately confer with flesh and blood (v. 16), nor did he come under the influence of those who were apostles before him (v.17).

These are all clear distinctions being made by the Spirit concerning the true gospel. More is seen further on in Galatians;

Gal. 3:16

"But to Abraham were the promises addressed, and to his seed: he does not say, And to seeds, as of many; but as of one, And to thy seed; which is Christ."

There are profound differences between the promises God made to Abraham's many seeds, his physical descendants, and the covenant of promise confirmed in his one Seed, who is Christ. In Christ are the spiritual seeds of Abraham, by faith his spiritual children (Gal. 3:7) and also called the sons of God (Gal. 3:26, 4:5-7). Christ, in resurrection glory, is the firstborn (from the dead) among many brethren (Rom. 8:29).

Sarah and Hagar – Children of Promise and Children of Bondage

In chapter four of Galatians there is another clear distinction made by the Spirit of God between these two groups -- the physical seeds and the spiritual seeds. And the importance of the differences is brought home in Gal. 4:21-31, were two types are used in comparison with each other:

Abraham: Galatians 4:21-31

Hagar, the bondwoman (v.22)	Sarah, the freewoman (v.22)
Ishmael, the slave son (v.22) – *the type*	Isaac, the free son (v.22) – *the type*
According to the flesh (v.23)	According to promise (v.23)
From Mt. Sinai – covenant of Moses, the law (v.24) – Judaism, leads to bondage	Covenant of promise in one Seed, which is Christ (v.24) – Christianity, leads to liberty, specifically from Judaism – Gal. 5:1
Earthly Jerusalem (in Paul's day, v.25)	Jerusalem above (heavenly) (v.26)
Children of slavery (the Jews) (v.25), *the fulfillment of the type*	Children of Promise (N.T. believers) (v.28), *the fulfillment of the type*
Born according to the flesh (the Jews, the nation of Israel) (v.29)	Born according to the Spirit (believer/ Body of Christ, v.29)
The children in bondage persecute the children of the Spirit (v.29)	Cast out the bondwoman and her son, they will not be heirs of God as His sons (v.30)

The differences between the two columns above are obvious and striking. It is the Spirit of God using the types in comparison and teaching the lesson. The children of promise are clearly distinguished from the children of bondage. The believer's understanding of these differences and maintaining them in our faith and doctrine is paramount to our Christian liberty (Gal. 5:1). This liberty is given up through the Judaizing of the believer's walk in this world. These are important distinctions or why would the Spirit bother? Again, in Galatians:

Gal. 5:1

"Stand fast therefore in the liberty by which Christ has made us free and do not be entangled again with a yoke of bondage."

The yoke of bondage not to be entangled with is Judaism, the Law of Moses. As I said previously, not one vestige of Judaism should be mixed in with the believers' faith and practice. This is basically the whole message of this epistle to the Galatians. To show this conclusively, and since we've been led in this direction, we can easily see this important truth in other Scriptures.

What reason did God have for giving the Law?

Gal. 3:19

"What purpose then does the law serve? It was added because of transgressions, till the Seed should come to whom the promise was made;"

Here we are looking for God's thoughts, intentions and reasons that will define for us the true purpose of God giving the law – it was because of transgressions. By the giving of the law to Israel, their committing of sins would no longer be known as lawlessness, but now as transgressions of the law. It tells us in Rom. 5:20 that sin abounded by producing many transgressions as a result of the law being given. *More than simply revealing sins, the law exposed the sin nature in man inherited from Adam* (Rom. 5:12, 7:7-8). *The law exposed the presence of sin in the flesh.* From the beginning death came in – the wages of the sin nature (Rom. 6:23, 7:10-13). The condemnation of God was attached to sins (Rom. 5:16, 18). This is why the law was a ministration of death and condemnation (II Cor. 3:6-9).

Israel Thought the Law Would Produce Righteousness and Life

Many more New Testament scriptures could be brought in as further proofs. But how did man actually see the purpose of the giving of the law by God? How did man in the flesh reason in his mind the intentions of God? Rom. 10:1-5 and Phil. 3:9 answer this question. Israel saw God giving the law to them as a means of producing life and righteousness. God says death and condemnation, while man reasons life and righteousness. It shouldn't be hard for anyone to see the disconnection. It is not merely a mistake, but an error in man's reasoning of monumental proportions. This is man in the flesh, man in Adam, and he reasons and perverts the thoughts and purposes of God.

There is another thought worth entertaining concerning Gal. 3:19, which we discussed earlier. It says the law was added...until the Seed should come... Well, I think we all know that the Seed has already come. If something was added for a certain period of time until another event, the coming of the true Seed, and that period of time is obviously ended, then why is the addition allowed to continue? And further, when the Seed came He brought with Himself the implementation of the covenant of promise -- that which was confirmed in Him previously. This raises a few questions. How can two covenants from God exist at the same time for the same people? If the covenant of law continues on, once the Seed has come with His covenant of promise and grace, how is it not considered an addition and a violation of the principles addressed in Gal. 3:15-17? We answer this question in a later chapter on covenants and dispensations – Israel, as a nation, never obtained the covenant of promise given to Abraham.

The Confidences of the Flesh

Man in the flesh and in Adam is all about having confidences in the flesh. For Paul these confidences were what his former life in the religion of the Jews represented. In Phil. 3:4-6 these confidences are detailed.

Phil. 3:4-6

"...though I also might have confidence in the flesh. If anyone else thinks he may have confidence in the flesh, I more so: circumcised the eighth day, of the stock of Israel, of the tribe of Benjamin, a Hebrew of the Hebrews;

concerning the law, a Pharisee; concerning zeal, persecuting the church; concerning the righteousness which is in the law, blameless."

This is his former life in Judaism before his life in Christ. It is quite impressive, that is, to man in the flesh and the carnal mind. But it isn't impressive to God in the least, as verses 7-9 plainly point out. So when Paul finds himself in Christ by the sovereign work and grace of God (Acts 9:1-19), the Spirit has Paul discard and cast out all vestige of his former religion, as all things counted as loss and, get this, simply rubbish.

Judaism is for man in the Flesh, a man in Adam, and man of the Earth

Judaism is the religion given by God to man in Adam, man in the flesh. We've already discussed God's reasons for giving it -- a testing, if you will, of man in Adam, to see if he could be responsible in the flesh to bear fruit before God and to see if man in the flesh could have a relationship with God. This all was proven impossible. God came to the fig tree desiring fruit and found none, only leaves (the outward show of the flesh). And what was said? "Let no fruit grow on you ever again." God was finished with testing man in the flesh, he could not be responsible, and he could not bear fruit (Matt. 21:18-19, 33-44). And at that time Jesus says in John 12:31, "Now is the judgment of this world..." Why now? Because God was finished with the world and He judged it.

Judaism is the religion of the earth, given to man in the flesh, and the religion of the earthly calling in God. Christianity isn't any of these things. Here in Phil. 3:3 as describing the believer, "...we are the circumcision, who worship God in the Spirit..." In John 4:20-24, Jesus connects Judaism with the earth in its worship in a permanent temple in Jerusalem and the patriarchs' worship on a mountain in Samaria (that which preceded Judaism). This He *contrasts* with the new worship. He would be the source and life of worship of the Father in spirit and truth by true worshipers. This thought is connected with Christ in the title of Son of Man. A permanent temple in Jerusalem and the earthly worship and religion of the Jews is connected with

Christ in the title of Messiah. And Jesus says in verse 23, the hour is coming, and now is (presently), for the new kind of worshipers that the Father is seeking.

I cannot overemphasize these two words that Jesus used in contrasting Christianity with Judaism -- spirit and truth (John 4:23). Believers alone worship God in the Spirit, because God is Spirit, and only true worship of God is done in the Spirit. We are talking about true worship as revealed in Scripture and by the Lord's very own words. Further, the believer is not in the flesh (as all unbelievers happen to be) but in the Spirit (Rom. 8:9). The Christian alone, being in the Spirit, can offer true worship of God, who is Spirit. Then there is the other word -- truth. Only Christianity is true worship of God, according to who and what God is, and has revealed concerning Himself. So we can conclude that Judaism is not true worship of God as He desires (Heb. 10:5-9), and never could be described as worship of God in spirit and truth. What we should also be able to conclude -- Judaism is set aside by God, if God was seeking something different.

The Judaizing of the Christian faith was a serious problem in the early church. Paul fought this corruption and evil influence at every turn. Its corruption took in many in the early church. The Galatians fell under this deception as we have seen, but this wasn't the first of it. It is clearly present in Acts 15 when it says at Antioch that certain men came down from Judea, teaching... At that time the Lord works by the Spirit through Paul and Peter to save the church from splitting into separate Jewish and Gentile bodies. But the problem didn't go away. And then later on, we see in Gal. 2:11-16 that Peter, Barnabas, and others of the Jews are swept up in this corruption and play the hypocrite, refusing to eat with the Gentile believers at Antioch. This leaven would not go away, but would take up roots and branch out, even early in the apostolic period.

The Leaven Continues to Spread

What had a corrupting presence working at the beginning of the age will only become a greater presence of evil towards the end of this period. *Evil, as a Biblical principle, only ripens and worsens through the passage of time.* The Judaizing of the Christian faith was one of the mysteries of lawlessness in the church world already at work in Paul's time (II Thess. 2:7). It was secret, hidden, subtle and deceptive. The three measures of meal, in the end, become all leavened (Matt.13:33). In the latter days, it will be so, but worse. How will it be secretive and hidden? Well, it will not be as obvious as circumcision in the flesh. But rather the mixing of the heavenly and earthly calling, the blurring of any distinction between the two, in the teachings and doctrines of the Christian faith, done unwittingly and naively by its ministers.

Romanism is a well- established pattern of the Judaizing of the Christian faith that has been in the church world for 1500 years. I'm sure there have been and continue to be many different forms and offshoots of this influence in Protestantism. But I'm not referring here to the obviousness of Romanism, although that has been firmly established in professing Christianity for a long time. What I refer to is a less obvious and more subtle Judaizing that has already inundated Evangelical Christianity. How has this happened? How was Satan able to come in secretly and work corruption? Satan sows tares because man failed in his responsibility. Satan comes in because men slept;

Matt. 13:25

"...but while men slept, his enemy came and sowed tares among the wheat and went his way. But when the grain had sprouted and produced a crop, then the tares also appeared."

We have already discussed the details of this parable. The understanding of it and its proper interpretation, as we know, is of the upmost importance for all believers. I simply point out this portion again to the reader. We are looking at professing Christianity, we see how evil comes in, and that there is failure in responsibility. Judaizing of the Christian faith and truths is an evil corrupting in Christianity today. And please understand this point – it is not just the Judaizing of truth by adding to Christ, who should stand alone, in justification by faith for the believer. It is the Judaizing of the Christian walk. It is the compromising of the truth that Christ alone is all you'll ever need as a believer, in your walk upon this earth. Peter and Barnabas were well- established Christians. It was their walk that they allowed to be Judaized.

It is the mixing, and as a result, the confusing of these two titles of Christ, that leads to so much misunderstanding of Scripture. Our failure to distinguish between the two, and failure to clearly understand how each is fulfilled in scripture, will continue to result in many misleading teachings. We see this lack of understanding in many of man's devised systems of doctrine. When you engage in the spiritualizing of Scripture, by making the body of Christ into earthly Israel, and no longer distinguish between the two, you give yourself carte blanche in teaching doctrine. This is a Judaizing of the Christian faith.

The spiritualizing is done to maintain man's systems of doctrine. It leads to the mixing of Israel with the church in scriptures, and then the mixing of the promises spoken to Israel with those of the church. There arises a blurring of the distinction between the heavenly calling of the church and the earthly calling of Israel. Worse, there is often a total lack of acknowledging the existence of the heavenly calling. And as so often we see, it drags the church back down to the earth. The church is then taught the teachings and instruction intended for Israel, and there is a broad mixing of the two distinct covenants. Confusion reigns or the simple minded are placated. It further leads to placing the body of Christ into the prophetic statements addressed to Israel, and connects it with this earth and world.

Why the Church is never the Proper Subject of Prophecy

You do not see teaching or prophetic statements concerning the church in the Old Testament, the main body of prophetic scripture. This is for two main reasons as previously discussed. The church is not of the earth and not of the world. Israel is of the earth and of the world. *The church's calling is heavenly; but prophecy concerns the events that happen on the earth, and of the world.*

The second reason comes directly from the first. The church, it's existence, it's nature and character, it's doctrine and calling, is all part of God's mystery (Eph.3:2-11, Col.1:24-27). This was hidden from the prophets of old, now revealed through Paul's revelation (II Cor.12:1-4, 7) and teachings. A dispensation of grace and truth given to Paul (Eph. 3:2, Col. 1:25), and he was given responsibility to unveil this mystery...the church, the body of the exalted Man, Christ Jesus, in glory (Eph. 1:22-23).

In the absence of having a better way of closing this chapter, I mention some study points of interest in Scripture that the believer may want to search out further than I've been able to do in this writing. Four examples are given, each showing how the carnality of the human mind in the flesh (in Adam), or the untrained spiritual mind, *tends to see the opposite of what God actually intends and His truth teaches.*

1.) Israel and the law (Rom. 9:30-10:5), is it for life or for death? The carnal mind says life. Israel, having the mind of the flesh, agrees it is for life and righteousness for their people. However the Scriptures say the opposite; that it is for death and condemnation (II Cor. 3:7, 9).

2.) Grace (its proper understanding through the Scriptures) and its actual deliverance of the believer from sin vs. the carnal mind mistaking the teaching of grace as a license to sin (Rom. 6)

3.) The choice of God in sovereignty – we see it as evil in God (Rom. 9:14) when really it is the choice of God in supreme special love (Eph. 1:3-6, Rom. 9:23-24, 8:29-32) because of the reality of sin and man being lost (John 8:34, Rom. 6:15-22, 8:7-8, 3:9-19, Eph. 2:1, 3, 5). [This topic we touched on in just a few paragraphs]

4.) Jesus Christ, His appearing and His kingdom through judgment in righteousness (Isaiah 5:16) vs. Kingdom now doctrines and philosophies and associated grandiose ideas about the success of preaching the gospel and its effects on changing the world. [This was somewhat explained in this chapter, but certainly a topic worth further study]

2 Timothy 1:9-10

"...who has saved us and called us with a holy calling, not according to our works, but according to His own purpose and grace which was given to us in Christ Jesus before time began, but has now been revealed by the appearing of our Savior Jesus Christ, who has abolished death and brought life and immortality to light through the gospel,"

I pray that the God of our Lord Jesus Christ, the Father of glory, may give to you the spirit of wisdom and revelation in the knowledge of Him, the eyes of your understanding being enlightened; that you may know what is the hope of His calling, and what are the riches of the glory of His inheritance in the saints (Eph. 1:17-18), -- God's blessings to you.

Chapter 16:

The Real Book of Acts

n a previous chapter I remarked that the gospel of the glory of Christ was the gospel that Paul preached. Understanding now why the gospel is called this, I want to bring out in greater light the history of its development in the book of Acts and its greatest connection with the apostle Paul. The conversion of Saul is simply a marvelous story of God's sovereign grace and glory in every way. His conversion experience fully shows forth the definitive choice of God as Sovereign. It was a choice absolutely apart from the will of the flesh, or the will of man (John 1:12-13). Saul's experience demonstrates, in a sense, the range and scope of God's choice, and becomes an example of the truth of God's ways for all believers.

I Timothy 1:11-16

"...according to the glorious gospel of the blessed God which was committed to my trust. And I thank Christ Jesus our Lord who has enabled me, because He counted me faithful, putting me into the ministry, although I was formerly a blasphemer, a persecutor, and an insolent man; but I obtained mercy because I did it ignorantly in unbelief. And the grace of our Lord was exceedingly abundant, with faith and love which are in Christ Jesus. This is a faithful saying and worthy of all acceptance, that Christ Jesus came into the world to save sinners, of whom I am chief. However, for this reason I

obtained mercy, that in me first Jesus Christ might show all longsuffering, as a pattern to those who are going to believe on Him for everlasting life."

Paul's conversion is a pattern and example for all. The range I refer to is exemplified by the differences between what might be thought of Paul as an unbeliever then as a believer. First, what you see in his former life before he met Christ on the road to Damascus:

The Confidence of the Flesh

Philippians 3:4-6

"...though I also might have confidence in the flesh. If anyone else thinks he may have confidence in the flesh, I more so: circumcised the eighth day, of the stock of Israel, of the tribe of Benjamin, a Hebrew of the Hebrews; concerning the law, a Pharisee; concerning zeal, persecuting the church; concerning the righteousness which is in the law, blameless."

Paul had thought highly of his own natural descent and accomplishments in the religion of the Jews. This gives you an idea of what Paul would have gloried in before Christ intervened. But his birth, his works, and the religion itself was all the product of the flesh, the natural man. I am convinced that Paul, at the time and in his thinking and conscience, felt he lived a life very pleasing and of great service to God. He most likely thought his persecution of believers, putting them in chains and responsible for their deaths, was religious service to God (John 16:2-3). It was all in the flesh and offensive to God.

After Paul was saved, he had a more enlightened view of his former life, and his testimony became quite different. He calls himself formerly a blasphemer, a persecutor, and a violently arrogant man. By his own witness he was the greatest of sinners. Nevertheless, Paul understood and realized the working of God, saying,

1 Corinthians 15:9-10

"For I am the least of the apostles, who am not worthy to be called an apostle, because I persecuted the church of God. But by the grace of God I am what I am, and His grace toward me was not in vain; but I labored

more abundantly than they all, yet not I, but the grace of God which was with me."

The Apostle of the Destruction of Christ becomes the Apostle of the Sovereign Grace of God

Paul was the enemy of the name of Jesus Christ and this new sect of Judaism called "the Way." He imprisoned and murdered many disciples, breathing out hatred and threats. He was the greatest of sinners against God right up to the point outside Damascus where he saw the glory. As a consequence, Paul knew he was not deserving of anything, but by the sovereign choice of God he was what he was, chosen and saved. And even in his labors for Christ he understood, saying, "Yet not I, but the grace of God working in me." Paul simply was a chosen instrument of God (Acts 9:15). He is now the apostle of the sovereign grace of God, which was his personal experience. Paul also, by experience, is the apostle of the glory of Christ, as being an eye-witness of His heavenly glory. Paul's gospel that he would preach is the gospel as he received it. It is not of man or from men, but by direct revelation from Christ in glory. The ministry of this apostle and the gospel he preached was directly related to his personal experience with Christ.

Galatians 1:11-17

"But I make known to you, brethren, that the gospel which was preached by me is not according to man. For I neither received it from man, nor was I taught it, but it came through the revelation of Jesus Christ.

For you have heard of my former conduct in Judaism, how I persecuted the church of God beyond measure and tried to destroy it. And I advanced in Judaism beyond many of my contemporaries in my own nation, being more exceedingly zealous for the traditions of my fathers.

But when it pleased God, who separated me from my mother's womb and called me through His grace, to reveal His Son in me, that I might preach Him among the Gentiles, I did not immediately confer with flesh and blood, nor did I go up to Jerusalem to those who were apostles before me; but I went to Arabia, and returned again to Damascus."

Paul becomes the apostle of the glory of Christ by virtue of seeing Christ in glory. He receives the gospel he preaches by direct revelation from Christ in glory. He makes the point that he did not receive anything from another man, especially the other apostles in Jerusalem. Paul's gospel is the gospel of the glory of Christ (II Cor. 3:18, 4:4-7).

Apostles Testify to what they are Eye-Witnesses of

What we find is that this is true of the other apostles. Their testimony was based on their personal experience with Christ. The other twelve certainly were chosen vessels as well (John 15:16, 19), and so, had personal knowledge of the sovereign grace of God in the gospel of Christ. But there was a distinction in their testimony from that of Paul's. This difference may be seen in John's gospel when Jesus is speaking of the Comforter.

John 15:26-27

"But when the Helper comes, whom I shall send to you from the Father, the Spirit of truth who proceeds from the Father, He will testify of Me. And you also will bear witness, because you have been with Me from the beginning."

Paul could have no part in this last verse, for he was not with Christ from the beginning, nor at any time did he know Christ in the flesh. His experience was seeing the Son of Man in heavenly glory. But the twelve certainly did have this distinction and difference in their experience, they walked with a Christ in the flesh from the beginning and they were witnesses to His resurrection. John and Peter give a certain emphasis concerning their testimony here:

1 John 1:1-3

"That which was from the beginning, which we have heard, which we have seen with our eyes, which we have looked upon, and our hands have handled, concerning the Word of life — the life was manifested, and we have seen, and bear witness, and declare to you that eternal life which was with the Father and was manifested to us — that which we have seen and

heard we declare to you, that you also may have fellowship with us; and truly our fellowship is with the Father and with His Son Jesus Christ."

2 Peter 1:16-18

"For we did not follow cunningly devised fables when we made known to you the power and coming of our Lord Jesus Christ, but were eyewitnesses of His majesty. For He received from God the Father honor and glory when such a voice came to Him from the Excellent Glory: "This is My beloved Son, in whom I am well pleased." And we heard this voice which came from heaven when we were with Him on the holy mountain."

The Testimony of the Twelve – a Christ in the Flesh and a Christ raised from the Dead

The twelve would bear witness to all that they saw and touched, as eyewitnesses of Christ in the flesh and then raised from the dead. After the resurrection, Christ appeared to them showing them His hands and His feet, saying, "Handle Me and see, for a spirit does not have flesh and bones as you see I have." He adds, "Have you any food here?" They gave Him a fish and honeycomb and He ate in their presence (Luke 24:36-45). They would bear witness of everything up to the time He was taken up from them into the cloud (Acts 1:9) and they lost sight of Him. After the Spirit was given on the day of Pentecost the testimony of Peter by the Spirit was according to their experience. It was the Man, Jesus of Nazareth, whom they walked with on this earth, raised up from the dead by the power of God (Acts 2:22-24, 3:15, 26);

Acts 2:32

"This Jesus God has raised up, of which we are all witnesses."

Acts 4:8-12

"Then Peter, filled with the Holy Spirit, said to them, "Rulers of the people and elders of Israel: If we this day are judged for a good deed done to a helpless man, by what means he has been made well, let it be known to you all, and to all the people of Israel, that by the name of Jesus Christ of Nazareth, whom you crucified, whom God raised from the dead, by

Him this man stands here before you whole. This is the 'stone which was rejected by you builders, which has become the chief cornerstone.' Nor is there salvation in any other, for there is no other name under heaven given among men by which we must be saved."

Acts 10:36-41

"The word which God sent to the children of Israel, preaching peace through Jesus Christ—He is Lord of all— 37 that word you know, which was proclaimed throughout all Judea, and began from Galilee after the baptism which John preached: 38 how God anointed Jesus of Nazareth with the Holy Spirit and with power, who went about doing good and healing all who were oppressed by the devil, for God was with Him. 39 And we are witnesses of all things which He did both in the land of the Jews and in Jerusalem, whom they killed by hanging on a tree. 40 Him God raised up on the third day, and showed Him openly, 41 not to all the people, but to witnesses chosen before by God, even to us who ate and drank with Him after He arose from the dead."

Jesus of Nazareth is always a reference to Christ as the Son of Man. As man He came as Jesus from this town in Galilee. The testimony was always related as such and according to their experience. In this last reference from Acts above, when Peter was sent by the Holy Spirit to Cornelius' household, he remarks that they were eyewitnesses to all the things Jesus did in the flesh. But further, he says that after Jesus was raised up, he was one of the few witnesses who ate and drank with Him. Clearly, the apostles were to testify of a Christ in the flesh and a Christ raised from the dead.

Paul's Testimony – a Christ in Glory

Paul's experience however is different than the twelve. As an apostle he too was an eyewitness, just from a different viewpoint. Paul's testimony starts where the twelve leave off, they losing sight of the risen Christ in the cloud. Paul only sees and knows Jesus Christ in heavenly glory.

Acts 9:3-6

"As he journeyed he came near Damascus, and suddenly a light shone around him from heaven. Then he fell to the ground, and heard a voice saying to him, "Saul, Saul, why are you persecuting Me?"

And he said, "Who are You, Lord?"

Then the Lord said, "I am Jesus, whom you are persecuting. It is hard for you to kick against the goads."

So he, trembling and astonished, said, "Lord, what do You want me to do?"

Then the Lord said to him, "Arise and go into the city, and you will be told what you must do."

The Gospel of the Glory

It isn't any wonder that Paul would say, by the inspiration of the Spirit, we know Christ no longer according to the flesh (2 Cor. 5:16). His would be the preaching of the gospel of the glory of God in the face of Jesus Christ (2 Cor. 4:4-6). The revelations received by him (2 Cor. 12:1, 7), the dispensation of grace given to him (Eph. 3:1-6), the filling up of the word of God (Col. 1:25), the unfolding of the mysteries of God (Eph. 3:3-4), and the doctrines of the body of Christ, all are part and parcel of his preaching this gospel of the glorified Son of Man.

When we read the first two chapters of Galatians we see Paul defend the legitimacy of his apostleship and gospel. In this defense, the Spirit makes clear the uniqueness of Paul's calling and ministry apart from that of Peter and the other eleven. The twelve in Jerusalem, among whom Peter and John were prominent, had an apostleship to the circumcised (the Jews), while Paul had one effective toward the uncircumcised (the Gentiles, Gal. 2:7-9). God had separated Paul from the twelve, so as not to come under their direct influence and authority, because of the importance of the work he was to do. God would have Paul independent from the others, so that He could fashion Paul as He pleased, a sovereign work of God, and not by the hands of men (Gal. 1:1).

Even when Saul was still breathing threats and murder against the disciples, we see the providential hand of God drawing him away from Jerusalem and the twelve located there (Acts 9:1-2). Upon his conversion he is blinded by the glory for three days, a time no doubt of introspection concerning the realities of his former life in Judaism and his now discovered enmity against God (Acts 9:9). God is doing all this work. The gospel Paul preached he never heard from another man, nor was he taught it, but he received it by direct revelation from Jesus Christ (Gal. 1:11-12). Now how special is this? Again it is the Sovereign God at work, and absolutely nothing of the product of the hands of flesh (also compare Eph. 2: 11 with Col. 2:11 and Phil. 3:3). Upon Paul's conversion he did not immediately confer with flesh and blood, nor did he go up to Jerusalem to those who were apostles before him (Gal. 1:16-17). The Spirit keeps him for three years in Arabia and Damascus. He only spends fifteen days with Peter in Jerusalem and then fourteen years away from Jerusalem in ministry to the Gentiles (Gal. 1:18-2:1).

The Testimony of the Spirit

Above we quoted from John's gospel where Jesus said, when the Comforter came, He would testify of Me (John 15:26). This testimony is the same principle as that of the apostles and Paul. The Spirit would testify of all He saw and heard. This, I believe, is the sense of the following passage.

John 16:12-15

"I still have many things to say to you, but you cannot bear them now. However, when He, the Spirit of truth, has come, He will guide you into all truth; for He will not speak on His own authority, but whatever He hears He will speak; and He will tell you things to come. He will glorify Me, for He will take of what is Mine and declare it to you. All things that the Father has are Mine. Therefore I said that He will take of Mine and declare it to you."

There is a deeper understanding implied in this passage than just the truth that the Spirit sent would testify of Christ. All things that the Father has are given to Jesus Christ. It is the ministry of the Holy Spirit to reveal these things to the believer. Why? What is the importance? Because in that day, after Christ had gone back to the Father and the Spirit was sent, the believer would have an association and union with Christ. We are sealed by the Spirit, we are sons of God. We are brethren with Him. It is His God and our God. It is His Father and our Father (John 20:17). We are His body. All things of the Father's are the Son's. By the redemptive work of the Son as the Son of Man, there are many more sons of God. These sons are co-heirs with Christ of all things. Jesus now has all things as the Son of Man glorified, and by His work the believer has been brought into the same position as Christ. This is why he says there are still many things remaining to tell them but they could not bear them now. These things would have to wait for the Spirit to reveal (John 16:7, 25).

The Story of the Book of Acts

It is interesting and exciting when the Spirit of God begins to enlighten and instruct the believer as to the truths of God in His counsels and ways. We are privileged to apprehend the purpose and means by which God sovereignly works His plans. Allow me to share a bit of a story here that I believe is given by the understanding of the Spirit. At the end you may disagree with my conclusions, but at the least it is an interesting perspective. I will go through it quickly without over- elaborating (as is my nature) various points, for the sake of time and space.

The Sin against the Son of Man

On the cross Jesus prayed, "Father, forgive them, for they do not know what they do." Do you think His request was granted? Absolutely it was. This was the forgiving of the nation of Israel for their sin against the Son of Man (Matt. 12:32, Luke 12:10). They nailed Him to the cross, but Jesus interceded for them. On the day of Pentecost the Holy Spirit was sent to testify of the Son of Man now raised from the dead (John 15:26). This testimony of the Holy Spirit would be

Israel's last chance before certain judgment on the nation. Peter and the eleven with him, under the power of the Spirit, preached to the house of Israel. This was their particular understanding – that if Israel listened, realizing they had crucified their own Messiah, repented of their sins and were baptized, that God would send Christ back to the nation. This would set the stage for the restoration of Israel and the Messianic kingdom. This perspective was on the hearts and minds of the disciples in the early history of the book of Acts, as we can see in the following passage:

Acts 1:6

"Therefore, when they had come together, they asked Him, saying, "Lord, will You at this time restore the kingdom to Israel?"

The disciples still expected the Lord to bring about the visible Messianic kingdom in Israel, the throwing off of the chains of the rule of the Roman Gentiles. Witnessing a resurrected Lord, they believed this had to be the time when God would fulfill all the promises and expected hopes of the nation. Note here that the Lord never tells them that the prophecies and promises are not true, nor that their desires were misplaced, but only that the times and seasons of this restoration do not concern them. This specific timing was solely in the Father's hands. The kingdom will certainly be restored to Israel, we simply do not know when. They knew that Jesus had promised the coming of the Comforter upon His departure from them. They were instructed to wait in Jerusalem for this. He then is taken up into the cloud out of their sight. The eleven would be eyewitnesses of the Lord, from the beginning up to this point (John 15:27).

Acts 2:22-24

"Men of Israel, hear these words: Jesus of Nazareth, a Man attested by God to you by miracles, wonders, and signs which God did through Him in your midst, as you yourselves also know— Him, being delivered by the determined purpose and foreknowledge of God, you have taken by lawless hands, have crucified, and put to death; whom God raised up, having loosed the pains of death, because it was not possible that He should be held by it."

By the Spirit, Peter's message on the day of Pentecost was to Israel concerning the Son of Man raised from the dead. Further on in his preaching he says, "Therefore let all the house of Israel know assuredly that God has made this Jesus, whom you crucified, both Lord and Christ." The nation was certainly being addressed (Acts 2:36). What is so remarkable is how the Spirit has Peter quoting the prophet Joel.

The Day of Pentecost and the Jewish Prophecy by the Prophet Joel

Acts 2:16-21

"But this is what was spoken by the prophet Joel:

'And it shall come to pass in the last days, says God,
That I will pour out of My Spirit on all flesh;
Your sons and your daughters shall prophesy,
Your young men shall see visions,
Your old men shall dream dreams.
And on My menservants and on My maidservants
I will pour out My Spirit in those days;
And they shall prophesy.
I will show wonders in heaven above
And signs in the earth beneath:
Blood and fire and vapor of smoke.
The sun shall be turned into darkness,
And the moon into blood,
Before the coming of the great and awesome day of the Lord.
And it shall come to pass
That whoever calls on the name of the Lord
Shall be saved.'"

This prophecy specifically speaks of the Spirit being poured out on the Jewish remnant in the last days before Jesus Christ returns as their Messiah – before the great and terrible day of the Lord (v. 20). The pouring out of the Spirit on Pentecost can only be seen as a partial fulfillment of Joel's prophecy. Reading the words of the prophecy should make this overwhelming clear. Pentecost is a precursor and foreshadowing of *the real and complete fulfillment* of these words that will take place before that awesome day. The fulfillment is yet future, of which, in a certain sense, this was only a shadow or type. But our understanding of this today is by using hindsight, which is of great advantage to us. Obviously, this advantage wasn't available to the disciples.

Now it is true that Pentecost is more than just a shadow. It is also the Comforter sent to live in believers, and unbeknown to the disciples then, the Holy Spirit on earth gathering the body of Christ (the beginnings of the church). But what we are addressing still remains, from the perspective of the nation of Israel and these present disciples – in the upper room there was a Jewish remnant on which the Spirit was poured out. This upper room remnant was still expecting and looking for a Messianic kingdom in Israel. This thought was still a possibility for the nation, albeit a remote one. Regardless, all the elements of the prophecy were present on the day of Pentecost for its fulfillment. If Israel did not repent, which they didn't, then Pentecost would become a foreshadowing of a future event in prophecy that Joel is actually speaking of. Allow me to point out a few more insights that I believe the Spirit leads us into here.

Joel's Prophecy – the Coming of Messiah and a Jewish Remnant

Concerning the use of this Jewish prophecy, was Peter making a mistake? Certainly not! He is inspired by the Spirit of God in all he is saying. "But this is what was spoken by the prophet Joel," he says. There is no mistake here, the Spirit is leading him. I believe we just have to admit that Joel's words, as an Old Testament prophet to Israel, are spoken directly to Israel. They are not words spoken to Gentiles. The great subject of all of prophecy is Israel, God's government of the earth and His judgments that will bring this back into place. We see all this in the words quoted from the prophet. The prophecy is for Israel and Peter is preaching to Israel. And it is Israel's last chance.

How then is the Spirit not guilty of making a mistake according to the words of the prophecy? It is because the Spirit was poured out on one hundred and twenty or so disciples in the upper room. All in the room were of Jewish decent, and in a certain important sense represented a Jewish remnant at the time (Rom. 11:5). There were no Gentiles involved. The character of prophecy in general is maintained and those that gathered outside were addressed as 'men of Israel, hear these words...' The words of the prophet apply to the event, and the Spirit was poured out on Israelites, albeit a foreshadowing only of the times of the last days.

How will the complete and real fulfillment come about? Generally speaking, all of prophecy points to the end times and Joel's words do this. Let me ask who will say to Jesus Christ in the end, "Blessed is He who comes in the name of the Lord!" It will be the Israeli remnant. Who will say in the end, "For unto us a Child is born, unto us a Son is given; and the government will be upon His shoulder." Again, it will be the Israeli remnant. In the last days who in Israel will God pour out His Spirit upon according to the prophet Joel? It will be the Jewish remnant (Rev. 14:1-5).

Of course our understanding gains a tremendous advantage by hindsight – we know the composition and number of the future Jewish remnant from visions recorded in Revelations (Rev. 7:1-8). But, for the upper room disciples, this knowledge was yet in the future.

Acts 3:19-21

"Repent therefore and be converted, that your sins may be blotted out, so that times of refreshing may come from the presence of the Lord, and that He may send Jesus Christ, who was preached to you before, whom heaven must receive until the times of restoration of all things, which God has spoken by the mouth of all His holy prophets since the world began."

Peter and the Disciples still expecting a Messianic Kingdom in their day

This is Peter on Solomon's porch in the temple after the healing of the lame man at the gate called Beautiful. He starts his message by

saying, 'Men of Israel' (Acts 3:12). But what is this *'times of refreshing'* *and sending Jesus back?* It is the Messianic kingdom restored to Israel that Peter is speaking of by the Spirit. It is still in consideration here. The nation needed to repent and be converted. But what came of this? Peter and John were arrested and dragged before the rulers and elders of Israel. They testified of the risen Man, Jesus of Nazareth, but then were threatened to speak no more in that name (Acts 4:1-21). This wasn't the nation repenting and expecting restoration. Jesus had asked for forgiveness on the cross. The offence against the Son of Man was forgiven. The Holy Spirit had been poured out in Israel, to testify of the risen Christ (John 15:26). It is the testimony of the Holy Spirit that is now rejected by Israel. As a whole the nation would become guilty of a sin that could not be forgiven them, sinning against the Holy Spirit (Mark 3:28-29, Matt. 12:31-32).

Acts 5:29-33

"But Peter and the other apostles answered and said: "We ought to obey God rather than men. The God of our fathers raised up Jesus whom you murdered by hanging on a tree. Him God has exalted to His right hand to be Prince and Savior, to give repentance to Israel and forgiveness of sins. And we are His witnesses to these things, and so also is the Holy Spirit whom God has given to those who obey Him." When they heard this, they were furious and plotted to kill them."

When the apostles were brought before the counsel they speak of repentance of Israel and forgiveness. They speak of Jesus being Prince and Savior of Israel which is Messianic in character. And from Pentecost on, it is the Holy Spirit witnessing with them to all these things. This testimony is rejected by the leaders of the nation, they wanting to kill the apostles. Then later there is the testimony of Stephen:

Acts 7:51

"You stiff-necked and uncircumcised in heart and ears! You always resist the Holy Spirit; as your fathers did, so do you."

The Sin against the Holy Spirit

This was Israel's last chance for restoration then. They constantly resisted the testimony of the Holy Spirit. This would not be forgiven of the nation. Certain judgment from God would come, on what remained of the nation, on Jerusalem and the temple. The people would be put to death or scattered into the Gentile nations, and not one stone would remain upon another. This is the consummation of the judgment of God pronounced in Hosea, the full setting aside of Israel all the way until the very end.

Hosea 1:9

"Then God said:

"Call his name Lo-Ammi,
For you are not My people,
And I will not be your God."

With Israel set aside, God turns to form a Gentile Body – the Mystery of Christ (Eph. 3:4-8)

The stoning of Stephen marks a huge transition point in the book of Acts and in the counsels of God. This pronouncement by God in Hosea was hundreds of years previous to this time. As for the government of God on the earth, Israel was set aside when God raised-up Nebuchadnezzar and Babylon to rule the earth. Morally speaking, Israel was not completely set aside until they rejected their Messiah and judgment came a second time in 70 AD. Obviously God is patient and longsuffering with Israel during this time.

It is always interesting and enlightening for me to see and understand the overall principles of God's ways in His counsels and plans. Often you can see remarkable parallels and connections being made that bring understanding by the Spirit of God. One such connection involves the two different times I speak of Israel being set aside.

❖ The first is concerning God's presence and government of the earth. This was set aside when God raised-up Babylon to rule the world.

❖ The second is when Messiah was rejected and Israel was morally set aside. Israel's house would remain desolate for a long time.

Both are Lo-Ammi experiences for Israel. Of significance is that both are soon followed by the total destruction of Jerusalem and the Jewish temple.

We see God being patient with Israel in the pronouncement of judgments in Isaiah 6:9-10. Years later God is bringing these very judgments of Israel to a head at the rejection of Messiah;

Matthew 13:10-17

"And the disciples came and said to Him, "Why do You speak to them in parables?"

11 He answered and said to them, "Because it has been given to you to know the mysteries of the kingdom of heaven, but to them it has not been given. 12 For whoever has, to him more will be given, and he will have abundance; but whoever does not have, even what he has will be taken away from him. 13 Therefore I speak to them in parables, because seeing they do not see, and hearing they do not hear, nor do they understand. 14 And in them the prophecy of Isaiah is fulfilled, which says:

'Hearing you will hear and shall not understand,
And seeing you will see and not perceive;
15 For the hearts of this people have grown dull.
Their ears are hard of hearing,
And their eyes they have closed,
Lest they should see with their eyes and hear with their ears,
Lest they should understand with their hearts and turn,
So that I should heal them.'

16 But blessed are your eyes for they see, and your ears for they hear; 17 for assuredly, I say to you that many prophets and righteous men desired to see what you see, and did not see it, and to hear what you hear, and did not hear it."

The Sovereign Choice of God (again)

In Israel at the time of Messiah the words would be fulfilled. But you say, didn't He have disciples out of Israel who could see and hear? Certainly! But how was this? Well, Jesus teaches and explains this in verse eleven. It is the choice of God. It is the sovereignty of God. It was given to the disciples, and not given to Israel. Given? Given by whom? The only answer here is the sovereign God. The disciples did not give this knowledge to themselves.

The choice of God is further addressed by Jesus in His words in verse sixteen and seventeen. Here the two groups in comparison have both been saved by God's choice and grace. The prophets and righteous men of the Old Testament were saved through a faith in God. His disciples' faith and those coming after would rest on redemptive work already completed. Still God is making a choice here that is pointed out by Jesus.

Blessed are those having not seen, and yet believe

I mentioned the disciples' faith and the faith of those coming in after as having the commonality of resting on the finished work of Christ. However there is a minor distinction the Lord makes even here. The disciples were eyewitnesses. Their testimony was of what they saw with their eyes, what they heard with their ears, what they handled and touched (I John 1:1-4). But Jesus said, "Blessed are those who have not seen and yet have believed." (John 20:29, I Pet. 1:7-9)

John 12:37-41

"But although He had done so many signs before them, they did not believe in Him, that the word of Isaiah the prophet might be fulfilled, which he spoke:

"Lord, who has believed our report?
And to whom has the arm of the Lord been revealed?"

Therefore they could not believe, because Isaiah said again:

"He has blinded their eyes and hardened their hearts,
Lest they should see with their eyes,
Lest they should understand with their hearts and turn,
So that I should heal them."

These things Isaiah said when he saw His glory and spoke of Him."

Eight hundred some years after Isaiah's pronouncement these words fit Israel's rejection of Messiah as quoted by the Spirit in John's gospel. An interesting sidebar is that Isaiah was looking at Christ in His glory. What? This is found in Isaiah six, where he sees Jehovah on the throne in heaven with the Seraphim.

The Turning Point in the Book of Acts

I believe the stoning of Stephen is the point in God's counsels where Israel is morally judged, sinning against the Holy Spirit, and completely set aside until the end. God turns to the Gentiles with the salvation of God (Acts 28:28, Rom. 11:11). And who is present at the stoning of Stephen? Saul is holding the garments, the future apostle to the Gentiles.

Look at the events that follow this as orchestrated by the Spirit of God. A great persecution arises in Jerusalem scattering the disciples out of that local; all except the twelve (Acts 8:1). In the scattering, Philip baptizes Samaritans after they believed his preaching Christ (Acts 8:4-12). The apostles in Jerusalem send Peter and John, and those baptized of the Samaritans receive the seal of the Holy Spirit by the apostles laying their hands on them. (Samaritans were not considered pure Jewish, but a mixture of Jewish and Gentile decent). After this, Philip is instructed by an angel to meet a Gentile Ethiopian. Then Saul is met by Christ on the road to Damascus. He would be a chosen vessel in the counsels of God for the bringing in of the Gentiles. Peter is given a vision that leads the most prominent of the original apostles to Cornelius' house and the opening of the door of the gospel to the Gentiles. There the Holy Spirit is given to them by the will of God, but not through Peter's hands (compare Acts

8:14-17 with 10:44-45). This all is the manifold wisdom of God in His sovereign choice manifesting His eternal counsels. God is turning to the Gentiles.

The 'Fullness of the Gentiles' begins

These events are all of significance. In Stephen's vision, when heaven is opened up to him, he sees the Son of Man *standing* at God's right hand. I believe Messiah would have come back as Peter preached, if Israel would have fully repented and received the testimony of the Holy Spirit. However, from this point forward I believe the Son of Man sits down, waiting. The fullness of the Gentiles begins in reference to the gathering of the body of Christ by the Holy Spirit (Rom. 11:25). This has been taking place for just short of two thousand years.

The importance of God's dealings with Peter, the Apostle of the Circumcision

The Spirit's dealing with Peter through Acts 10-11 is remarkable. It is as if the Holy Spirit is taking him by the hand and pulling him along as to the plan of God. And Peter's resistance is undeniable (Acts 10:14). Why would the Spirit repeat three times the words of the vision if it wasn't for Peter continuing his same response (Acts 10:16)? While Peter contemplates what he heard and saw, the Spirit speaks directly to him in a very pointed manner saying, "...go with these men, doubting nothing, for I have sent them." The angel appearing to Cornelius in Caesarea gave him a detailed description as to whom and where Peter was. God was turning to the Gentiles with His salvation. In His wisdom, the leader of the apostles would have to be involved in the first calling of them. Do we not see the divine wisdom in this?

Why did the Spirit have to speak to Peter again after the vision? Shouldn't it have been enough for Peter that these men, who had never before met him, knew his name and surname and exactly where he was lodging? God knows exactly all He has to do in every situation to accomplish His will and counsels. When Peter arrives at the house he first speaks this to those gathered:

Acts 10:28

"Then he said to them, "You know how unlawful it is for a Jewish man to keep company with or go to one of another nation. But God has shown me that I should not call any man common or unclean."

What Peter was doing here, by the Law of Moses, was unlawful. It simply was the breaking of the law. Peter identifies himself as a Jewish man. Now I could talk about whether Peter was really a Jewish man any more, being a believer in Jesus Christ, but the doctrines and teachings about the body of Christ had yet to be revealed by the Spirit. Peter didn't know that 'in Christ' there is neither Jew nor Gentile. He wasn't aware that the wall of separation had been abolished in the flesh of Christ (Eph. 2:14-15). Peter would not be responsible for what hadn't been revealed yet. He was having enough issues in dealing with understanding the vision of the scroll and how he would explain being in the house of a Gentile. But on the surface I can understand how someone might say the Holy Spirit is forcing Peter to break God's law. Some type of understanding is needed in this.

Israel Morally set aside, the Law of Moses set aside

Israel as a nation and people had been set aside by God. He was giving the nation one last chance, but His patience was soon to end. At the stoning of Stephen, God morally sets aside Israel as a people, they rejecting the testimony of the Holy Spirit. Messiah is set aside, and all promises to Israel set aside. Prophecy stops. Time stops being counted. Even the intercession of Christ on the cross for their forgiveness doesn't change their blindness. Peter's preaching to the house of Israel doesn't change anything, only a small remnant in Israel is saved. Christ sits down at the right hand of God. He would not be coming back at this time as Messiah to Israel. All this is set aside. The Law of Moses, the religion of the Jews, is set aside as well by God. The Father would be seeking true worshipers who worship Him in spirit and truth. He no longer would tolerate the worship of the flesh that He found no pleasure in (Heb. 10:8). God would have Jerusalem and the temple destroyed. He would effectively end the practice of Judaism. These things had to be, for God was turning to the Gentiles, revealing His mystery, and by the Holy Spirit gathering a Gentile body.

Peter, no doubt, was breaking the Law of Moses. You see this same issue with the law when the Jewish elders refused to come into Pilate's house. But if God had set aside the law, then the Holy Spirit's acting on Peter was not a violation at all. And it had to be set aside, otherwise not only was Peter breaking the law but the Holy Spirit is guilty. How do we understand these things? Do we see what God's counsels are in this experience?

God Never Gave the Law of Moses to the Gentiles

Let me pursue this further. Many people feel that the Law of Moses is for everybody -- all mankind. They reason that if it is the Law of God, then it must be for everybody. This is where we lose sight of God's counsels and start inventing our own. I have never found in all of scripture that God gave the law to the Gentiles. He simply never did. He gave the law to Israel, and they kept it to themselves for over a thousand years. In giving it to them He had a very specific purpose. Israel is who He brought out of Egypt to meet Him at Mt. Sinai. If God had intended His law for all mankind, He would have given it to Cain and Abel, after their parents disobeyed. But this didn't happen. He gave it to Israel and Israel alone. If God did intend His law for the Gentiles and He failed to make sure the Gentiles were given it, then something is very wrong with this picture – unrighteousness in God? It would be if this was true, but this is human thinking and not the thoughts of God.

God never gave His law to the Gentiles. God never had any intention of doing so. If the law had the stipulation that Jews were forbidden to associate with Gentiles, eat with Gentiles, or enter even the thresholds of their homes, tell me, how was a Gentile to obey this? Our human thinking and impressions would only create contradictions.

The law was given to Israel. Sure enough, God is responsible for giving it. He does not give it to the Gentiles though. The law is a test. It is given for the testing of Israel. They are the test-case. They represent all mankind in the testing. Israel had advantages as the test-case, all the advantages God could give. There was no reason to give the others the test. If the test was given to the ones with all the advantages, that would do to prove the outcome. Israel failed the testing. They were accountable in responsibility by the law. God was looking for the fruit of righteousness (Matt. 21:33-34), but found none (the law was always the measure of human righteousness before God). When the test was failed by Israel, there was no reason for God to keep the test papers around. When the case was proven and closed, He nailed the test papers to the cross of Christ (Col. 2:14). This effectively ended the testing of man in responsibility forever. The case was finished, and Jesus declares, "Now is the judgment of the world." (John 12:31)

The Principle of the Law

The law is viewed in Scripture as a whole entity having one overriding principle – the man who does those things shall live by them. The principle is clear – the doing of responsibility first, and then you are promised life.

Romans 10:5

"For Moses lays down in writing the righteousness which is of the law, "The man who has practiced those things shall live by them."

It is a whole entity because you must do it all and do it perfectly before you get the life. This wholeness of the law is easily seen here;

Galatians 3:10

"For as many as are on the principle of works of law are under curse. For it is written, "Cursed is everyone who does not continue in all things which are written in the book of the law to do them;"

Cursing is the only outcome for fallen man being given this law. This cursing includes judgment, condemnation, and wrath from God. The measure is all the law being done perfectly as a whole. Fallen man could not attain this and he could not have the promise of life from the law as the blessing at its end. There was only a curse for him, and that was on his head sooner than later. The law could not give life, and could not produce the fruit of true righteousness in man (Gal. 3:21). The law was not of faith, not of the principle of faith at all (Gal. 3:12). The law was not grace, and again, in principle these two are mutually exclusive (Rom. 6:14). The law is the works of man, and as such is not compatible with grace (Rom. 11:6). All of these scriptures describe the principle and character of the law, and we find nothing there that produces fruit in man. The basis of it is responsibility in man, and in this principle man has always failed.

Is Peter Breaking the Law? Is Peter a Jewish Man? Is the Spirit Leading Him?

It is the thought of the wholeness of the entire law that I address here. When I am told I must still keep the law, it is always with this stipulation – that I cannot pick and choose what parts to keep, but I must keep everything. Now I agree that the law is a whole, and for someone of the law, to break one part is to be guilty of all. But don't look at me; let us look at Peter.

Acts 10:28

Then he said to them, "You know how unlawful it is for a Jewish man to keep company with or go to one of another nation. But God has shown me that I should not call any man common or unclean.

As a Jewish man he is breaking a part of the law, and so, is guilty of it all, the Holy Spirit complicit in the offence. Are we allowing Peter to pick and choose? No, Peter isn't picking and choosing anything. God has set aside the Law of Moses and has set aside Judaism as a religion. The Gentiles are not unclean, and neither are all the animals on the sheet in his previous vision. It all has to have been set aside by God, or there is a transgression of the law being committed.

Look at all the animals on the sheet (Acts 10:11-16). In the Law of Moses they simply are all unclean. Eating them is a transgression of the law of God for a Jewish man. But this is what the Spirit says:

Acts 10:15

"And a voice spoke to him again the second time, "What God has cleansed you must not call common."

Question: Are the animals Peter saw on the sheet let down from heaven clean or unclean? *They are all now clean contrary to the law.* The only explanation for this is that God has set aside the law, so that it is now permissible for Peter to eat such things if he chooses. He is also allowed to associate and eat with Gentiles, which he does. Again, is this picking and choosing? No, it is the setting aside of the whole law.

In the same way that Messiah was a promise to Israel alone, and not to the Gentiles, so was the Law of Moses given only to the Jews. All of this together was set aside at the same general time at the stoning of Stephen. In 70 AD, through physical judgment, God brings an end to the practice of Judaism. The city and temple are destroyed by the Romans, and the Jewish people scattered to the nations. All of these things are related to each other. The law is related to Messiah, and the promises in Him. The law is related to the land, as well as the earthly calling of Israel that will be the remnant in the end. Messiah is associated with the land and physical restoration, and a future temple in Jerusalem. It is all set aside by God until then. When Israel is recognized again by God and Messiah returns to them, the law will be taken up again by the earthly calling. But then God will, by His sovereign power, work a slight difference concerning the final remnant and His law. Restored in the land at the beginning of the millennium, the remnant will have His law written on their hearts and minds (Jer. 31:31-34, Heb. 8:8-12).

The Two Main Covenants from God

The law as a testing would continue until the Seed appeared (Gal. 3:19). And this brings us to another line of thought concerning the law that is equally interesting and revealing. We can find this in Galatians 3-4. Let me start with this statement: it is obvious in Scripture and in the history of God's dealings with man (fallen man removed from paradise) that the involvement between God and man relates to two main covenants. We find these two covenants contrasted with each other by the Spirit of God in Galatians. It is the covenant of promise given to Abraham and the covenant of Law given to Israel at Mt. Sinai.

The Contrasts and Distinctions between the Two Covenants

Allow me to point out all the contrasts between the two. For starters the covenant of promise preceded law by 430 years. The covenant of promise is to Abraham, while the law is given through Moses to Israel. Promise is the principle of calling and grace, and so, involves only the choice of God and the working of God, as He alone is responsible. It is God making promises, and God alone responsible for fulfilling these promises. It is the faithfulness of God as an attribute, which simply cannot fail. Promise does not look at man as being responsible, nor does it test responsibility in man, but is God being responsible and faithful to keep His promises. Therefore, the covenant of promise had no mediator, being solely dependent on God's unchanging nature (Gal. 3:20).

When the reader understands the above paragraph as defining promise and the principle of calling and grace, then we see how God alone is truly glorified. God alone is choosing, God alone is working, and God alone is faithful. God confirms this covenant of promise in the one Seed of Abraham, which is Christ (Gal. 3:15-16). Isaac only served as a shadow in this. But as we saw in the Types and Shadows chapter, Isaac is offered up at the time of confirmation. The type he becomes is shadowing a crucified and resurrected Christ (Heb. 11:17-19). The one Seed of Abraham, in whom the covenant of promise is confirmed by God, is the resurrected Christ, the Son of Man glorified. The redemptive work is the shedding of the blood of the Last Man – this speaks of His death as the propitiation, the payment of the debt (God's righteousness not only being maintained, but fully glorified and exonerated by His death, Rom. 3:24-26).

Grace Preceded Testing in Responsibility

The covenant of promise preceded the covenant of Law. This is another connection and pattern in God's ways as displaying His counsels. Before the creating of the world the individual believer and body of Christ are found in God's counsels as "in Christ" (Eph. 1:4, 2 Tim. 1:9, and Titus 1:2). Before the world began, we are in grace by the choice of God. When God created the world, we see man in paradise, being tested in responsibility. In the very same way the covenant of promise precedes the covenant that tests man in responsibility, this covenant of Law.

It would be impossible for Israel to have two covenants from God at the same time. We know for certainty that Israel was given the covenant of law at Mt. Sinai. We have established earlier in this chapter that the law was given to Israel alone, and it was never intended for the Gentiles. This was the covenant Israel definitely had for over 1500 years from Sinai to the coming of the Seed (Gal. 3:17-19). However, the covenant of promise to Abraham, once confirmed back in Genesis 22, could not be annulled or changed or added to in any way by another covenant given after it (Gal. 3:15-17). So what is going on here? Israel was never given nor did they ever have the covenant of promise. They rejected the one Seed of Abraham, putting Him to death. They still reject the One Seed of their father Abraham.

The covenant of promise is through the resurrected Christ, and it is God working in grace towards those He places "in Christ". God is drawing, and the Holy Spirit is gathering. A body is being formed that will be united to the glorified Man, the body of Christ. The faith of Abraham is characteristic of this covenant of promise and grace, as well as characteristic of those being gathered in the covenant. Abraham's faith is unique and pleasing to God;

The Faith of Abraham is in a God who raises the Dead

Romans 4:16-25

16 *"Therefore it is of faith that it might be according to grace, so that the promise might be sure to all the seed, not only to those who are of the law, but also to those who are of the faith of Abraham, who is the father of us all 17 (as it is written, "I have made you a father of many nations") in the presence of Him whom he believed—God, <u>who gives life to the dead and calls those things which do not exist as though they did;</u> 18 who, contrary to hope, in hope believed, so that he became the father of many nations, according to what was spoken, "So shall your descendants be." 19 And not being weak in faith, he did not consider his own body, already dead (since he was about a hundred years old), and the deadness of Sarah's womb. 20 He did not waver at the promise of God through unbelief, but was strengthened in faith, giving glory to God, 21 and being fully convinced that what He had promised He was also able to perform. 22 And therefore "it was accounted to him for righteousness."*

23 *Now it was not written for his sake alone that it was imputed to him, 24 but also for us. It shall be imputed to <u>us who believe in Him who raised up Jesus our Lord from the dead</u>. 25 who was delivered up because of our offenses, <u>and was raised because of our justification</u>."*

Hebrews 11:17-19

"By faith Abraham, when he was tested, offered up Isaac, and he who had received the promises offered up his only begotten son, of whom it was said, "In Isaac your seed shall be called," <u>concluding that God was able to raise him up, even from the dead,</u> from which he also received him in a figurative sense."

The underlined parts above show that Abraham's faith was truly in a God whom raises the dead. Those gathered by the Spirit in this covenant of promise have the same character of faith as Abraham, and by it are made sons of God through faith in a resurrected Seed. Also our faith is in a God who not only raises the Seed, but who raises the believer with Him.

Ephesians 2:5-6

"...even when we were dead in trespasses, made us alive together with Christ (by grace you have been saved), and raised us up together, and made us sit together in the heavenly places in Christ Jesus,"

Sons of Abraham, Sons of God

Galatians 3:7

"Therefore know that only those who are of faith are sons of Abraham."

Galatians 3:9

"So then those who are of faith are blessed with believing Abraham."

Galatians 3:26

"For you are all sons of God through faith in Christ Jesus."

Galatians 3:29

"And if you are Christ's, then you are Abraham's seed, and heirs according to the promise."

These are the many sons of God that are partakers of the covenant of promise. Christ resurrected is the firstborn from the dead among many brethren. The brethren will be conformed to this glorified Man's image by resurrection. These truths and realities are the sovereign working of the God who raises the dead and in this work is alone to be glorified.

Romans 10:8-9

"But what does it say? "The word is near you, in your mouth and in your heart" (that is, the word of faith which we preach): that if you confess with your mouth the Lord Jesus and believe in your heart that God has raised Him from the dead, you will be saved."

The Resurrection – God's Seal of Approval and Acceptance of the Redemptive Work

Our faith is in God who raised Christ from the dead. The resurrection of the Son of Man from the dead is the centerpiece of the Christian faith. When Jesus sat down at God's right hand, the work of redemption was entirely finished (Heb. 10:11-12). But His sitting down brings out another important truth. The work of redemption was entirely acceptable and pleasing to God. God simply and absolutely will have nothing else but the death of Christ. God has shown that He has accepted this death, in that He has raised-up this Man from the dead, and has set Him, as Man, at His right hand in glory. God has made Christ's blood the propitiation of the redemption of man. This is the absolute sufficiency and perfection of the work of Christ, the Son of Man.

The Christ of Glory

This is the promised Seed of the woman from the beginning of the creation of God. This is the one Seed of Abraham resurrected, in whom the covenant was confirmed. This is the Son of Man come down from heaven. He is the second Adam, the last Adam, of which the first was just a type. He is the glorified Man of Psalm eight, for a time made a little lower than the angels. Christ is the Son of Man lifted up. He is the one who, being in the form of God, did not consider it as something to be grasped, but came in the likeness of men for the reason of death, even the death of the cross. Christ is the Head of all creation, as well as the Head of the church, His body. He is the centerpiece of all the counsels of God, and God will gather all things in Him, both in the heavens and on the earth. In Christ, all the promises of God are yes and amen, regardless as to whether they are heavenly or earthly. This is the glory of the Son of Man. This is the Christ of glory.

[Please note; in this chapter I never say that the church did not have its beginnings on the day of Pentecost. If Saul, in Judaism, persecuted the church of God, then it existed from that day (Gal. 1:13). That does not mean that the Messianic Kingdom wasn't still being presented by the apostles to Israel, and that the Jews weren't being given a last chance at the intercession of Christ on the cross. When Christ came in the flesh to Israel, He presented Himself as their Messiah in Luke 4. This also was the possibility of the Messianic kingdom. But this wasn't well received at that time – they took Him outside to throw Him off a cliff. He never embraced this title much, knowing the counsels of God, and knowing the reason why the Son of Man came down from heaven. The same can be said concerning Israel's last chance in the early chapters of Acts. What comes later is the full setting aside of the nation of Israel and God turning to the Gentiles, as well as all the teachings and doctrines concerning the church in Paul's epistles.]

Chapter 17:

Covenants and Dispensations

eformed theology is also referred to as Covenant theology. This, along with Dispensational theology seems to be the two major players in human thought and doctrine, as far as attempts by man in finding or creating a system of understanding Scripture. As you may surmise, I am not a big fan of human teachings and systems of doctrine. I would prefer God's thoughts, and that we search for them. I would prefer the Holy Spirit doing the teaching, if we will allow Him. And the ministers and teachers try to be mere vessels and instruments of God's working and grace (II Cor. 4:7, Phil. 2:13).

There are many broad biblical principles discussed in these chapters. When you understand them and agree that they have basis in God's Word, then you truly begin to see the forest instead of always staring at the trees. You really can understand better the length of scriptures. I am excited by what God is willing to teach through His Spirit and Word. I'm amazed at how God never is in error and never makes mistakes. When our eyes are opened, it all makes sense. It all fits. God's counsels are truly amazing.

Covenants and Dispensations are both found in the scriptures, and so we should talk about them. I'm not convinced either one is the best way of viewing the scope of Scripture, at least in how these two systems are set up by men. In discussing here these two doctrinal systems I will have to assume some familiarity with them on the part of the reader. In this chapter I'll also discuss what I believe to be God's way of viewing Scripture. But first we'll say a few things about both.

The Two Sons of Abraham -- the Two Main Covenants Involving God and Man

Galatians 4:22-24

"For it is written that Abraham had two sons: the one by a bondwoman, the other by a freewoman. But he who was of the bondwoman was born according to the flesh, and he of the freewoman through promise, which things are symbolic. For these are the two covenants: the one from Mount Sinai which gives birth to bondage, which is Hagar."

Some of the detail from our discussion in the last chapter concerning the covenants and Galatians 3-4 is repeated here. Please forgive me for the redundancy. There are only two covenants that the Spirit of God through Paul sees fit to discuss in Galatians. When we count covenants, only three are discussed in any detail in all the New Testament. We'll get to the third one shortly. However, these two covenants are the main ones we need to see and understand. One was given to Abraham and confirmed in his one Seed. The other was given to Israel at Mt. Sinai -- the Law of Moses. But simply, two covenants worth discussing.

Is there a Covenant in Paradise? Not Likely

Right away we should notice we are not discussing a covenant with Adam and Eve in paradise. There was no covenant then. There was no Law of Moses or Law of God given to Adam. The thought of a covenant in the garden is a creation of the human mind. Adam had no neighbors and could not love his neighbor as himself, or covet his neighbor's wife or possessions. There was no law of God. Adam was in innocence – without the knowledge of good and evil. If he was given laws, he would not have been able to apply them without such a conscience and knowledge. Adam was given a command by his Creator that required obedience – do not eat the fruit of this certain tree. He did not look at the fruit and think it was evil, he wouldn't have known this. Eve did not know the serpent was evil, nor did she know what he was saying was evil. Adam was required to obey one command. To be sure it was a testing of man in responsibility, and failure was soon in coming. But this is not a covenant. It is not the law spelling out evil and transgressions. And it was not work for Adam, for there was no work for man in paradise. It was the rest of God on the earth.

A Covenant Before the World Existed? Again, not likely

Also we do not see the existence of a covenant before the foundations of the world. That would fall into the category of the thoughts of men as well. Where in scripture is another covenant spelled out, as we see done concerning these two covenants in Galatians 3-4? The fuller truth of God concerning the Trinity was not revealed until the Son became flesh and came into this world. Are we to take this revelation back before the world was created, and say they made a covenant with each other? Why do we think the Trinity of the Godhead even needed an agreement with each other?

Before the Foundation of the World – the Counsels of God

What do the scriptures reveal concerning things from before the foundations of the world? It's not a covenant. Rather it is that the eternal God existed, and that He had His very own counsels. Also we see a 'Lamb slain' before the foundations of the world (Rev. 13:8), which alone is the basis and foundation for all God's counsels. The Lamb slain is not part of these counsels, but is the redemptive work in view by which God accomplishes all His plans. However what is revealed as part of God's counsels is the believer chosen and accepted in Christ before time began (II Tim. 1:9, Titus 1:2, Eph. 1:4).

The counsels are the plans God made. The plans speak of the work God would do on behalf of His creation. God works and God rests. The counsels of God are His plans that describe all His working. The death of the Lamb is the means of reconciling all things back to God (Col. 1:20), by which God, in turn, shows grace and blessing according to His own good pleasure and counsels (Eph. 1:9).

Also it is revealed that the Son and the Father shared a divine glory together in eternity past before the world existed (John 17:5). This is not part of the counsels of God. The Godhead did not plan and counsel their own divinity, nor the eternal glory associated with it. What is part, however, is Christ re-entering this previous glory as the glorified Man. There is more to the subject of God's counsels than simply this understanding. What I shared here concerning 'before time began' is what is revealed in the Word.

There is another principle displayed in the phrase 'before the foundation of the world.' It involves the understanding of the above points overlaid with a certain spiritual perspective. Here is a list of the thoughts involved:

❖ Everything that God reveals as a truth existing 'before the foundation of the world' stands on its own completely separated from the world, having no association or relationship with the world.

❖ The slain Lamb is a revealed truth that preceded the existence of the world (Rev. 13:8). More accurately, the book of the slain Lamb with names written in it is what existed. However this only affirms the truth that the thought of the slain Lamb was present.

❖ The Son of Man title identifies Jesus Christ as the slain Lamb (John 12:23-24). When the Son of Man is lifted up from the earth as the slain Lamb, it is in this understanding – as apart from the world (John 12:32). At this time the world was judged and condemned by God (John 12:31). [This is not the same truth that is taught in John 3:14. The lifting up of the Son of Man in that passage is Christ condemned by God as being made sin on our behalf – the serpent lifted up in type. However John 12 is the separation of the Son of Man from the world, as in relationship and association.]

❖ The individual believer and the Body of Christ are revealed in Scripture as 'before the foundation of the world,' (Eph. 1:4, II Tim. 1:9, Titus 1:2). The phrase 'before time began' carries the same meaning as the phrase 'before the foundation of the world.'

❖ Jesus taught this, "They are not of the world, just as I am not of the world." (John 17:16) In John 15:19 He says this, "...you are not of the world, *but I chose you out of the world*..." He repeats essentially the same thing here – John 17:14. This completes the specific revelation of this Biblical truth. However the associated truths around this principle go further. If the believer is apart from the world and earth, it is because we are 'in Christ' through a heavenly calling with a heavenly citizenship, etc.

❖ The revelation of Israel and separate Gentile nations is 'after the foundation of the world.' This establishes them as part of the world. The same understandings are true concerning Judaism as a religion. It is God's religion of the earth and world.

❖ Christianity is the religion of the slain Lamb and believers found 'in Christ.' It is the religion that is apart from this world. It is the religion and faith of the heavenly calling in Christ Jesus (Heb. 3:1)

The Rest of God – man in the garden

God worked for six days bringing forth the original physical creation. He rested on the seventh day. If there was an eighth day God was resting then as well -- and a ninth, tenth, and so on. The rest (sabbath) of God was man in paradise in innocence. God wasn't working and neither was man. I do not see a covenant of works existing between God and man in the garden.

Man's disobedience and sin ruined the rest of God on the earth. Adam was chased out of paradise, forcibly removed from the sabbath of God. In simple human terms, when this happened, God had to go back to work, and He has been working ever since. Was there a covenant of works man had with God after the fall? That would mean laws were given from God to man to obey. I do not see this existing in the world that was between Adam and the flood. Sin filled up that world (Gen. 6:5-7), and it could be best described as lawlessness (Rom. 2:12).

In dispensationalism they call this period of time 'conscience.' Man certainly now had a conscience from Adam's disobedience, but it was always defiled by the presence of sin in the flesh. There doesn't seem to be a progressive revelation of God at this time. God doesn't have a foothold into the earth, but just an occasional testimony in Abel, Enoch and Noah. The dispensationalists name the first two periods of time innocence and conscience. However, if we listen to Peter, the world that existed then was destroyed (II Pet. 2:5-6). What we have when Noah came out of the ark is a new world (II Pet. 2:7). This would be the first mild objection I would have concerning these first two commonly recognized dispensations in their theological system. I would have to think that a dispensation has some connection with this present earth.

What Man Inherits from Adam

Instead of conscience describing a dispensation of time and an existing economy and revelation from God, it better describes part of what all men inherit by natural birth from the first man Adam. And conscience was defiled by something else we receive from Adam – the presence of sin in the flesh. These two things are passed from Adam to all mankind – a defiled conscience and sin in the flesh. What are the fruits of these two things? The committing of sins is one of the fruits – lawlessness without the law or transgressions of the law if you have the law. The other fruits are death and condemnation. All of this, throughout time still is the over-riding problem of the entire human race. By natural birth we are all 'in Adam' with no exceptions. These types of understandings and generalized principles of scripture are the truths not adequately addressed in dispensations.

All the products and fruits of the disobedience of Adam were still in Noah and his family when the flood waters receded. What came out of the ark was man in Adam – fallen man. Israel was given the law at Mt. Sinai -- the start of another new dispensation called Mosaic Law – and they failed from the outset. Why? At the bottom of the mountain making a golden calf was man in Adam – fallen man. When Messiah was presented to Israel, the nation rejected Him outright. Why? They were "in Adam" as fallen man. In the commonly divided dispensations, this over-riding issue starts in the first and continues through the last, making the various divisions a bit arbitrary.

From Adam man possesses a conscience that knows the difference between right and wrong. There is nothing evil about this knowledge, and the tree with its fruit in paradise was not evil either. It was a testing of responsibility and a matter of obedience. Adam, before the fall, had no need of this knowledge. As long as man obeyed the one command he would have stayed in a state of innocence and remained in the rest of God. But calling the time from the fall to Noah a dispensation of conscience is a bit misleading as far as describing an economy given to man by God. It's more Adam's economy given to mankind than anything else, and it did not end at the flood. If Mosaic Law is a dispensation, it is strictly a Jewish one, because the law was never given to anyone else. The dispensations are never as neat and tidy as the dispensationalists would like them to be.

After the flood God makes a covenant with creation and places His sign of covenant in the sky. The curse over creation will be lifted at the beginning of the millennium at the revelation of the sons of God (Rom. 8:19). After the millennium, the new heavens and the new earth come about by fire (II Pet. 3:7, 10, 12). God's covenantal promise to not destroy this present creation again by water will be kept.

These are the Two Covenants – Galatians 4:24

It is the two covenants of Galatians 3-4 that are of great significance for man, the Spirit saying through Paul, 'these are the two covenants.' The first is the covenant of promise given to Abraham, while the second is the covenant of law given to Israel. I have discussed details about both in different chapters throughout this book, so I will only discuss here certain points of interest.

The covenant of promise is one of sovereign choice and grace by God and is dependent on the faithfulness of God. It was confirmed in Isaac in type when his father offered him up (Gen. 22). In type, because the true Seed in whom the covenant was actually confirmed, is Jesus Christ – the Son of Man raised from the dead. When Jesus tells the disciples this is the new covenant in My blood, it is this covenant of promise and sovereign grace. It is given to Abraham, confirmed in Christ, but does not function as a covenant until after the Son of Man is raised up. This is the covenant the true Christian possesses. Through faith we are sons of Abraham (Gal. 3:7) and sons of God (Gal. 3:26).

The Principle of the Law

How different is the second covenant – the Law of Moses – from the covenant of promise? Different almost in every way except that they are both actually covenants given by God. For starters, the principle of the law is quite different than the principle of promise. It is, do this and live. This is entirely based on the responsibility and performance of man (Rom. 10:5, Luke 10:26-28, Gal. 3:10-12). The covenant of promise first gives you eternal life (Gal. 3:11), sets you in a relationship of sonship (Gal. 3:26), and then your responsibilities are based on the relationship you find yourself in as a son. The principles of the two covenants are opposite each other. Further, the law was a ministry of death and condemnation, while the covenant of promise was a ministry of life and righteousness. It is eternal life and the righteousness of God. So we also see the outcomes of both covenants are opposite.

In the pages of this book we have had numerous discussions concerning the Law of Moses. These discussions are from the scriptures, taught by the Spirit, having great scriptural support. They are profound in their arguments. They show you how to look at the Law of Moses the way that God looks at it, and they teach you God's reasons and intentions for giving it. And they show you the broad principles concerning the law instead of staring at four hundred laws and ordinances and numerous different sacrifices trying to figure out the inherent spiritual character of each. For example, let us consider the part of the law involving the sacrifices.

Hebrews 10:1-7

"For the law, having a shadow of the good things to come, and not the very image of the things, can never with these same sacrifices, which they offer continually year by year, make those who approach perfect. For then would they not have ceased to be offered? For the worshipers, once purified, would have had no more consciousness of sins. But in those sacrifices there is a reminder of sins every year. For it is not possible that the blood of bulls and goats could take away sins.

Therefore, when He came into the world, He said:

"Sacrifice and offering You did not desire,
But a body You have prepared for Me.
In burnt offerings and sacrifices for sin
You had no pleasure.
Then I said, 'Behold, I have come—
In the volume of the book it is written of Me—
To do Your will, O God.'"

God had No Desire or Pleasure in the Sacrifices of the Law

The first understanding is that the law is a whole entity together. It is the commandments, ordinances, washings, eating of foods, feast days, sabbaths, sacrifices, priesthood, tabernacle furniture etc. You cannot legitimately separate out anything. It is one entire entity. All of Israel became debtors to keep the whole law (Gal. 5:3). In this passage the discussion of the law refers specifically to all the sacrifices, the tabernacle, and the priesthood.

It wasn't necessarily meant to be this from the beginning for Israel. God's intention at first was pure law to be given to the Jews. When Moses came down the mountain the first time he had the tablets of stone, but they never made it into the camp (Ex. 32:19). The law was already broken by Israel by the making of the golden calf. The survival of Israel as a nation was dependent on God making additions to pure law in order for Him to show mercy and compassion through atonement (covering of sin). You see this all in the conversations with Moses at the tabernacle outside the camp and the second time he goes up the mountain (Ex. 32:31- 34:9). Israel would not have survived under pure law – God would have wiped them from the face of the earth and would have raised up a new nation unto Moses (Ex. 32:1-10).

The other important understanding to learn is that the sacrifices offered according to the law were never desired by God or pleasing to Him. Though we can gain some spiritual insights by looking at the many different sacrifices and offerings, they are only as shadows and non-realities. And you have to remember this over-riding principle when you are concentrating on the details of the sacrifices, or else they become something to the believer that they really are not. This is the covenant of law. This is Judaism.

Important Understandings Concerning the Law

Other important understandings concerning the Law of Moses are listed below. We have already discussed many of them at length in this book. Put together they bring tremendous insight:

- It was a testing of responsibility in man by God.

- It was given to man in the flesh, man in the first Adam, and sinners already. The law and Judaism are tailored by God for man in the flesh. It is a walk in the flesh and by the senses.

- It exposes the presence of sin in the flesh by becoming the strength of sin (I Cor. 15:56), and allowing sin to abound more and more (Rom. 7:5-17, 5:20).

- It was given to Israel as a nation. It was never given to the Gentiles. Israel had it alone for over 1400 years. It is their covenant and theirs alone.

- Israel was the test case for all mankind, because they were the most privileged nation by God (Rom. 3:1-2). They failed miserably in responsibility (Matt. 21:33-40), proving the abject depravity of all mankind's nature in Adam. When the testing was complete, God condemned the entire world (John 12:31), nailed the test papers to the cross (Col. 2:14, Eph. 2:15), and stopped the practice of the law by destroying Jerusalem and the temple.

- It is worship of God according to the flesh and the senses. It is worship according to the weak and beggarly elements of the world (Gal. 4:9). It is not worship of God in spirit and truth (John 4:23-24). This is a direct contrast of Judaism and Christianity. Judaism is a walk by sight, while Christianity is a walk of faith (II Cor. 5:7).

- The law, as a covenant, only gives birth to bondage and only could produce children in bondage and slavery (Gal. 4:24-25, 5:1).

- The law given to Israel placed all those who practice it, under a curse automatically (Gal. 3:10). This curse is judgment, condemnation and wrath from God. The scripture says, "...as many as are of the works of the law are under the curse..." This would be all Israel without exception.

- The covenant of law to Israel at Mt. Sinai was proven to be weak and flawed (Heb. 8:7). It had to be set aside. It presently is set aside by God, as well as the nation of Israel as a people.

What was proved by the Testing of Israel?

Of importance, mentioned in the list above, is that the law was a testing in responsibility. It is important that you understand the parameters of the testing so you fully understand what was proved by the testing – the outcome and results. It is not enough to say that the law was a testing of Israel. There are many questions you have to consider and properly answer that explain this testing by God, so you have a proper understanding.

Why just Israel? God had no reason to test the Gentiles, because if Israel, the most favored and privileged nation by God, failed the testing, then Gentile failure was guaranteed. So Israel is the test case representing mankind.

The State and Condition of Mankind

What was Israel's state and condition going into the testing? They were sinners. They are set apart sinners, separated from the Gentile sinners in the rest of the world. But in nature and by birth, they were descendants of Adam just like the Gentiles. Now the scriptures describe this state and condition. It is the state of being in the flesh. It is being a slave of sin and dead in sin. It is, by nature, a child of wrath – that is, appointed for wrath and headed for it. As for righteousness -- "There is none righteous, no not one." As for seeking God – "There is none who seeks after God."

Romans 3:12

"They have all turned aside;
They have together become unprofitable;
There is none who does good, no, not one."

This is the abject depravity of all mankind by birth in Adam. All of this is the definite result of the fall of man. It has left all men, Israel included, without God and without hope in this world. It is a state where man is without strength and resource, and simply put, is lost. And so, this was Israel's state and condition going in.

And how did they emerge from the testing? They were still all sinners, and totally depraved. You see, any testing would test what you have going in. Naturally speaking, a test would not give you the answers or give you resources. The law, as the test, required and demanded of man what he ought to be, with God and with his neighbor. But it never gave him anything so he could be different than what he was already – a sinner in Adam. He was an Israelite for sure, but still a sinner in Adam.

This is what the testing proved – the human race's state and condition in Adam. It is a desperate state, one needing to be recognized and understood. God tested for a reason – to show and fully prove man's state and condition. But man will not admit or recognize his proven position in Adam. The overwhelming majority of believers do not understand this position, this testing and its results, while all along we are the ones who have been privileged by God taking us out of Adam and placing us in Christ! Often because we do not have this understanding, as believers, we will judge all things by sight and circumstances instead of by God's Word and by seeking God's thoughts. We may ask, "Are we better than they?"

The Coming of Messiah – the Last Testing of Mankind

When Christ came to Israel as their Messiah, this was the last testing by God of mankind. Israel was still the test case. He was their Messiah according to their prophetic scriptures, and the nation was looking for Him. But they could not recognize Him. They could not receive Him. Their state and condition in Adam was proven again! At His rejection, Jesus says, "Now is the judgment of the world." (John 12:31) Notice – it is the judgment and condemnation of the whole world, not just the Jews. This is also expressed in Romans.

Romans 3:19

"Now we know that whatever the law says, it says to those who are under the law, that every mouth may be stopped, and all the world may become guilty before God."

When Israel failed all its testing by God, then every mouth in the entire world was stopped. The world now was fully proven guilty and condemned.

Judaism – God's Religion of the Earth

There are two distinct perspectives, from God's viewpoint and scripture, involving the Law of Moses and Israel's responsibility. It is almost as if there are two Jewish dispensations to consider. One is close to what we discussed above, but with an important difference. Instead of looking at the law as a test proving the utter depravity of mankind, in this Jewish dispensation, the law is God's choice of Judaism as His religion of the earth. It was worship of the one true God, as opposed to all the other religions of man on the earth. And God gave it to Israel.

From the time of Israel before Mt. Sinai through the coming of Messiah, the law was practiced in Israel with few exceptions. This ended in 70 AD with the destruction of Jerusalem and the temple. Israel and their law are set aside by God. The sacrifices stopped. There was no tabernacle, no temple, no veil, etc. Now most dispensationalists like to draw lines, ending one dispensation and starting the next. But here, I believe, is a dispensation that God sets aside for a time. The law is abolished for any individual in Christ (Eph. 2:15). But it is not abolished for the nation of Israel on the earth. It is their religion. It is God's religion of the earth. It is simply set aside for now, as Israel is set aside.

In the end, when God recognizes Israel as a people again by saving a Jewish remnant, the Law of Moses, Judaism, will be practiced again in a new temple in Jerusalem (Ez. 40-48). Throughout the length of the millennium Judaism will be practiced as the religion of the earth, and by the earthly calling. It will be accomplished in the remnant by the sovereign power of God. And if I'm not mistaken, Israel will teach the law of God to the Gentile nations. Nevertheless, the dispensation seems to restart, which is contrary to most common dispensational teaching.

God's Government of the Earth

The other Jewish dispensation involves the direct government of God on the earth with His presence in the midst of Israel. This also started at Mt. Sinai and continued through Solomon's temple, until the time of Jeremiah and Ezekiel. When the prophets of God could no longer call Israel back to the law, and their idolatry and rebellion became too much for God to continue to honor with His presence, the glory leaves the temple, the city, and the earth. Interesting enough, there is a destruction of Jerusalem and the Solomon temple at this time (sound familiar?). It is a setting aside of Israel by God – they are no longer His people (Hos. 1:9). This also seems like a Jewish dispensation suspended. It will restart at the beginning of the millennium with the kingdom of the Son of Man over the entire earth, and the Messianic kingdom as a subset of it. Israel will become the most exalted nation on earth. So again, a Jewish dispensation is set aside and at a later time restarted.

But you say Israel rebuilt a temple under Nehemiah. That is certainly true, and they restarted the practice of the law with the priesthood and sacrifices. But what was always missing from their new temple? Missing was the Ark of the Covenant, the throne of God. Also the presence and glory of God never returned. This Jewish dispensation of the government of God over the earth by His presence in the midst of Israel was suspended. God now brought the Gentiles in for world government.

Isn't there a Gentile Dispensation? Four Gentile World Empires

This Jewish dispensation concerning the government of God is interrupted by what would seem to be a Gentile dispensation of world civil government and the four beasts of Daniel 7. Why this isn't considered a dispensation by the dispensationalists, I'm not sure. It has revelation and prophecy concerning it, responsibility given to the Gentiles, failure of that responsibility, and judgment from God. This looks like a dispensation.

God Deals with Israel as a Nation, as a People

A principle that is often missed that I believe is an important understanding is how God always seems to deal with Israel as a nation and a people. Rarely does He deal with them individually. They were delivered out of Egypt as one people and one nation. They are given the covenant at Mt. Sinai as a nation. Messiah comes to and ministers to the house of Israel. Their house is made desolate by God, the nation set aside. Whenever God saves in Israel, it always seems to be a remnant representing the nation – in the time of Elijah (Rom. 11:1-4), the time of the beginnings of the church (Rom. 11:5), and the Jewish remnant in the end (Rev. 7:1-8). We know that in the doctrines concerning the heavenly calling in Christ there are no nationalities. But Israel on the earth is always either 'My people,' or 'not My people,' in the mind and counsels of God.

When Israel is restored in the Promised Land during the millennium, it will be the Messianic kingdom ruling over twelve tribes. At that time a new covenant is given to the Jewish remnant that is placed in the land (Jer. 31:31-34). This promise of a new covenant with Israel is spoken of in the book of Hebrews.

Hebrews 8:7-13

7 "For if that first covenant had been faultless, then no place would have been sought for a second. 8 Because finding fault with them, He says: "Behold, the days are coming, says the Lord, when I will make a new covenant with the house of Israel and with the house of Judah— 9 not according to the covenant that I made with their fathers in the day when I took them by the hand to lead them out of the land of Egypt; because they did not continue in My covenant, and I disregarded them, says the Lord. 10 For this is the covenant that I will make with the house of Israel after those days, says the Lord: I will put My laws in their mind and write them on their hearts; and I will be their God, and they shall be My people. 11 None of them shall teach his neighbor, and none his brother, saying, 'Know the Lord,' for all shall know Me, from the least of them to the greatest of them. 12 For I will be merciful to their unrighteousness, and their sins and their lawless deeds I will remember no more."

13 In that He says, "A new covenant," He has made the first obsolete. Now what is becoming obsolete and growing old is ready to vanish away."

The Divided Kingdoms of Judah and Israel become One Nation

It is very clear that this covenant is with the two formerly divided kingdoms – the house of Israel and the house of Judah. In the millennium the two become one Messianic Kingdom (Jer. 3:18, 23:6, Ez. 37:15-28, Hos. 1:11), one people and one nation. It is clear that this is 'a new covenant' with Israel, because the first covenant with that nation was insufficient. Israel's old covenant, given at Mt. Sinai, was written on tablets of stone. It is described as mere copies and shadows of the true (Heb. 8:1-5). As shadows, it always lacked a certain reality and power to change the worshiper. It left them with a continual consciousness of sins (Heb. 10:2).

God gives the Nation of Israel a New Covenant

This new covenant is not for the Gentiles. It is a new covenant with a united Israel. This is not the new covenant for New Testament believers. This is not for the body of Christ. This covenant for Israel does not exist today. It will only exist when Israel is acknowledged again by God as His people. He says, "...and I will be their God, and they shall be My People." (Heb. 8:10). Presently Israel is Lo-Ammi (Hosea 1:9). As a people Israel is set aside (Heb. 8:9 – I disregarded them). God has set aside their law, their religion. Their covenant is described as obsolete and growing old – vanishing away (Heb. 8:13). In the sight of God they are not a people at this time, and they have no covenant. The above passage starts with the weakness and failure of the covenant from Sinai. Then it is "Behold, the days are coming..." This is the millennium. It is the sovereign work and power of God at that time.

This new covenant for Israel is the same law of God they were given back at Mt. Sinai. The difference is the finger of God writing on hearts of flesh, instead of tablets of stone (Ex. 31:18, Heb. 8:10). "I will put My laws in their mind and write them on their hearts."

Israel at this time will perfectly obey the law of God. They will have a new temple in Jerusalem and be making sacrifices and offerings according to the law written in their hearts and minds (Ez. 40-48). All previous sins will be totally removed from them (Heb. 8:12). From that point on they will sin no more by the sovereign power of God. A significant understanding of this is they perfectly obey while still being in the flesh and in Adam. This new covenant is the law written on their hearts and minds – it is not the removal of sin from their flesh. What we've said about Israel's new covenant brings up some interesting thoughts when we consider the covenants discussed in Galatians 3 and 4.

The question for the theologians should be what are the thoughts of God, and are we teaching what God reveals and speaks in His word by His Spirit? When considering Galatians, we are discussing two distinct and legitimate covenants from God (Gal. 4:22-24). These are the two covenants of greatest importance concerning the counsels of God toward man. The covenant of promise was given to Abraham, and confirmed in his one Seed, who is Christ. We have discussed previously that the confirmation of this covenant was through a resurrected Christ, the Son of Man (Heb. 11:17-19, Gal. 3:16). The other covenant was the Law of Moses given to Israel at Mt. Sinai.

Galatians 3:15-18

"Brethren, I speak in the manner of men: Though it is only a man's covenant, yet if it is confirmed, no one annuls or adds to it. Now to Abraham and his Seed were the promises made. He does not say, "And to seeds," as of many, but as of one, "And to your Seed," who is Christ. And this I say, that the law, which was four hundred and thirty years later, cannot annul the covenant that was confirmed before by God in Christ, that it should make the promise of no effect. For if the inheritance is of the law, it is no longer of promise; but God gave it to Abraham by promise."

The Covenant of Promise -- Confirmed in the Son of Man Resurrected

The covenant of promise was confirmed in the resurrected Son of Man. This covenant did not exist until Jesus Christ came and completed the work of redemption, the death of the Son of Man on the cross. God, being fully satisfied and fully glorified, raises Jesus from the dead. It is in this glorified Man that the blessings and grace of the covenant of promise reside. It is being in this glorified Man, in Christ, that the believer is positioned, and enjoys all the privileges as being sons of God (Gal. 3:26, 4:5-7). This covenant was to Abraham and his Seed. It is for no one else, except the believer chosen and hidden in Christ (Gal. 3:26-29).

In a general sense this covenant of promise involves all the promises of God, whether earthly promises or heavenly promises. Jesus Christ, the one Seed of Abraham, secured every single promise and blessing by His death and shed blood. As I said in an earlier chapter, even the new heavens and the new earth after the millennium are based upon the shed blood of Christ. "For all the promises of God in Him are yes, and in Him Amen, to the glory of God..." The death of the Son of Man has simply paid the price for everything that God has promised and everything God will do (II Cor. 1:20).

The earthly promises were given to Abraham for his 'many seeds' after the flesh – the nation of Israel. They cannot have the earthly promises presently because, as a nation, they rejected the one Seed and crucified Him. These promises remain set aside, because Messiah is set aside as well as the nation of Israel itself. In the end, in His sovereignty, God is faithful to fulfill all. He sends their Messiah to them a second time. God will again acknowledge Israel as His people and He as their God.

I mentioned earlier in this chapter that God's dealings with Israel are always as a people and a nation. This is an important point to notice and this principle has its connections to the earth and Israel's earthly calling. As a nation they were delivered out of Egypt and given the law. They wandered in the wilderness for forty years as a nation, even those among them who had the good report. They went into captivity as a people. When God acknowledges them, it is as a people, as a nation. And when He doesn't, it is they are not my people (Hos. 1:9). This is how you may recognize some of the prophecies concerning Israel restored in the end, simply because in the language of the prophecy Jehovah once again acknowledges them (Ez. 34:23-31, 36:23-28, Jer. 30:18-22). In the end the Jewish remnant represents what Jehovah sovereignly saves as the nation of Israel, twelve tribes numbered and sealed by the hand of God (Rev. 7:1-8, Rom. 11:25-29).

Romans 15:8

"Now I say that Jesus Christ has become a servant to the circumcision for the truth of God, to confirm the promises made to the fathers,"

Acts 13:34

"And that He raised Him from the dead, no more to return to corruption, He has spoken thus:

'I will give you the sure mercies of David.'"

The sure mercies of David are all God's promises made to the fathers of Israel. These promises are physical and earthly in nature. They are tied to the Promised Land and restoration, a throne of David, and a son of David reigning over twelve tribes (Ez. 34:23-24). These earthly promises are obviously confirmed by the Son of Man raised up from the dead, the One Seed of Abraham.

This does not mean that Israel is partakers of the covenant of promise. Rather, quite the contrary. All it means is that Israel's promises are secured for them, by the shed blood of Christ and the unchanging faithfulness of the God who made the promises. When they are restored in the land and enjoy the physical blessings and prosperity of Jehovah, it is not the covenant of promise He makes with them (Heb. 8:6-12).

The covenant of promise characterizes the Christian believer as 'in Christ' by faith and a son of God (Gal. 3:26, 4:5-7). Being of faith we are sons of Abraham (Gal. 3:7, 9). The promise of the Spirit, who is the guarantee of the inheritance, is given to us through faith (Gal. 3:2, 14, 29, 4:6-7). These truths and more are benefits to being 'in Christ' and partakers of the covenant of promise. We individually have sonship with the Father, and Christ is our brother. We are members one of another, the body of Christ and His bride. We are seated in heavenly places 'in Christ' and blessed with every spiritual blessing in the heavens. Our citizenship is in heaven and not on this earth or of this world. The point is the many seeds of Abraham according to the flesh (Gal. 3:16) cannot claim any of these truths. They are connected to the earth, having rejected the one Seed of Abraham.

Abraham had Promise, Israel had Law

The other covenant was four hundred and thirty years later. It was the covenant of law. Who was it given to? -- Israel at Mt. Sinai. Now we see in the counsels of God concerning the earth and what He saves and restores in the land in the end. It is a remnant of Israel. Jehovah will write His law on their hearts and in their minds. During the millennium they will obey it perfectly, by the sovereign power of God. They will live in the land; they will grow and prosper (Deut. 28:1-14). Israel and Jerusalem will be the center of the earth and the center of the government of God over the earth.

Was the covenant of Law given to Abraham? No, he wasn't there. Besides he already had a covenant. The truth of the matter is once the covenant of promise was confirmed in Christ (Gen. 22:15-18), it could not be annulled or added to or changed in any way. Its promises and blessings depended on the character of God alone – His faithfulness. It remains fairly obvious then that Abraham had one covenant, and Israel had the other. And never did the two meet (Gal. 4:28-31). The covenant of law could not annul, or add to, or change the previous covenant of promise (Gal. 3:15-18). It could not touch it in any way.

Promise – God's Sovereign Choice and Grace

The covenant of promise has the character of God's sovereign choice and grace. This is the same character of the calling of Abraham out of Ur of the Chaldeans.

Genesis 12:1

"Now the Lord had said to Abram:

"Get out of your country,
From your family
And from your father's house,
To a land that I will show you."

God chose Abram out of the idolatry that surrounded him in his home country. God's calling of him was a separation from father, family, and country. He was sent to a place that God would give him. In this calling, Abram is a type of the believer, for he left all to sojourn in a foreign land as a stranger and pilgrim (Heb. 11:8-9, 13). With the calling of Abram, God has an entrance back into the earth among man. It is an entrance of promise founded in God's very own faithfulness.

Where the covenant of promise has the character of God's grace and choice, the covenant of law is the opposite. It is a testing of man -- can man be righteous before God? Man's responsibility is looked at and tested in his relationship with God and with his neighbor. It was only Israel that was tested, as the test case for all mankind. The failure of the law was immediate. Israel made a golden calf. The failure of the law was certain. It was given to man in the first Adam, already sinners. So we should be able to reason, knowing that God knew this beforehand, that He had different intentions for giving the law than what is usually thought by man. It was a ministration of death and condemnation (II Cor. 3:7, 9).

With their Covenant of Law Israel always a Bond Servant

The covenant of promise resulted in many sons of God (Gal. 3:26). The covenant of law produced slaves and servants (Gal. 4:22-25). This is always what Israel was with the law – a slave to sin in Adam, and a servant in the house of God.

John 8:34-36

"Jesus answered them, "Most assuredly, I say to you, whoever commits sin is a slave of sin. And a slave does not abide in the house forever, but a son abides forever. Therefore if the Son makes you free, you shall be free indeed."

The sons of God by the covenant of promise abide in the house of God forever. We are the ones in Christ, who the Son has made free from slavery and servant hood. And we are free indeed. But the law could not do this for Israel. Rather, by the covenant of law, Israel was a slave to the power of sin – the law only making sin to abound all the more (Rom. 5:20). By the law they were always servants in the house, not ever knowing what the master was doing (John 15:15), and with no chance of abiding forever. The covenant of promise is about God, and who He is in faithfulness. The covenant of law is about man, and what he is in Adam.

Israel is Set Aside, and so is the Law

I have spoken repeatedly in these chapters of how Israel was set aside by God. I have shown this through the scriptures. When Stephen was murdered, Israel was guilty of sinning against the Holy Spirit. This is Israel morally set aside, and God, in 70 AD, destroys Jerusalem and the temple. If Israel is set aside, then God no longer recognizes them as a nation, as a people. In God's eyes they are as the Gentiles, and that is where He scattered them. With the destruction of the temple, God stops the practice of Judaism – the Law of Moses. What purpose does the law serve? It was added because of transgressions – it was very good at this, exposing sin and sins (Gal. 3:19). It was added until the Seed should come – the Seed came and went, and God stopped the practice of the law. As a covenant, the law isn't recognized by God, just as He doesn't recognize Israel as a nation. As a covenant, the law basically doesn't exist presently.

It doesn't matter what man acknowledges. It only truly matters what God acknowledges. I've tried to make this point as well. It doesn't matter what man's thoughts are, it only truly matters what God's thoughts are. It doesn't matter what man does, what he builds, what he teaches, and on and on. The only thing that matters is the counsels of God – His one plan, and how He sovereignly brings it to pass. The only works that will last are those which God alone is working. This is so His own glory will always remain untarnished, and so man will never have a reason to boast. This is far from the present reasoning of man, and even that of many believers. In the end however, this will be proven to be so, and God will be the one doing the proving.

The Personal Stewardship (Dispensation) given to Paul

This present age is about the Holy Spirit sent down from heaven after the Son of Man was glorified (John 13:31-32). It is the time of the 'fullness of the Gentiles' coming in, the Spirit gathering the body of the glorified Man (Rom. 11:25). The earth and prophecy has been set aside presently, and these are only heavenly things now (John 3:12). As a dispensation, it is hard to make heavenly things and the heavenly calling into one. It isn't of the present earth, it's hidden from prophecy, and it's not the counting of time. When Paul speaks of a dispensation of grace, it seems to me to be a personal stewardship of responsibility (Eph. 3:1-2). He says,"...which was given to me for you..." That would be his personal responsibility to make known the mystery of Christ to the Gentiles and fill up the remainder of the word of God (Col. 1:25). A personal stewardship that would only last the length of his life.

If the defining characteristic of a dispensationalist is maintaining the distinct separation between Israel and the church, then I am overwhelmingly guilty of being one. This distinction is critical to any proper understanding of scripture. The teaching of this book focuses on the separation between the earthly and heavenly callings. The 'plain or normal interpretation' of scripture brings forth God's thoughts, and should always be maintained. Mostly it isn't a matter of interpretation, but a good translation with an understanding of the meaning of words put together by the inspiration of the Holy Spirit. This is what they mean by literal interpretation. I would rather call it a literal understanding of a good translation. As indicated in the first chapter, the use of interpretation should be reserved for parables, types, and symbolic prophetic language. But this should be the legitimate extent of its use. The spiritualization of scripture, in my opinion, becomes the manipulation of scripture in the effort to make everything fit nicely into doctrinal systems.

The endpoint of all God's counsels is the absolute glory of God. Doctrinal systems should never compromise this understanding. There are some great Biblical principles that all doctrinal systems should fully address. Listed below are some notable examples that we have discussed in this book:

- The rest or sabbath of God – this is where man started, in paradise. It was the rest of God because there was no presence of sin in man. Adam's disobedience ruined this. Now sin was in the flesh of man. The future rest of God will always be after sin in the flesh is removed. For the body of Christ and the heavenly calling, this is when it is removed from the earth, and our bodies glorified. For the earthly calling it is after the great white throne judgment by the Son of Man, and the beginning of the eternal state in the new heavens and the new earth. There are types and shadows in the Old Testament concerning the rest of God that the believer enters into. These types are dealt with in Hebrews 3-4.

- The Law of Moses was a testing of mankind. What God proved by the testing was the utter depravity of man in Adam. This gives you the real reason why God gave this covenant to Israel. This understanding shows God's intentions and thoughts behind the law. When we romanticize the law, we make it into something that it isn't, and false doctrines soon follow. As it was given, written on tablets of stone, it was only ever an administration of death and condemnation.

■ There are heavenly things and earthly things, and great biblical principles concerning both (John 3:12, Eph. 1:10). For example: the government of the earth and its development in scripture, and its relationship to the gathering in the end of all things on earth in Christ, the Son of Man. This began with Jehovah's presence in Israel from Mt. Sinai and progressed through the 'times of the Gentiles.' In the millennium it is the kingdom and power of the Son of Man.

■ The understanding of the Biblical principle of God acknowledging Israel as His people and He as their God. This is contrasted with times when He sets Israel aside (Hos. 1:9) – first, relating to God's government of the earth. Second as relating to a group of subjects: Messiah, Messianic promises, prophecy, earthly things, and the counting of time. This entire grouping was set aside when Israel was set aside morally at the rejection of Christ as their Messianic King.

These are just some of the important Biblical principles that a doctrinal system should explain.

A Better Understanding of Scripture – the First Adam and the Last Adam

When I look for a means of dividing scriptures, I find the understandings surrounding the first Adam and the last Adam to be invaluable. The first man started it all and brought ruin to the human race. The last Adam is Jesus Christ, the Son of Man. The redemptive work of this Man is the foundation of all the work that God accomplishes. In the end God's work gathers all things in Jesus Christ, the Son of Man – things distinctly in the heavens first, and then things distinctly on the earth (Eph. 1:10). The overriding purpose of the glory of God is magnified in all God does to glorify the Son of Man (John 13:31-32) – that is, after the Son of Man glorified God by His one act of obedience (Rom. 5:18), His death.

It all can be explained by the two Adams, and the understanding spans the length of Scripture. The first Adam is a type of Jesus Christ, the Son of Man. This Man, the Son of Man come down from heaven, is the Seed of the woman that would eventually crush the serpent's head. We have shown conclusively in this book that the Son of Man raised from the dead is the Seed of Abraham in whom the Covenant of Promise was confirmed. In Abraham were the many seeds according to the flesh (Israel – the earthly calling), but also the one Seed of Promise. In this one Seed, in Christ, are all the many sons of God, those of the heavenly calling. They are those that He is not ashamed to call His brethren. They are the many sons He brings to glory.

In the second Adam and based upon His death, are absolutely all the promises of God confirmed. The sum total of these promises is the counsels of God. It does not matter whether we speak of heavenly promises in the heavenly calling or earthly promises in the earthly calling. All the promises of God in Him are Yes, and in Him Amen, to the glory of God (II Cor. 1:20). It is all gathered into Jesus Christ, the last Adam, the Son of Man.

From paradise, through the fall of man, all the way to the coming of Messiah, it was the economy of the first Adam. Man was sold under sin, with death and condemnation as the only result (Rom. 5:12-14). All of it was the consequence of the disobedience of the first man. Sure enough, we can divide this time up between man without law practicing lawlessness (Rom. 5:14) and Israel, given the law, practicing transgressions (Rom. 5:20). After God had fully tested and condemned the entire world in the first Adam (John 12:31, Rom. 3:9-19, 23), He brings in the second Adam, the Son of Man – that His death and His blood would be the propitiation for it all (Rom. 3:24-26). Now God brings forth the working out of all His counsels based simply on nothing else, but the death of this Man – Jesus Christ, Son of God as the Son of Man.

Scripture Notes on the Revelation of the Father

A general scriptural point which should be beyond any dispute among believers is that Jesus, the Son of God, was sent by the Father to reveal the Father (Matt. 11:27, Luke 10:22, John 6:46).

Matthew 11:27

"All things have been delivered to me by my Father, and no one knows the Son but the Father, nor does anyone know the Father, but the Son, and he to whom the Son may be pleased to reveal him."

John 17:26

"And I have made known to them thy name, and will make it known; that the love with which thou hast loved me may be in them and I in them."

John 20:17

"Jesus says to her, Touch me not, for I have not yet ascended to my Father; but go to my brethren and say to them, I ascend to my Father and your Father, and to my God and your God."

This revelation was started by Jesus in person in the gospels, but finished by Jesus in the epistles through the Spirit of truth (John 16:25). It is in the epistles that we have the doctrine of the adoption of sons by the seal of the Spirit and that we are brethren with Christ. This, in the gospels and further on in the epistles, establishes the relationship of the Father with the many sons in His household. I intend to bring this out clearly, starting in the gospel of John.

John 14, 15, 16, and 17 are filled with the revelation of the Father and His heart, His love. It didn't start there; Jesus spoke to the nation of Israel at large previously to this, but the people did not have ears to hear and refused it outright (John 8:42-47 as well as many other places).

In John 14:2 we have "in my Father's house" (which requires sonship to be in this house)

In v. 6 we have "coming to the Father", v. 7 knowing the Father

In v. 9, if you've seen Me, you've seen the Father; v. 11, I am in the Father and the Father in Me

In v. 12, I go to the Father; in v. 16, the Father gives you another Helper

In v. 21, the love of the Father is that He and Christ together will come to the believer and make their abode with him

In v. 24, the Father's word; v. 26, whom the Father will send; v. 28 the Father is greater than I (Jesus speaking as the Son of Man)

In John 15:2 the Father prunes; v. 8, by this the Father is glorified, you bearing much fruit

In v. 9, the same love of the Father on us; v. 16, whatever you ask the Father

In John 16:23, whatever you ask the Father in My Name, He will give you

In v. 25, at His speaking here (at the last supper), Jesus says that so far, up to this point, His revealing of the Father has been with figurative language, **but,** the time is coming (future) when I will tell you plainly about the Father

In v. 27, the Father Himself loves you

In John 17:2, 6, 9, 10, 11, 12, 24, the Father gives certain ones to Christ, as ones chosen by the Father, elected by the Father, those as the possession of the Father

In v. 21, the believer in the Father (in Us); v. 23 the Father loves the believer just the same as He loves Jesus (v. 26)

And further, the epistle to the Ephesians, where the heart of the Father is clearly revealed;

Eph. 1:3, the Father has blessed us with every spiritual blessing in the heavens in Christ (the calling is all heavenly)

In v. 4, the Father chose us in Christ before the foundation of the world

In vs. 4-5, the Father, in love, predestined us to adoption as sons by Jesus Christ to Himself (and sons then are those who have a relationship in love with the Father). It was the good pleasure of the Father's will that did this – that is, the Father's will delighted in predestining us.

In v.6, the Father has made us excepted in the Beloved (Christ) by the glory of the Father's (sovereign) grace

In v.7, In Him (Christ, the Beloved One) we have redemption through His (Christ, the Son of Man) blood, the forgiveness of sins, according to the riches of His (the Father's) grace

In V. 8, which He (the Father) made to abound..., v. 9, having made known to us the mystery of His (the Father's) will, according to His (the Father's) good pleasure, which He (the Father) purposed in Himself (the Father)

In v. 10, ...He (the Father) might gather together in one all things in Christ...in Him (Christ)

In v. 11, in whom (Christ) also we have obtained an inheritance, being predestined according to the purpose of Him (the Father), who (the Father) works all things according to the council of His (the Father's) will

In v. 12, that we who first trusted in Christ should be to the praise of His (the Father's) glory

In v. 14, ...to the praise of His (the Father's) glory v. 17, ...the Father of glory may give you...the knowledge of Him (the Father)

In v. 18, His (the Father's) calling...His (the Father's) inheritance v. 19, His (the Father) power toward us...the working of His (the Father's) mighty power

In v. 20, which He (the Father) worked in Christ when He (the Father) raised Him (Christ) from the dead and seated Him (Christ) at His (the Father's) right hand in the heavenlies

In v. 22, and He (the Father) put all things under His (Christ's) feet, and gave (the Father gave) Him (Christ) to be head over all things to the church (the Father places the church over all things as with Him – Christ)

In Eph. 2:1, and you He (the Father) made alive... v. 4, But God (the Father), Who is rich in mercy, because of His (the Father's) great love with which He (the Father) loved us

In v. 5, (the Father) made us alive together with Christ v. 6, (the Father) raised us up together and (the Father) made us sit together in the heavens in Christ Jesus

In v. 7, that in the ages to come He (the Father) might show the exceeding riches of His (the Father's) grace in His (the Father's) kindness

In v. 8, that not of yourselves; it is the gift of God (the Father) v. 10, we are His (the Father's) workmanship...which He (the Father) prepared

In vs. 11-18 we have all Jesus Christ, but v. 18 ends, "...access by one Spirit to the Father."

In v. 19, God (the Father) house, we members in it (as sons) v. 22, we are the habitation of God (the Father) through the Spirit.

One Final Thought...

Now is the judgment of this world; now the ruler of this world will be cast out.

Jesus said this before He went to the cross to give His life. If you have read this book then you should know that God judged and condemned the entire world at that time. This was nearly two thousand years ago.

Up to that point God had been testing mankind in the first Adam. He gave Israel His law and they failed miserably in responsibility before Him. He later sent His Son as Israel's Messiah, yet they rejected Him and would not have Him as their King. The most privileged nation on the face of the earth, in representing all mankind, had failed all the testing. God had proven that man in the first Adam was utterly lost and ruined.

This is what you are in the first Adam – a sinner. You are this, not only by the frequency of sins you commit – be they many or few -- but also because you were born in sin and it exists in your flesh. And there is no getting away from this. You are by birth, by nature, a child of wrath. You are in the flesh and of the world. You are lost, without God and without any true hope in the world. This is your actual state and position. It is who you are. It is how the holy God sees you. You could argue with Him, but that would be pointless. In the end many unbelievers intend to do just that – stand before God someday and argue with Him that He is wrong.

Maybe you think that God will wink at your sin? Somehow excuse it or not bring it up. Do you really believe the holy and righteous God will pass by and not have you give account? I'm sorry, but there's no chance at that happening – I believe you know, deep down, you will have to answer. Possibly you're thinking somehow in that day God will show you favor, and you're willing to take your chances. Sounds like a very risky bet. Again you're wagering that God will be willing to compromise Himself on your behalf. Not likely.

Most of the time unbelievers do everything they can to hide from God. He is too much light. Darkness is always a better cover for the works and thoughts of man. Better to be done in darkness than to be exposed in the light. But God is light and in Him there is no darkness at all. He is the God who knows the thoughts and intentions of the human heart. All things are naked and open to the eyes of Him to whom we must give account (Heb. 4:12-13). You must know that you will 'have to do' with God. Yet this very thing we so easily forget, or lose sight of. Our natural instinct is always to get out of the presence of God, and then to distain and dread it from that point on. In His presence there is no possibility of hiding anything. Yet just like Adam and Eve after they sinned, you hide in the bushes and trees hoping God will not see you. The end will be the same – cast out of the presence of God forever.

As a sinner, you will never truly believe in Jesus Christ unless you see your desperate need for Him. You do not acknowledge yourself having any need unless your conscience has been touched and enlightened as to your real state and condition before God. Just like the prodigal had to come to his senses, your conscience must be quickened as well (Luke 15:17). Quickened as to an understanding of your condition in sin and that you will surely perish if you remain (Luke 15:14-17). This is the story of the prodigal. His conscience was made alive to understand his true state and condition in sin and in the world. And then he is drawn to God (John 6:44).

John 3:18

"He who believes in Him is not condemned; but he who does not believe is condemned already, because he has not believed in the name of the only begotten Son of God.

For you, your judgment is decided at this present time. It is now in this life. It is not at some future time when you actually stand before God. Then it is too late. You are putting off God's judgment to some indefinite future time when you hope things will go well and in your favor. You say now that you are not ready, or it is not for you yet. I have heard all these excuses. But more than that, they are the words of an unbelieving world that is perishing. "...he who does not believe is condemned already..."

When the world is saying peace and security, then sudden destruction will come upon them (I Thess. 5:2-3). There is no hope for a good outcome for the world. They will be eating and drinking, this and that, but for the world the judgment is always described as coming like a thief in the night. Do you want to be part of this foolishness and presumption? Going merrily on in life while judgment for you is at the door? You say this cannot possibly be true, but it is the exact same mindset that does say, 'peace and safety!'

If you are an unbeliever and you have read this book, then God is dealing with you. He has quickened you. Your conscience has been made to feel the guilt and weight of your position in Adam, in the flesh, and in sin. But God is doing a work in you and He is drawing you to faith in Jesus Christ. The blood of Christ is the propitiation for all your judgment and condemnation due to you from God. God condemned Him to death and wrath instead of you. This not only shows God's righteousness in judging your sin (Rom. 3:22-26), but also shows His love toward you (Rom. 5:5-10).

When you are quickened by the Spirit of God and your conscience becomes aware, the Scriptures become an authority for you. What God says you have to know, what God has done you have to find out. To be uninformed and in the dark is no longer an option for you. You are being drawn to Christ. The blood of Christ will wash away all your sins and guilt. The death of Christ is where you in the first Adam die; God condemning sin in the flesh by Christ's death (Rom. 8:3). You will be justified by faith in Christ (Rom. 5:1, Gal. 2:16) and will then be sealed by the Holy Spirit (Eph. 1:13). You are then a son of God (Gal. 3:26), His workmanship, created in Christ Jesus (Eph. 2:10). This is your new state and position – a new creation in Christ Jesus. It is out of the first Adam and into the second Adam as a new creature born of God.

The matter is all decided now. "He who believes in Him is not condemned; but he who does not believe is condemned already..."